应用翻译实务
PRAGMATIC TRANSLATION
（第二版）

谢工曲　编著
（暨南大学）

中山大学出版社
SUN YAT-SEN UNIVERSITY PRESS

· 广州 ·

版权所有　翻印必究

图书在版编目（CIP）数据

应用翻译实务/谢工曲编著．—2 版．—广州：中山大学出版社，2017.8

ISBN 978-7-306-06097-6

Ⅰ．①应⋯　Ⅱ．①谢⋯　Ⅲ．①英语—翻译—高等学校—教材　Ⅳ．①H315.9

中国版本图书馆 CIP 数据核字（2017）第 168879 号

出版人： 徐　劲
策划编辑： 林彩云
责任编辑： 林彩云
封面设计： 林绵华
责任校对： 刘学谦
责任技编： 何雅涛
出版发行： 中山大学出版社
电　　话： 编辑部 020-84111996，84113349，84111997，84110779
　　　　　　发行部 020-84111998，84111981，84111160
地　　址： 广州市新港西路 135 号
邮　　编： 510275　　　　**传　真：** 020-84036565
网　　址： http://www.zsup.com.cn　　**E-mail:** zdcbs@mail.sysu.edu.cn
印　刷　者： 佛山市浩文彩色印刷有限公司
规　　格： 787mm×1092mm　1/16　13 印张　320 千字
版次印次： 2014 年 6 月第 1 版　2017 年 8 月第 2 版　2022 年 8 月第 4 次印刷
印　　数： 5001～6000 册　　**定　价：** 35.00 元

如发现本书因印装质量影响阅读，请与出版社发行部联系调换

前　言

　　《应用翻译实务》修订版以"中国企业与中国文化走出去"战略为指南，聚焦全球化环境下需要完成的译写任务，旨在培养译者的对外交流和信息传播能力。内容包括：城市宣传、企业宣传、产品与服务宣传、旅游与文化宣传、投资指南、学术论文摘要译写、技术写作在应用翻译中的应用、信息查询技巧、求职求学申请和简历译写等。本教材试图运用翻译理论与策略解决工作中的实际问题，目的是加强翻译学习的实用性和针对性，提高译者用英汉双语完成实际工作的能力。

　　本教材以职业需求和语言服务的发展为导向，其特点是：

　　（1）应对智库发展需求，提供针对信息库建设所需的翻译策略与译写技巧，包括如何确定目标读者及其信息需求，如何挖掘信息的潜在价值，从而实现翻译服务的增值。

　　（2）将技术写作引入应用翻译实践，旨在提高译文的可读性、针对性与适用性，满足目标读者的信息需求。

　　（3）将信息查询技巧运用于应用翻译实践，包括如何确定和运用关键词搜索信息，提高译者获取相关专业知识和信息的能力，从而帮助译者沿着原作的思路译写，产生贴近原文的译文。

　　（4）如何利用图片信息和平行文本帮助译写。

　　（5）加强旅游宣传的主题化及其文化内涵，通过对信息的甄别，传递实质性信息，提高旅游文本的感召力。

　　（6）通过对国外工程和经管类部分学术期刊论文摘要各要素的归纳总结，规范学术论文摘要译写，方便信息查询，促进学术成果的传播。

目　录

第一章　应用翻译基本知识与技能 …………………………………… 1
　一、引言 ………………………………………………………………… 1
　二、学习翻译的方法 …………………………………………………… 2
　三、翻译对译者素养的要求 …………………………………………… 11

第二章　应用文本的特征与翻译策略 ………………………………… 18
　一、概述 ………………………………………………………………… 18
　二、应用文本翻译的目的与策略原则 ………………………………… 19
　三、应用翻译译例解析 ………………………………………………… 24

第三章　信息查询技巧在应用文本翻译中的作用 …………………… 39
　一、引言 ………………………………………………………………… 39
　二、从语境中获取专业信息 …………………………………………… 39
　三、如何查找和筛选信息 ……………………………………………… 45

第四章　技术写作对应用文本翻译的借鉴作用 ……………………… 55
　一、引言 ………………………………………………………………… 55
　二、技术写作 …………………………………………………………… 55
　三、技术写作对外宣文本翻译的借鉴作用 …………………………… 56

第五章　外宣翻译的目的与策略原则 ………………………………… 64
　一、概述 ………………………………………………………………… 64
　二、对外宣传翻译的目的论原则 ……………………………………… 67
　三、"外宣三贴近"原则 ………………………………………………… 72
　四、实例分析 …………………………………………………………… 73

第六章　旅游文本翻译 ………………………………………………… 82
　一、概述 ………………………………………………………………… 82

二、旅游指南的主题信息性质与分类 …………………………… 83
　　三、主题关联信息突出策略原则及其可操作性 ………………… 87
　　四、英汉旅游文体特色及其风格差异 …………………………… 93
　　五、酒店文宣的文体特点 ………………………………………… 104

第七章　企业外宣文本翻译 ………………………………………… 111
　　一、企业外宣的目的 ……………………………………………… 111
　　二、英汉企业外宣特点 …………………………………………… 111
　　三、平行文本对企业外宣英译的启示 …………………………… 118
　　四、企业产品译介 ………………………………………………… 124

第八章　投资指南翻译 ……………………………………………… 129
　　一、英汉投资指南的特点 ………………………………………… 129
　　二、投资指南的汉英翻译原则 …………………………………… 134
　　三、相关平行文本 ………………………………………………… 150

第九章　英语学术论文摘要译写 …………………………………… 153
　　一、概述：学术论文摘要的一般语体结构特征 ………………… 153
　　二、英汉论文标题和摘要的差异与翻译 ………………………… 155
　　三、英语学术论文摘要解析 ……………………………………… 158
　　四、摘要修改 ……………………………………………………… 170

第十章　简历、求职信写译 ………………………………………… 175
　　一、什么是个人简历 ……………………………………………… 175
　　二、如何制作个人简历 …………………………………………… 176
　　三、如何写求职信 ………………………………………………… 186
　　四、留学申请 ……………………………………………………… 189

参考文献 ……………………………………………………………… 201

第一章 应用翻译基本知识与技能

一、引言

根据文秋芳等人（2008，2）对职场英语需求的调查，培养学生的说、写、译表达技能比培养听、读接受性技能更具社会功能，尤其是口、笔译技能。体现职场英语交际活动成效的终结形式是说、写、译活动，而且，调查发现，口、笔译出现的频率远远高于说和写。

在全球化、信息化时代，随着中国企业和中国文化走出去战略的进程加快，翻译行业面临着前所未有的发展机遇和挑战。传播中国声音、树立国家形象，让世界真切地了解中国，感受中华文化的魅力和现代中国蓬勃发展的生机是译者肩负的重要使命。同时，如何让国际社会接受与认可中国话语、倾听中国故事是译者面临的巨大挑战。

由于中西方社会环境不同，文化语境存在显著的差异，我国的对外宣传存在相当大的"文化折扣"现象。要实现中国文化走出去战略，讲好中国故事，让世界关注中国话题，听清中国声音，让中国声音赢得国际社会的广泛理解和认同，让世界知道中国为人类文明进步做出的重要贡献，译者需要学会使用国际通用的话语体系，掌握相关语言特色和表达习惯，从而提高中国文化的传播力、影响力、引导力和公信力，提升国家文化软实力。因此，"翻译是一种工具，更是一种战略；翻译工作者是专一人才，更是跨文化沟通与管理人才"。（冯晞）

（一）应用翻译的性质和特点

应用翻译（pragmatic translation），又称实用翻译（practical translation 或 applied translation），是一种实用性文本的翻译，内容涵盖政治、经济、社会、文化、科技、生活等各个方面，几乎包括了除文学翻译之外的所有文本。因此，应用翻译是一种以传递信息为主要目的，同时又注重信息传递效果的实用型翻译。

应用翻译涉及的文本包罗万象，但是，这些文本的翻译又具有相当的共性：实用性、目的性、专业性和匿名信等。

1. 实用性

应用翻译具有很强的实用性，是为了向译文读者（target language readers）传递有价值的、实用的信息，如科技知识、新闻资讯、产品说明、旅游项目介绍等。应用翻译的实用性要求译者充分考虑译入语的文化背景、读者的认知能力和信息需求，使译文的实用价值得以充分体现。

2. 目的性

应用翻译具有明确的目的性。

（1）传递信息（科技、新闻、经贸等），注重信息传递的有效性，在原文与译文的关系上，为了提高信息传递的效果需要改变原文的形式。

（2）诱导行动（对外宣传、广告等），注重译文的可读性和译文读者的理解和接受能力，意在唤起读者去体验、去行动。应用文本的目的性既可以由文本自身的功能决定，也可以由翻译委托人（commissioner）决定。例如，产品说明书是以信息功能为主的文本，翻译委托人可以要求译文增强诱导功能，以便促进产品销售。

应用翻译的目的性要求译者把握好译文的文本功能，使原文的文本功能在译文中得以实现；或者改变原文的文本功能，以达到翻译委托人的要求。应用翻译的目的性还要求译者改变原有的翻译观念，即翻译只能全译，而是根据翻译的目的和具体要求，采用改译、编译等变译技巧。

3. 专业性

专业性强是应用翻译不同于文学翻译的又一特点。从语言和文体特点看，应用翻译涉及专门用途英语（English for Specific Purpose，即 ESP），专业性和规范性很强，例如，法律、科技文本的翻译。因此，译者不仅要掌握相关文本的语言和文体特征，而且要熟悉所翻译的专业领域的知识。

4. 匿名性

应用文本的匿名性是指这类文本大都缺少个性，作者的身份往往处于匿名（anonymous）状态，作者的个人风格无从体现，在原文与译文的关系上，大多按照译文固有的格式和规范行文，原文的作用是提供信息。同样，译者在翻译的过程中也不能过多地发挥自己的个性和创造性。

二、学习翻译的方法

翻译是一门实践性很强的学科，但是，单靠自己的实践是不够的，还必须借助于别人的翻译实践经验。因此，学习者在使用翻译教材时，不仅要学习翻译理论,而且要学会分析与借鉴别人的翻译实践,在此过程中,要先看别人在这种情况下怎么译。具体步骤是:首先阅读原文,找出原文中的难点,如生词、短语、难句和陌生的信息与知识点,借助工具书或网络查询,根据上下文内容,突破这些难点;然后再读译文,在遣词造句、文章风格、信息查询与筛选等方面得到启发,并以此指导自己的翻译实践。同时,要注意收集整理相关专题的文本范例,作为翻译的参考与借鉴。

(一)认识阅读理解的重要性

阅读理解能力决定了译者是否能够准确把握原文的主旨,正确传递信息。

例 1

原文:

"You're always going to **have** the **basics**, such as banners, bags, badge holders, receptions and the like," says Nancy Largay, former vice president of media sales for Penton Media of Cleveland, **the organizer** of shows such as Internet World. But new options are emerging, as well. A company now can sponsor a new product **showcase** or a live Internet broadcast from a show.

这里的 basics 指的是什么?线索在哪里?have 怎么译?同位语 the organizer 怎么译?showcase 怎样理解?

分析:

(1) 第一句话的线索在 such as banners, bags, badge holders, receptions and the like,它们是赞助方式,按照费用由低到高、形式从简单到复杂排列。因此,basics 在这里指的是基本的赞助方式,那么,have the basics 就是从基本的赞助方式做起。

(2) the organizer 是 Penton Media of Cleveland 的同位语,它进一步说明 Penton Media of Cleveland 是一家什么样的公司/机构,在业界所处的地位,而 Internet World(因特网世界)是一个品牌展览,Penton Media of Cleveland 又是这个品牌展览的主办方,这里的关系需要搞清楚。

(3) showcase 的词典释义是 case for displaying articles in a shop, museum, etc 或 any means of showing sth. favourably。根据后面 a live Internet broadcast from a show(一个展会的现场网络直播)来看,此处,

product showcase 意指产品展示或者产品展示会。

译文：

"你总是可以从基本的赞助做起,例如彩旗、资料袋、徽章别针和招待会等赞助形式,"克利夫兰市 Penton 传媒公司媒体营销部前副总裁 Nancy Largay 说。Penton 传媒公司也是因特网世界这类展览的主办者。然而,新的赞助方式层出不穷。企业可以赞助一个新产品展示,或者赞助一个展会的现场网络直播权。

例2

原文：

"They're really an important consumer segment for companies like Mercedes and American Express." He **points to** the high household income, technological **sophistication** and early-adopter attitudes of typical attendees at events such as Comdex.

points to, sophistication 怎样译?

分析：

(1) 第一句中的 They 是指 typical attendees at events（出席展会的典型观众）,他们是 an important consumer segment for companies like Mercedes and American Express（奔驰和美国捷运这类公司的重要客户群）。

(2) sophistication 的词典释义是 quality of being sophisticated（世故、复杂性）,early-adopter attitudes 的意思是易于接受新事物。那么,什么样的人易于接受新事物呢? high household income, technological sophistication（高收入、高技术人群）。

(3) 因此,He points to 可译为"他指出"。

译文：

"他们是奔驰和美国捷运这类公司的重要客户群。"他指出,高收入、高技术背景和易于接受新事物是参与 Comdex 这类展览观众的典型特征。

例3

原文：

Most show producers are reluctant to talk about how they calculate the price of sponsorship opportunities. David Korse, CEO of Imark Communications, shows **proprietary** formula that includes material costs, attendees' buying power and the "**quantity of visibility**", which may include exposure on the show's

Web site, through direct mail, and at the show itself.

"**Then you put it all in a cuisine**," Korse says, "and let the market come up with a price **that makes sense**." He explains that once Imark has determined a tentative price for a sponsorship, the company compares it to what **competitive events** charge for similar opportunities. The price is raised or lowered accordingly.

怎样译"Then you put it all in a cuisine", that makes sense, competitive events?

分析：

（1）proprietary 的词典释义是 of or relating to an owner or ownership（私有的、所有权的），此处意为某公司所有的。

（2）quantity of visibility 意为访问量、点击量/率，这里特指赞助商的曝光率。

（3）"Then you put it all in a cuisine"，it 指所有这些因素（材料费、观众购买力、赞助商曝光率），就像一盘菜中的所有食材，这是一个形象化的比喻。

（4）that makes sense 意为"有意义"，在此处意为"合理的"。

（5）competitive events 意为"有可比性的、同类的"。

译文：

多数策展商（或展会主办方）都不愿透露他们如何计算展会的赞助费用（或赞助商收费）。Imark Communications 的首席执行官 David Korse 公开了该公司计算赞助费的公式，涉及材料费、观众购买力和赞助商曝光率，包括展会官网的访问量、邮件传播量以及展会期间的访问量。

"然后，你把所有这些原料放在一盘菜里，让市场决定一个合适的价格。"Korse 说，一旦 Imark 制定了一个赞助项目的初步价格，就会将其与同类展览的同类赞助费进行比较，做出相应的调整。

例4

原文：

Actually one of the disadvantages of the Global Strategy is that **integrated competitive moves** can **lead to the sacrificing of revenues, profits, or competitive positions in individual countries** — especially when the **subsidiary** in one country is told to attack a global competitor in order to convey a signal or divert that competitor's resources from another nation.（韩素音青年

翻译竞赛，2013)

分析：

(1) integrated competitive moves 是指跨国公司可以凝聚与整合总公司与旗下位于其他国家子公司的资源，形成综合的竞争力；moves 是行动、举措。

(2) lead to the sacrificing of revenues, profits, or competitive positions in individual countries 直译：导致个别国家在收入、利润和竞争地位方面受损，但是下面一句提到 the subsidiary，因此可译为"海外子公司在收入、利润和竞争地位方面受损"。

译文：

实际上，全球化战略的一个负面影响是，跨国企业凝聚的竞争力及其商业运作会导致海外子公司在收入、利润和竞争地位方面受损，尤其是当企业为了传递某个信号或者迫使一个全球竞争对手转移其在另一个国家的资源，要求旗下位于某国的子公司挑战这个竞争对手时，情况更是如此。

(二) 重视语言对比

翻译实践要想取得好的效果，必须对英汉两种语言进行对比，找出各自的特点，这样就知道同样的意思，用汉语应当怎么说，用英语应当怎么说，而不至于在翻译时过分受原文的影响，避免中式英语。

1. 句式结构差异

在汉译英中常出现"英语词语，汉语结构"的现象，即英语译文呈现出汉语的句式结构。显然，这是因为译者对英汉两种语言在句法结构或思维与表达方面的差异认识不足。英语句式呈现主句+多个从属结构的形式，体现从属关系；而汉语句式缺少从属连接成分，在形式上并列分置，其语义层次依靠上下文的语境来体现。因此，如果将汉语一一对应地译成英语，其语际间的逻辑关系可能失去，译文就难以准确传达原文意旨。

例5

原文：

三峡大坝曾经是毛主席"截断巫山云雨"的梦想，但是在核电出现之后，相形之下，水电对环境的破坏显得触目惊心。三峡大坝彰显大国国力的政治意义更大于经济利益，这是政治决策的内在逻辑。

三峡大坝为库区环境提供了不破不立的机会，水坝的浩大决定了城市设计的基调，一张生态改造的大幕开始拉起。

原译：

Chairman Mao had a dream to build a great dam at Three Gorges of Yangtze River. The water power station damage environment horribly compared with the nuclear power station. Three Gorges Dam project symbolizes prosperity of China. Due to the logic of politics, the political significance of Three Gorges Dam project is more important than its economic significance.

Three Gorges Dam project has destructed the environment while it gives chance to rebuild the area drastically. The tremendous dam needs splendid urban design. Ecological reconstruction begins at same time.

分析：

原文委婉地表达了作者对三峡大坝带来的环境破坏的担忧，如果依照中文的行文方式一一对应地译成英文，看似"忠实"的译文会让英语读者不知所云，原文的文本功能失去。

仔细分析原文，看似并列或独立的中文句式之间存在着因果、转折和对比关系。因此，根据英语语际衔接特点，恰当调节句式结构，运用或添加合适的语篇衔接手段，使译文连贯、逻辑明了，通过英语的句法结构再现中文的语义层次，原作意旨一目了然。

改译：

Chairman Mao once dreamed of building a great dam at the Three Gorges of Yangtze River. However, compared with nuclear power, the water power station has severely damaged the environment. Obviously, the political significance of the Three Gorges Dam exceeds its economic benefits, based on the political consideration of showing off the national power.

While destroying the environment, the Three Gorges Dam has created an opportunity to rebuild the ecosystem of the area. The huge project has initiated a large-scale urban design and reconstruction of the ecosystem at the same time.

2. 写作风格差异

汉语行文讲究工整对仗、文采华丽，因而使用过多修饰词，而且，用词中有很多同义重复现象，有些修饰词实际意义不大，与英语形成很大反差。例如，"彻底粉碎"（smash）、"走南闯北"（travel a lot）、"平淡无奇"（featureless/ ordinary）、"更加圆满"（perfect）等，这些表达都有明显的同义重复现象，译成英语时常常需要使用"省译"的手法对原文进行处理。与之形成鲜明对比的是，英语行文用词注重上下文搭配，语言表达简洁客观,层次清晰,逻辑性强,最忌重复堆砌的表达。因而,汉语中那些被认为是必不可少的甚至是富有文采的表达在英语中常常被视为累赘多余,不合语法,不合逻辑。

例6

原文:

这是一个千帆竞渡、百舸争流的伟大时代。万里昆仑谁凿破,无边波浪拍天来。纵观当今世界风起云涌的国际经济贸易浪潮,波浪壮阔,气象万千,逆水行舟,不进则退,唯有革故鼎新,方能永不衰败。山东东方公司……

分析:

这是比较典型的中文开头方式,辞藻华丽,描述宏大,色彩浓烈,对汉语读者来说,这也许是一篇成功的企业宣传,如果直接译成英文就显得夸张、浮艳;而且,从第3句才能看出这是一家外贸公司的介绍,前面是过度的渲染,并没有提供实质性信息。考虑到译文读者的思维习惯和译文的交际效果,在翻译时可对过多的修饰做出弱化处理或删除。

译文:

This is an era of severe competition where every organization has to be enterprising at its best in order to provide services satisfactory to Chinese companies seeking successful access to the global market. (引自《商务汉英翻译》)

或者直接译成:

Shandong Oriental Corporation specializes in …/ operates in the field (business; trade) of…

3. 文化差异

中西文化上的差异,导致思维习惯和表达方式上的明显不同。许多中文里约定俗成的词句原封不动地翻译成英文后,不但难以达到忠实传达原作的目的,反而会引起不必要的误解。比如,中国人特别习惯使用军事化的语言。例如,中国参加奥运会的体育代表团被称为"奥运军团",我们几乎每天都在不同领域里进行着"一场攻坚战",一个工程的收尾阶段常常是"一场决战"。中文里这样的词句很能鼓舞"士气"和"斗志",但是翻译成外文就显得"火药味"十足。又比如,中国的学者注重谦虚和含蓄,在写好一本书后,即使是倾毕生之力写成的学术著作,也往往在前言里说:"由于本人水平有限,书中谬误肯定不少,敬请读者批评指正。"如果照译过去,不了解中国文化的外国读者可能会问:"既然你知道有错误,为什么自己不纠正以后再发表?"因为在英美等国出版的图书中,人们习惯于说"这是迄今为止,在这个领域中最为权威的著作"。而实际上很可能是一本普通的大路货图书(黄友义,2004)。

例7

原文:

If you want to develop your perceptual and creative skills to their utmost, you will want to follow the strategies outlined in Visual Notes for Architects and Designers. It is a valuable guide for architects, landscape architects, designers, and anyone interested in recording experience in sketch form.

译文:

如果你想最大限度地提高自己的悟性和创造力,就请参照《建筑师和设计师的视觉笔记》提出的策略。这本书不愧是建筑师、景观建筑师、设计师以及所有喜欢用图像记录亲身体验的人士之宝典(Visual Notes for Architects and Designers,2012)。

(三) 注重借鉴平行文本

平行文本(parallel text)是指在相似的交际情景中产生的具有相似信息的不同语言的文本,也就是与原文内容相关的译入语参考资料。译者要注意收集相关专题的文本范例,作为翻译的参考与借鉴,通过平行文本获得准确可靠的译法,提高译文的可读性,使译文的信息传递效果与原文基本相同。

在研究翻译时,要细心观察外国人在这种场合怎样使用英语,怎样表达才是地道的英语,这样做对提高译文质量很有好处。

例8

原文:

And while some popular Buzz Feed posts — like the recent "Is this the most embarrassing interview Fox News has ever done?" — might do their best to elicit shares through anger, both BuzzFeed and Upworthy recognize that their main success lies in creating positive viral material. (韩素音青年翻译竞赛,2014)

译文：

虽然 BuzzFeed 上的一些热门帖子——像最近发布的"这是福克斯新闻史上最囧的采访吗?"——不遗余力地通过表达愤怒情绪博取<u>转发次数</u>,BuzzFeed 和 Upworthy 都认识到他们的成功主要在于创造能<u>以病毒方式传播</u>的正面信息。

例9

原文:

In a recent study from the Massachusetts Institute of Technology, researchers found that "<u>up votes</u>," showing that a visitor liked a comment or story, begat more up votes on comments on the site, but "<u>down votes</u>" did not do the same. In fact, a single up vote increased the likelihood that someone else would like a comment by 32%, whereas a down vote had no effect. (韩素音青年翻译竞赛,2014)

译文:

麻省理工学院最近的一份研究报告表明,表示网友喜欢某一评论或故事而投的<u>"顶"票</u>,会引来更多网友点"顶",而投"踩"票不会产生这样的响应。事实上,<u>一个点"顶"</u>就会使其他访问者对该评论的喜欢概率增加32%,<u>而点"踩"</u>就没有这个效应。

分析:

观察中英文中是否有对应的表达方式,直接使用。

例10

原文:

Although not a "<u>first tier</u>" economic global city, such as New York, London, or Tokyo, Chicago is a <u>world city</u> from the perspective of immigration, culture, control of capital, and command over a vast region of agricultural and industrial production. Its universities participate in the global economy through the work produced on their campuses. As Arjun Appadurai noted, the academic world participates in its own forms of "<u>knowledge transfer</u>" throughout a global network of scholars. These <u>flows of information</u> may not have a significant physical presence, but the institutions that house these scholars and their work do.

译文:

虽然芝加哥不像纽约、伦敦和东京那样属于经济全球化的<u>一线城市</u>,但它在移民、文化和资本操控方面绝对是<u>世界级城市</u>,控制了大片工农业生产区。芝加哥的大学以其校内产出的学术成果参与全球经济。正如阿尔让·阿帕杜莱所指出的那样,学术界通过全球学者网络,以其知识输出方式参与其中。这些<u>信息流</u>也许是无形的,但是拥有学者及其成果的学术机构却是有形的。

例 11

原文:

新型手机产品除了加强基本功能外,越来越趋向多功能化,甚至融合其他行业高技术于一身,无论是造型设计,还是使用效果,各大品牌各显神通,纷纷打造更具个性化的手机产品。

译文:

In addition to the basic functions, the innovation in the designing and manufacturing of new mobile phones is increasingly oriented towards <u>versatility and functionality</u>, <u>merging the top-notch industrial technologies</u>. In terms of both styling design and utility effects, the top mobile phone manufacturers are <u>vying with each other</u>, striving to bring out new mobile phones with more <u>conspicuous personality</u>.(引自《商务汉英翻译》)

三、翻译对译者素养的要求

(一)语言功底

对汉英两种语言正确的理解和纯熟的运用能力,英语语感和英语表达能力对翻译结果起决定性作用。英语语感包括语法意识(sense of grammar)、惯用法意识(sense of idiomaticness)和连贯意识(sense of coherence)。英语表达能力是用自然、地道、合乎语法规范的英语进行表达的能力,要有丰富的词汇积累,纯熟的句式变化,语体风格的恰当运用。

例 12

原文：

从中国家族企业的发展现状来看，家族企业发展到一定阶段后，其人力资本问题日益突现，尤其是在用人问题方面，表现出了很大的局限，阻碍了企业的发展。

译文 1：

Looking at the development status of the Chinese family business developed to a certain stage, which highlighted the growing problem of human capital. Especially in the employment problem, which show a lot of constraints and hinder the development of enterprises.

译文 2：

Examining the family business, we can see that when it has developed to a certain stage, the family business will be experiencing the problem of human capital. The most obvious problem in this regard is human resources management, which demonstrates many inadequacies, hindering corporate growth.

译文 3：

A family business as it is will experience difficulties in its human capital after some time of operation. Human resources deployment, in particular, has been handicapped to many restraints that hinder the development of a company.

（引自《商务汉英翻译》）

分析：

译文 1 看似与原文一一对应，但都是无主句，不符合英语表达习惯；译文 2 符合英语语法，但是语言表达不够简练紧凑；译文 3 词的搭配和语句的连贯性更好，更符合英语表达习惯。

例 13

原文：

联合调查组深入一些省市的高新技术产品出口工业园和一部分高新技术产品出口企业进行了调查研究。

译文 1：

The joint researching group visited some high-tech and new-tech product export industrial zones in some provinces and cities and some enterprises of the export of high-tech and new-tech products to make investigation and research.

译文2：

Joint teams toured provinces and municipalities where they visited and surveyed high-tech exporters and industrial zones.（引自《商务汉英翻译》）

分析：

译文1虽然没有什么语法错误，但是不符合英语表达习惯；译文2更加简练紧凑。而且，汉语排序习惯是从大到小，而英语排序则是从小到大。

（二）广博的文化知识

翻译家应该是一个杂学家，除了深厚的语言功底外，还应该具备广博的文化知识。文化知识包括三个方面：一是相关国家的文化背景知识，涉及历史、地理、风土人情、自然风貌、文学艺术、宗教信仰等方面。知识面越广，对翻译的帮助越大。二是汉英两种语言所反映的中西文化差异的知识，在汉译英中，译者要有文化差异和文化传递意识，要考虑英语读者对译文所传达的汉文化的接受程度，反之亦然。三是翻译理论以及与翻译研究相关的科学知识。

当然，一个人的知识积累总是有限的，面对众多的信息文本，译者还需要掌握一些信息查询技巧，解决翻译中的难题。在翻译实践中，译者经常会遇到因文化背景知识缺乏所致的翻译困难。有些问题看似简单，但是想当然就会出错，为了传递准确可靠的信息，译者需要查询信息。

例14

原文：

The proposed site was sufficiently convenient for omnibus passengers coming from the Bank.（The Crystal Palace and the Great Exhibition）

分析：

这句话看似简单，这个文本讲述的是1850年第一届国际博览会，因此，这里的the proposed site指的是拟定的会址，但是1850年的omnibus和the Bank应当怎样理解和翻译？

怎样查询信息：

在Yahoo上输入the bank London 1850，同时输入地名和时间，限制查询范围；再输入omnibus London 1850，同时输入地名和时间，限制查询范围。

在 wikipedia 上搜到以下两则信息：

(1) The Bank of England, formally the Governor and Company of the Bank of England, is the central bank of the United Kingdom and the model on which most modern central banks have been based. Established in 1694, it is the second oldest central bank in the world.

从这段文字和历史图片上判断，那时的英格兰银行已成为伦敦的一个地标。

(2) Buses have been used on the streets of London since 1829, when George Shillibeer started operating his horse-drawn omnibus service from Paddington to the City of London. In 1850 Thomas Tilling started horse bus services, and in 1855 the London General Omnibus Company or LGOC was founded to amalgamate and regulate the horse-drawn omnibus services then operating in London.

从这段文字和历史图片上判断，那时的 bus 就是马车。

因此这句话可译为：选定的博览会场址对从英格兰银行乘公共交通到达的游客很方便。

例 15

原文：

Since cleaving off CeBIT from Hannover Messe in 1986, both shows have become the trendsetters for industry and the flagship tradeshows among the many different trade fairs and exhibitions staged by DMAG (Deutsche Industric-Messe).

分析：

怎样理解和翻译 cleaving off CeBIT from Hannover Messe in 1986？

在 Yahoo 上输入 cleaving off CeBIT from Hannover Messe in 1986，可以搜寻到这样一则信息：

Throughout the past 20 years, thousands of suppliers and users from all over the world have come together every year in the early spring at CeBIT in Hannover, Germany. Looking back, the birth of CeBIT on 12 March 1986 was the outcome of a long and complicated decision-making process. The computer industry had become a key feature of HANNOVER MESSE and had contributed to its unique status as the world's biggest trade show for capital goods. However, the computer exhibitors were having to contend with an increasing number of non-specialists at their stands.

从这段文字可以看出，信息技术展示原是汉诺威工业博览会的一部分，但是，随着信息技术产业的发展，它在博览会中的地位越显突出，举办专门的信息技术专业博览会成为必然，从而改变了展商不得不面对大量非专业观众的局面。

cleave—to divide into two parts by or as if by cutting forcefully

Hannover Messe 汉诺威工业博览会

CeBIT 汉诺威办公室设备博览会，也称之为汉诺威信息技术博览会。

这段文字可译为：1986 年信息技术博览会（CeBIT）从工业博览会（Hannover Messe）划分出来以后，这两个博览会已经成为工业界的开拓者，是德意志博览会公司举办的众多展览中的旗舰展。

例 16

原文：

Speaking to the promise of better times for the region and the country, the Official Guide stated the firm's purpose: "to give the visitor a glimpse, a pre-vision of what the future holds for the <u>Far West</u>" as the federal government financed such projects as "<u>Boulder Dam</u>, its <u>All American Canal</u>, its <u>Grand Coulee Project</u>, and a host of other activities that mark a new era".

分析：

翻译此段，画线部分需要上网查找信息，译文要符合中文读者的认知能力，不能将 Boulder Dam 译成 Boulder 水坝，将 its Grand Coulee Project 译成 Grand Coulee 项目。通过网络信息查询可知：Boulder Dam 又称为胡佛水坝，以纪念胡佛当选美国总统之前为此做出的重要贡献；All American Canal 是一条沿着美墨边界开凿的输水渠；Grand Coulee Project 是一座位于美国西北部的水坝。

译文：

世博官方指南在展望国家和地区的发展机遇时说，世博公司的目的是"让观众一睹为快，预览未来西部的发展前景"，因为联邦政府投资兴建了一批大型项目，包括<u>胡佛水坝</u>、<u>全美运河</u>、<u>大古力水坝</u>和其他一些项目，标志着一个新时代的开始。

（三）高度的责任感

1. 译前准备

（1）仔细通读全文，了解原文的相关知识，查阅背景资料。

（2）了解译文的文本功能和预期达到的目标，了解译文的目标读者群。

2．翻译过程

全面透彻理解原文，理解原文语言和文化的意义，理解原文的逻辑关系，再用准确得体的语言表达出来。对没有把握的地方要求助工具书和网络查询，尽量避免不该发生的错误。

例 17

2010 年 6 月，中国科技馆与瑞士伯尔尼历史博物馆联合举办"爱因斯坦展"。其中，有一个醒目的标题："爱因斯坦——大众情人？"接下来是"爱因斯坦和他的 14 个女人"，下面有一段煽情的译文让人产生不好的观感。

"他爱过的人包括物理学家、侦探、图书管理员甚至夜总会的舞女。"

而原文是：The women he loved included a physicist, a spy, a librarian and perhaps even a nightclub dancer. "也许还可能是……"

接下来的中文译文是："当他在公司指挥女性员工时，感到最自在，而女性也总是觉得他很有魅力。"

而原文是：He felt most at his ease in the company of dominating women, and they too often found him very attractive. "当他与强势的女性在一起时……"

又如："他在 16 岁时就要参加工学院的入学考试，但却不能提供离校证明。"

而原文是：He was supposed to take his entrance exam to the Polytechnic at the age of only 16 and without school-leaving certificate. "他被允许在只有 16 岁并且没有中学毕业证时就参加工学院的入学考试。"

（引自《南方周末》）

第二章 应用文本的特征与翻译策略

一、概述

（一）应用文本的范围和文本特征

应用文本的范围很广，内容涉及政治、经济、社会、文化、科技、生活等方面，几乎涵盖了除文学之外的所有文本，"包括政府文件、告示、科技论文、新闻报道、法律文书、商贸信函、产品说明书、使用手册、广告、技术文本、科普读物、旅游指南等各类文本"（方梦之，2003）。

应用文本的文体特征大多可归属于纽马克界定的"信息型"和"呼唤型"文本。文本的"信息"功能指传递真实客观的信息，强调信息传递的效果，因而需要对原文进行调整与修改；文本的"呼唤"功能（或称之为"诱导"功能）指这类文本大都具有宣传性，意在唤起读者去行动、去思考、去感受，注重文本的可读性和被接受程度。

应用文本的文体特征决定了原文在翻译的过程中只是起到提供信息的作用，译者可以根据译文功能需要提取信息。

虽然汉语和英语都有应用文体，各自的文本体裁差异也不大，但是，由于语言与文化上的差异，两种文本在语篇组合和行文风格上有很大差异。

（二）中文应用文本的文本特征

中文应用文本，尤其是对外宣传类文本，例如，各级政府的信息通报、投资指南、旅游指南、城市/企业/公司的宣传介绍、各种大型国际性活动宣传、产品/服务广告宣传等，主要体现了作者的个人风格和中国传统文化思维在语言表达中的特征。大多数应用文本是企事业单位工作经验丰富的秘书所写，需要迎合领导的语言风格，故容易出现套话空话或公文程式性语言，或有追求辞藻华丽、句式新奇、刻意渲染等倾向。

同时，由于中文句式讲究工整对仗，过多使用修饰词，使表达平衡对称，但这类词语实际意义并不大，因而造成句式冗长繁复，国内读者对此大都已经习以为常，但是译成英语时难以为译文读者所接受，可读性差，影响信息传递效果。

二、应用文本翻译的目的与策略原则

（一）国外用于指导应用翻译的主要翻译理论与策略

在国外翻译理论中，对应用翻译具有很大指导意义的是功能翻译理论，以德国功能翻译学派为主流，还包括英国学者纽马克（Newmark）和美国学者奈达（Nida）等人的语言功能与翻译研究。对于什么是功能翻译理论，德国学者诺德（Nord, 2001）的定义是："翻译的'功能主义'就是指专注于文本与翻译的一种或多种功能的研究。"（"Functionalist" means focusing on function or functions of texts and translation.）

德国功能学派翻译理论的代表人物赖斯（Reiss）、费米尔（Vermeer）和诺德（Nord）等学者提出的翻译"目的论"（Skopos Theory），从20世纪70年代开始，经过不断丰富完善，成为功能翻译理论的主流。

"目的论"认为，翻译是一种有目的的跨文化交际活动，在翻译的过程中，译文预期目的或功能决定了翻译方法和翻译策略，原文和译文是两种独立的具有不同价值的文本，会有不同的目的和功能，原文在翻译中只是起到提供信息的作用，作者通过原文提供信息，译者则将原文的语言和文化信息有条件地传递给译语读者。译者根据客户或委托人的要求，结合翻译的目的和译语读者的具体情况，选择原文信息、翻译策略以及译文的表现形式。因为"文本只有被接受者理解并且要让他们理解才有意义"。（A text is made meaningful by the receiver and for the receiver.）（Nord, 2001）目的论的核心在于翻译的目的和译文的功能。

翻译目的论将翻译视为一种人际间的互动活动，涉及译文发起者、译者、原文作者、译文读者等。翻译活动的发起者确定翻译目的和翻译要求（Translation Brief），包括文本功能、译文的目标读者、译文使用时间及场合、译文的传播媒介等。费米尔认为译文读者对于翻译过程起着重要的作用。

翻译目的论的三项基本原则分别是目的原则（Skopos Rule）、连贯原则（Coherence Rule）和忠实原则（Loyalty Principle）。目的原则是决定翻译过程的最主要原则，一切翻译活动都由其目的决定；连贯原则要求译文具有可读性和可接受性，并在译语文化及其交际环境中有意义；忠实原则要求译文与原文之间应具有连贯性，这种忠实不仅意味着忠实传达原文内容，还包括在分析原文的基础上，为实现译文预期功能所进行的必要调整，包括删减甚至改写，使译文被译语语言文化系统所接受，并达到与语篇类型和功能相一致的得体性。这三条原则的关系是：忠实原则服从于连贯原则，而这两者都必须服从于目的原则。

除德国功能翻译学派以外，英国当代翻译理论家纽马克也把翻译与语言功能结合起来进行研究，他将文本分为三种类型。一是表达型（expressive），如文学作品；二是信息型（informative），如报刊文章、学术论文和技术报告；三是呼唤型（vocative），如广告、企业推介等宣传文本。纽马克认为，很少有文本只具备一种功能，大多数文本以一种功能为主，兼有其他功能，如宣传文本具有信息型与呼唤型双重功能，翻译应着重于意义和精神，而不是拘泥于原文的语言形式。纽马克的文本功能分类（text-type）为译者针对不同类型的文本采用不同的翻译策略和方法提供了依据，说明翻译方法和翻译标准是多元化的，没有固定模式。

美国学者奈达同样也从语言功能的角度提出了"功能对等"翻译原则。他指出，由于语言文化上的差异，翻译不可能求得原文与译文的形式对应，而只能是功能上的对等。检验翻译质量优劣的标准是看译文读者与原文读者的感受是否一致。他的功能对等论原则的合理之处在于翻译的服务对象是读者，评判译文质量的优劣，必须看读者的反应如何。奈达认为，"作为职业翻译，最重要的是有效地传递意义，因为意义才是客户确切想要和需要的东西。他们所关心的不是文本的形式特征，而是文本的内容"。

上述功能翻译方面的观点都将翻译活动与文本功能和翻译目的紧密结合在一起，从语言功能的角度说明了文本类型与翻译的关系，形成了功能翻译理论的总体框架。

（二）国内有关应用翻译的研究

近年来，国内有关应用翻译的研究也相当丰富。由于应用翻译的功能性和目的性十分突出，翻译策略大多从文本功能和翻译目的入手。

应用翻译的本质是准确清楚地传达信息。"准确理解，通顺表达"是职业翻译的标准。"准确理解"是指对原文深入、透彻的理解，包括对每一个细节的理解；"通顺表达"是指译文对读者产生的效果与原文相同（李长栓，2009）。

应用翻译是一种以传递信息为主要目的、又注重信息传递效果的实用型翻译，与强调艺术审美和文学欣赏的文学翻译相比，应用文本翻译的本质是传达信息，侧重于事实性信息，其美学和文化信息处于次要的地位，应用文本的翻译要考虑信息传递的效果，因此要对文本信息性质进行辨析，对不同信息的价值度做出判断，决定取舍。

因此，在翻译策略上，应用翻译传递信息往往是有选择性的，或综合地或概要性地或部分地传递。应用翻译，无论是在译法上，还是在译品形式上，可变性更大（方梦之，2003）。

1. 对翻译的诠释

对于翻译的本质，许多学者从不同角度对其做了多种诠释，但其本质是传递信息：

（1）翻译实际上也是用另一种文字对原作进行改写和重写（郭建中，2005）。

（2）汉译英就是"有条件地英文写作"。中国人学习汉译英时，是分析理解用母语写成的原文，按与习惯的思维方式相对立的较陌生的思维方式（外语的思维方式），以较母语能力差的外语能力写成一篇与原文意义相符、功能相似的英语作文（陈宏薇，1998）。

（3）汉英翻译实践模式：A—B—C（Adopt—Borrow—Create，即模仿——借用——创新）。

英语中如果有对应的表达方式，不妨采取拿来主义的态度，照搬不误；英语中如果没有直接对应的表达，可以借鉴参考英语中类似的表达，进行移植和嫁接；英语中如果根本没有对应表达，也就是说需要翻译的词语在英语中属于意义空缺，就需要按照英语的表达习惯进行创造性翻译（丁衡祁，2005）。

例1

<u>原文：</u>

中国有句俗语"赶得早不如赶得巧"，赶上地坛庙会那就是巧。这里蕴含着浓郁的京味文化，教北京人和外地人都喜爱。

<u>译文：</u>

The Earth Temple Fair is a collection of local culture in Beijing and has a strong appeal to people in and outside Beijing.

<u>分析：</u>

原文中所用俗语"赶得早不如赶得巧"只是为了引入一个话题，或

强调作者自己"赶上地坛庙会就是巧"的观点,而"地坛庙会蕴含着京味文化"才是信息传递的重点。英语的景物描写注重客观真实,翻译的本质是传递信息,因此,译者需要根据译文读者的信息需求对原文进行改写。

例2

原文:

中国是世界上第一个以大自然为原型进行园林设计的国家。不仅如此,中国人对大自然的深情挚爱、对大自然的领悟、对自然美的敏感,是极其广泛地渗透到哲学、艺术、文学、绘画的所有文化领域之中,<u>至少已有三千年的历史</u>。中国的这种讴歌大自然的风景园林规划设计的传统美学观念,曾经对全世界产生过巨大影响。

中国雄奇瑰丽的自然风光,是中国古代园林艺术灵感的源泉,值得当今全世界大地规划工作者学习!

译文:

China is the first country in the world to design gardens <u>based on the prototype of nature</u>, <u>with a gardening history of 3000 years</u>. Chinese <u>enthusiasm for</u> and understanding of nature as well as perception of natural beauty have <u>integrated into Chinese culture</u>, in the aspect of philosophy, art, literature, painting and etc. Chinese traditional aesthetics of landscape/garden planning and design, which <u>represent and highlight natural beauty</u>, has exerted a huge influence on the world.

The splendid landscapes in China <u>are the source of inspiration for</u> ancient Chinese gardening art, which <u>is enlightening for</u> the landscape planners worldwide.

分析:

既然汉译英是有条件的英文写作,译文应当符合英语段落发展的习惯。例如,"中国是世界上第一个……的国家"需要事实加以证实,因此"三千年的历史"提前。同时,中文比较喜欢用抽象或空泛的修饰词,译成英文需要用固定搭配的句式表达。

例3

原文:

In the 1990s, the group of industries categorized as education and knowledge creation ranked second in the United States, after business services, in the number of jobs added, as most manufacturing industries continued to decline.

译文：

20世纪90年代，随着大多数制造业的持续衰落，从事教育与知识创新的企业在创造就业机会方面，在美国排名第二，仅次于服务业。

分析：

由于中英文在句型结构与表达方面的差异，译文需要根据译入语的习惯调整句式结构和语序。在英语中，状语位置的变化不影响表达习惯，只是强调的重点不同，而汉语则不同。此处，英文原文强调的是"从事教育与知识创新的企业在创造就业机会方面"的排位。

例4

1999年国庆节之前，我们几个单位的外宣翻译曾研讨过一个看似很小的问题：怎样翻译阅兵仪式上中央领导向部队官兵的问候："同志们好！同志们辛苦了！"和"首长好！"。大家认为，西方国家首长检阅部队时，只敬礼，不讲话，官兵也不喊口号。换句话说，英文中根本不存在相对应的词汇。我们于是决定，不应该用直接引语的方式翻译这三句话，而宜用间接引语的方式说"军委主席向部队官兵问候，官兵向他们的首长致礼"。

遗憾的是，当天还是有国内报道单位机械地把三句话译成："Hello, comrades!" "Comrades, you have worked hard!" 和 "Hello, leader!"。英国朋友指出，这种翻译法无异于说"伙计们，干得不错"和"头儿，您受累了！"（黄友义）。

分析：

英文中没有对应的表达方式，需要变通。

（三）应用文本翻译的目的与策略原则

从应用文本的内容、形式和特征看，应用文本翻译的本质就是传递信息。因此，应用翻译讲究"客观真实""言之有物"，而不是"艺术创造"和"审美体验"；语言表达"准确地道"和"通俗流畅"，注重实用性和交际性，引发读者的阅读意愿，方便读者阅读和获取信息，最大限度地传递信息。

在应用文本的翻译过程中，译者应根据应用翻译的特点，采用相应的翻译策略，而不必在传统的"忠实、通顺"或"信、达、雅"等标准的制约下权衡翻译策略的选择。

不同文本的功能和目的不一样，翻译的要求和标准也不一样。应用文本翻译信息传达的效果取决于读者的民族语言文化、思维方式、期待心理、认知能力等因素，只有充分考虑这些因素的影响，翻译才能达到信息传递的最佳效果。因此，应用文本翻译是一种动态的、可调节的信息传递过程，并非一个简单的"忠实"原则可以概括。

在应用翻译中，译者需要根据不同的文本类型，采取不同的翻译策略，使之适合一般读者阅读。同时，为了提高译文的可读性，便于读者理解掌握，对不完全适合译入语表达的原文和对不符合译入语读者欣赏习惯的描写进行必要的删节或改写，包括简化、虚化、弱化、淡化、改译、调节、移动、增补、删节、阐释、修正等方法，不必对原文进行逐字逐句的翻译。翻译之前，译者需要了解译文的文本功能与目的、目标读者以及信息传播方式等因素，制定相应的翻译策略，或是了解委托人或客户对翻译的要求，根据翻译要求（translation brief）制定翻译策略。

根据上述原则，我们可对应用翻译的可操作性作如下总结：

（1）删略对基本信息不提供实质内容的文字；
（2）删略或简化不必要的解释性文字或读者已知的信息；
（3）删略一般读者易于从文字中推出的信息内容；
（4）删略复合型词组的语义重复性文字；
（5）当出现多项描述或评价性文字说明某个事物时，删略或简化内容比较虚的文字；
（6）当同一或相邻语段内出现两处以上的相同或相似的文字信息，酌情压缩信息。

三、应用翻译译例解析

（一）准确理解原文，包括对每一细节的理解

例5

原文：
Universities do not direct the project of the touristic city, but they are key indicators of its health. The popularity of university campuses and their often

famous buildings as sites of architectural tourism is indicated by Princeton Architectural Press's popular Campus Guide series.

译文1：

虽然大学并不能主导旅游城市的发展，但它们却是城市旅游发展良好与否的关键指标。普林斯顿建筑出版社出版的热门校园导游丛书，公布了作为建筑类旅游景点的大学校园及其著名建筑的受欢迎程度。

译文2：

虽然大学并不能主导旅游城市的发展，但它们却是旅游城市是否健康发展的关键指标，因为大学校园及其建筑已经成为热门旅游景点，普林斯顿建筑出版社出版的热门《校园指南系列丛书》就是最好的例证。

分析：

译文1看似准确，但是第一句与第二句之间似乎没有什么联系，仔细阅读原文可以看出两句话之间有相当的关联性，因此，译文2更能准确传达原文旨意。

（二）掌握文本的主要信息，对原文进行重组、压缩或删减冗余文字和信息

例6

原文：

……首先，从经济上来说，在改革搞活经济中［1］，当前中国正处在计划经济和向计划与市场相结合的商品经济转变过程［2］。旧体制开始松动，商品经济混沌初开［3］，出现经济成分与交往的多样化［4］，人们收入来源的多元化［5］，经济出现了前所未有的活力［6］，社会上出现拜金主义倾向［7］，加之经济管理法制还没相应健全起来［8］，一些牟取暴利的人钻空子，乘机大肆贪污、行贿受贿，腐败现象突然剧增［9］。由于目前新旧经济管理体制并存，在企业与市场上存在价格的双轨制［10］，一些掌握有紧俏商品的实权者，便利用价格差把平价商品改为高价卖出，从中牟利，大发横财［11］。

分析：

译文要做到易于读者获取信息，必须做到经济简明，主题信息突出，因此，译者需要考虑原文的信息价值度和读者的信息需求，同时又要考虑读者的认知能力和语言文化差异。

从信息价值度看，语言单位［1］的信息内容已是国外读者所熟知的

信息，属于冗余信息，而且［1］的信息已被语言单位［2］所蕴含。

语言单位［3］的信息内容同样被［2］所蕴含：既然中国正在向商品经济转型，就必然意味着"旧体制开始松动，商品经济混沌初开"，故［3］为冗余信息。

语言单位［7］中"拜金主义"（贪钱财）是对语言单位［9］信息内容"腐败现象"的评价，属于评价性信息，价值度低，这种评价性信息是不言而喻的：搞腐败的人谁不贪钱财？

语言单位［9］中的"腐败"是一个抽象概括性词语，其语义已经蕴含了贪污、行贿、受贿的信息，corruption 的语义为 dishonest, esp. through accepting bribe（*Oxford Advanced Learners Dictionary*）；dishonest：intended to deceive or cheat；(of money) not honestly obtained（指金钱来路不正）。在语义上，"腐败"是上义词，"贪污、行贿、受贿"等是下义词。在对外宣传翻译中，为了经济简明起见，只要译出其上义词即可，不必将其下义词一一译出。其次，"一些……人钻空子"亦可推论为冗余信息，故不必译出。

另外，仅仅将"双轨制"译成 two-level price systems，英语读者是无法理解的，需要增补信息和释译：the state-owned and the private enterprises compete for materials at different-level prices, for some of the state-owned ones enjoy quota at lower prices under the state plans。

综上所述，对上述原文的翻译应做到信息突出，要做到信息突出就必须语言表达经济简明，弱化或虚化次要信息，避免冗长繁复，以适应译文读者的思维方式和阅读习惯。

译者可综合语言单位［2］、［4］、［6］、［10］、［11］的信息性质生成以下译文。

译文：

China is experiencing an economic shift from an ultra-centralized planned economy to a mixed economy characteristic of the planned and market-oriented elements. As a result, a varied economic practice leads to unprecedented vitality accompanied with a variety of income-making channels for the citizens. However, corruption finds its way in a number of people due to the loose legal systems. Moreover, the co-existence of the old and new economic systems allows the two-level price systems in practice (in which the state-owned and the private enterprises compete for materials at different-level prices, for some of the state-owned ones enjoy quota at lower prices under the state plans), which provides chances for those with power over goods-allocation to profiteer by selling the goods at higher prices. （引自《应用翻译讲义》）

例7

原文：

在中国一提到孔子，<u>上至白发苍苍的老人，下至天真幼稚的顽童，无人不知，无人不晓</u>，人们为了纪念他，在许多地方都建有祭祀他的寺庙，天津也不例外。

译文：

Confucius is <u>a household name</u> in China. Temples in memory of him could be found everywhere in China and Tianjin is no exception. （引自《新编实用翻译教程》）

分析：

译文需要压缩或删减语义重复或冗余的文字，此外，中文画线部分可用一短语 a household name 概括。

例8

原文：

Many academics might be troubled by Campbell's instrumental analysis—<u>certainly, Mario Savio would be</u>—but it would appear that most cities are not. Cities are willing to take the risk of accommodating the expanding power of universities in exchange for access to their capital, managerial skills, and initiative, which their own agencies, hampered by decreased federal and state funding, years of postindustrial decline and disinvestment, and a loss of public trust, cannot bring together.

译文：

很多学者也许会受到坎贝尔分析的困扰，但是大多数城市似乎并不在意。许多城市甘冒风险接纳大学不断扩张势力，以换取大学的资本、管理技能和创意，而这些恰恰是市政当局因为联邦和州政府的财政支持减少、后工业时代多年的衰落、企业撤资和公众信任丧失等原因无法聚集的资源。

分析：

因为这篇文章讨论的是芝加哥大学与所在城市的合作互动，作者在此处想要说明的是其他城市为什么不介意大学扩张势力，但全篇并没有补充说明 Mario Savio 为什么肯定会受其困扰，而且，certainly, Mario Savio would be 与主题关联性不强，中文读者对 Mario Savio 也不熟悉。为了不阻断信息内容或意义的连续性，在这里可以省略不译；如果要译，就需要加注 Mario Savio 的相关信息，否则难以达到传递信息的目的。

例9

原文：
我院拥有一大批具有<u>国内领先水平、国际一流水准</u>的实验室，共有10个国家级重点实验室、15个区域性中心实验室和5个合资合作实验室。

译文：
The Academy operates laboratories of different sizes, 10 of which are recognized as national key labs, 15 are regional laboratory centers, and 5 are joint-venture labs.（引自《商务汉英翻译》）

分析：
"国内领先水平、国际一流水准"的表述太抽象空泛，具体用"国家级重点实验室"和"区域性中心实验室"来体现。

（三）增补与阐释

增补就是在译文中添加一些原文中没有的文字。在原文简约，照直译出不能产生相应的译文效果时，为使译文通顺达意，翻译时常常需要从修辞的角度，按照译语的行文习惯，在译文中适当增词，调整词序以及一些变通手法，增强译文的修辞效果和感染力，称之为"修辞增译"，常用于英译汉。

有时，为了让译文读者更清楚地理解原文的信息，需要将原文的内涵意义加以引申，或添加一定的信息，便于读者理解掌握，称之为"信息增译"，常用于汉译英。

例10

原文：
The expansion of these relationships leads to an intersection of the needs and goals of both the city and the academy "on the ground" (in neighborhoods and communities) and within a "global network" (the space of exchange of goods, services, knowledge, information, an international elite, and large migrating groups).

译文：

这种关系的拓展会导致所在城市与大学在需求与目标方面的对接，这种对接可以是物质层面的（如所在的社区和社群），也可以是全球网络层面的（如货物和服务的<u>交换空间</u>、知识信息的<u>交流空间</u>、国际人才<u>流动和移民迁徙的空间</u>）。

分析：

（1）此处，the space of exchange of 与不同的名词搭配，产生不同的"……空间"。

（2）"on the ground"与 within a "global network"形成对比，"global network"译为全球网络，是虚拟空间或抽象的空间概念，那么"on the ground"就是"物质空间"或"现实空间"。

例 11

原文：

Recording your ideas and observations primarily in pictures instead of words can help you become more creative and <u>constructive on the job</u>, no matter what your level of artistic ability. This <u>show-by-example</u> sourcebook clearly illustrates proven methods and procedures for keeping a highly useful visual notebook.

Crowe and Laseau examine the relationship between note-taking, <u>visualization</u>, and creativity. They give <u>practical guidance on how to develop</u>:

Visual acuity—the ability to see more in what you experience

Visual literacy—expressing yourself clearly and accurately with sketches

Graphic analysis—using sketches to analyze <u>observations</u>

译文：

无论艺术水平高低，用图像而不是文字记录你的思路和观察，可以提高你的创造力和<u>工作成效</u>。这本资料图集，<u>通过实例</u>介绍了如何做视觉笔记的成熟方法和步骤。

Crowe 和 Laseau 通过研究做笔记与形象<u>思维</u>和创造力之间的关系，对开发以下三种<u>能力</u>提出了现实的指导意见：

视觉的敏锐度——从视觉体验中获取更多信息的能力

视觉的表现力——用草图清晰准确地表达自我的能力

图像分析能力——用草图对观察对象进行分析的能力

分析：

此文选自《建筑师和设计师的视觉笔记》一书封底上的图书简介，

语言表达具有很强的宣传风格，根据上下文情景，通过增补与阐释，形成汉语中常用的四字和六字结构词组，从而产生一定的节奏和韵律，读起来朗朗上口，达到句子结构的平衡。例如：

  constructive on the job——工作成效
  show-by-example——通过实例
  observation——观察对象
  visualization——形象思维
  visual acuity——视觉的敏锐度
  visual literacy——视觉的表现力
  graphic analysis——图像分析能力

例 12

  原文：

  Correspondent: When Percy Barnevik became head of the international engineering group ABB, his task was to make globalization work. He decided to divide the business into over a thousand smaller companies. In this way he believed the company could be both global and local. In answering the question "How do you make globalization work?", Percy Barnevik describes the "global glue" that keeps the many different people in ABB together. He then looks at the need to manage the three contradictions of company: it is decentralized but centrally controlled; <u>it is big and small at the same time</u> and it is both global and local.

  Percy Barnevik: We have now for ten years after our big merger created a "global glue" where people are tied together, where they don't internally compete, but support each other, and you have global leaders with global responsibility and your local managers working with their profit centers, and if you have the right, so to say, <u>agenda</u> for these people and the right structure, you can use a scale of economy and <u>your advantages of bigness but being small</u>.
（韩素音青年翻译竞赛，2013）

  分析：

  （1）it is decentralized but centrally controlled 与前面提到的 divide the business into over a thousand smaller companies 相关，将业务划分到千余家分公司运作，便于分散经营和集中控制，这样，it is big and small at the same time 可以理解为大小规模并存、大有规模优势、小有灵活性；而且，

与后面提到的 your advantages of bigness but being small 意义关联。

（2）agenda 直译为"议程"。此处将人才划分为全球性领导者和区域性经理，因此可以理解为"业务分工"。

译文：

记者： 珀西·巴内维克担任国际工程集团 ABB 总裁后，他的任务就是实现全球化运作。他决定将业务划分到千余家子公司运作，相信这样会使公司既全球化又本地化。在回答"您是怎样进行全球化运作的？"这个问题时，珀西·巴内维克描述了他的"全球胶"理念，也就是将各路人才汇聚于 ABB 旗下。接下来他要解决公司面临的三大矛盾：分散经营与集中控制、大小规模并存（既大又小）、全球化与本地化。

珀西·巴内维克： 我们经过大型兼并已经 10 年，创造了一种"全球胶"，我们将人们凝聚在一起，不是相互竞争，而是相互支持。我们有承担全球责任的商业领袖和负责利润中心的地区经理；也就是说，如果我们将人才的业务分工安排得当，管理结构合理，就可以利用规模经济，发挥大企业的规模优势和小企业的灵活性（或者大小规模并存的优势）。

例 13

原文：

琼岛东北部有"琼岛春荫"碑，为 1751 年所建，附近风光秀丽，过去是燕京八景之一。

译文：

In the northeast of Qiongdao Island, there is a stone tablet, erected in 1751, with "Qiong Dao Chun Yin" (Spring Shade on the Qiongdao Island) engraved on it. It is said the inscription was written by Emperor Qianlong (with his reign from 1736 to 1796). This area, noted for its beautiful scenery, was counted as one of the eight outstanding views of Beijing. （引自《实用旅游英语翻译教程》）

分析：

除了对"琼岛春荫"注释外，还增加了 It is said the inscription was written by Emperor Qianlong 这一信息，旨在说明石碑和景点的历史文化价值。

（四）编译

翻译与传媒、写作和说话等方式一样，是获取资讯、交流信息的方式之一,翻译也是信息加工的方式之一。在信息浩繁、工作与生活节奏加快的时代,许多文本需要编译或译写,也就是译者依据原文提供的信息用译入语进行写作,而不应当循规蹈矩地翻译。在此过程中,面对客户的要求和目标读者的实际需求,译者对信息的选取与加工拥有相当大的决定权和编辑权。

编译就是选择最新、相关性最大、目标读者最有可能需要的信息,而将铺垫性的、读者可能已知的或关联性弱的信息省略,便于读者快速获取、掌握和使用信息。译文的使用方法不同,服务的交际目的不同,译文删减和增译的幅度也不同,译文的形式也可以多样化。同时,无论加工幅度大小,编译形成的译文都要确保语法和用词正确。

由于中西文化背景和价值观念存在巨大差异,有些词句和"中国特色"的表述很难翻译,即便费尽心思勉强译出,也不一定能为译文读者所理解与接受,在此情况下,需要对原文有所取舍,不可生搬硬译,有些文本的部分内容最好不译。例如,a former appointed factory of the Ministry of Machinery(原机械工业部所属/指定企业),中文原文是要说明企业实力强、级别高,而直译成英文带来的负面效果是给人以中国市场化程度不高的印象。

在当今智库建设的热潮中,编译在智库的信息建设中发挥着重要作用,关键是要理清用户的信息需求,甄别信息的价值度与关联性,深入挖掘信息的潜在价值,加强信息的适用性和针对性,提高语言服务的质量与效益。

编译是应用翻译的一个重要方式。目前,以编译方式传播的信息量越来越大,缩写英语原文、摘译或编译的新闻与信息、业界动态、相关领域的信息库建设等都是编译的产品,国内的对外宣传也常常采取中英文双语版,针对不同的读者群,制作不同的文本,编译已成为常用的信息处理方式。

例 14

原文:

我们两个公司彼此之间的合作,多年来非常友好。因为我们之间,通过合作能够使得我们带来特别独特的增值。你们在推出新产品,以及在市场大规模推广方面做得非常好。我们非常了解本地的市场,能够把你们的产品推向本地市场,而且能够充分发挥渠道方面的优势。如果这两个公司进行合作的话,确实能够带来很多增值。也就是说我们所做的一切,可以补充你们的工作,你们的工作也能够补充我们的工作,成为中国市场发展的强大的推动力。

译文:

For many years, the cooperation between the two companies is remarkable, which has brought unique increment/added value. Intel does extremely well in introducing new products, upgrading computer platform systems/infrastructure and promoting sales. Thanks to its sufficient knowledge of the local market, our company is capable to localize global products and give full play to its advantages in sale channels. Therefore, the cooperation of the two companies will surely bring more increment because of economic complementarities and therefore become the powerful driving force in the Chinese PC market. (引自《商务汉英翻译》)

分析:

编译是一个梳理、缩写、简化、释义原文的过程,但是,编译并不意味着编译后的译文总是比原文简短,编译的目的是使信息更容易为读者理解掌握。这个实例中,中文文本在语言表达上淡化商业利益,从宏观上谈合作,为了加强信息的针对性,英文文本需要使双方的合作与受益具体化。

例 15

原文:

http://www.factcheck.org/2012/02/did-obama-approve-bridge-work-for-chinese-firms/

FactCheck. org

A Project of the Annenberg Public Policy Center

Did Obama "Approve" Bridge Work for Chinese Firms?

Posted on February 17, 2012

1 Q: Is President Obama responsible for Chinese companies building U.S. bridges with stimulus money, as reported by ABC News?

2 A: No. A viral email distorts an ABC News report. California officials hired a Chinese contractor and rejected federal money to avoid federal "Buy American" laws.

3　FULL QUESTION

4　Is this true?

5　Diane Sawyer reporting on U. S. bridge projects going to the Chinese... NOT Americans.

6　The bridges are right here in the U. S. and yet Obama has approved for Chinese contractors to come in and do the work. What about jobs for Americans?

7　U. S. A. Bridges and Roads Being Built by Chinese Firms

8　FULL ANSWER

9　This email is an example of how things get distorted and go viral — even when the facts are just a click away. It's true that ABC News did a <u>report</u> on Chinese firms winning contracts to repair U. S. bridges. But the report pointedly said states were to blame. It didn't mention federal funds — let alone stimulus funds — except to note that California turned down federal money to avoid federal "Buy American" laws and hire a Chinese firm.

10　In a Sept. 23, 2011, broadcast, ABC News reported on bridge repair contracts going to Chinese firms in three states: Alaska, New York and California. But it gave details on only one project — a $7. 2 billion repair of the San Francisco-Oakland Bay Bridge. ABC News explained how and why the Chinese firm wound up with the contract, beginning with a decision by the California transportation department not to accept federal funds.

11　ABC News, Sept. 23, 2011: U. S. law actually requires major infrastructure projects to Buy America when the cost difference is reasonable. In California, U. S. firms say they would have met those guidelines. But state officials decided to turn down federal money for a major part of the bridge, allowing a Chinese company to get the job.

12　ABC News interviewed a CalTrans official who said the Chinese firm could provide the fabricated bridge decks more quickly because U. S. firms don't have enough welders. The broadcast failed to note, however, that only some jobs, not all, will go to China as a result. And taxpayers saved a bundle. From a <u>story</u> in the *New York Times* last year:

13　*New York Times*, June 25, 2011: The assembly work in California, and the pouring of the concrete road surface, will be done by Americans. But construction of the bridge decks and the materials that went into them are a

Made in China affair. California officials say the state saved hundreds of millions of dollars by turning to China.

14 California decided not to apply for federal funding for the project because the "Buy America" provisos would probably have required purchasing more expensive steel and fabrication from United States manufacturers.

15 At the end of his report, ABC News reporter Chris Cuomo says, "That's why the Buy America laws were passed. If states can get around them, Diane, we'll never bring America back." (By the way, Cuomo is the son of former New York Gov. Mario Cuomo, a Democrat.)

16 The broadcast mentioned a $400 million project to repair the Alexander Hamilton Bridge in New York, but it provided no details on it.

17 The New York Times did a short story on China Construction America, the company that won the Alexander Hamilton Bridge contract. The Times story said the logo of the company—a New Jersey-based subsidiary of a state-controlled construction company in China — "is becoming a familiar sight at public works projects around New York City." It also said the company employs 500 employees in the U.S. and hires only union workers at New York City job sites. *The Times* did not, however, say whether any federal funding was involved.

18 The third project — a $190 million project in Alaska—went unnamed in the ABC News broadcast. However, it was named in a longer, print version of Cuomo's report that ran on ABC News' website that same day. In that report, ABC News said Alaska was "set to spend millions on foreign materials for the Tanana River Bridge Crossing and would largely fabricate the bridge overseas." The article did not say whether any federal money would be used on the Alaska project. However, we found that it does involve federal money…

译文：

宾夕法尼亚大学安嫩伯格公共政策研究中心调查报告——

奥巴马是否"批准"将美国的桥梁工程承包给中国企业

2012 年 2 月 17 日

问题：奥巴马是否应当对美国桥梁工程被中国企业承包负责？而且涉及联邦刺激经济专项资金，ABC 的报道是否属实？

答案：否。一个病毒邮件歪曲了 ABC 的报道。加州官方为了规避"购买美国货"的法案，拒绝联邦资金，选择了中国承包商。

2011年9月23日，ABC新闻报道了中国企业承担了美国三个州的桥梁维修工程，包括阿拉斯加、纽约州和加利福尼亚州。但是，ABC只详细报道了旧金山的奥克兰海湾大桥维修项目，造价72亿美元，中国公司最终获得该项目是因为加州交通部门决定不接受联邦资金，以摆脱联邦法律"购买美国货"的限制。

根据ABC的报道：美国法律要求，在价格差异合理的情况下，重大基础设施项目必须购买美国货。加州的一些公司表示，他们原本可以达到这些标准，但是加州政府决定拒绝联邦资金，让中国公司承担桥梁主体维修工程。

加州交通局的一位官员表示，中国公司可以更快地提供桥面预制板，而美国公司没有足够的焊工。然而，该报道没有提到，并非所有工程都由中国公司承包。结果是，为纳税人节省了一大笔钱，这一点可以从去年的《纽约时报》看到。

2011年6月25日《纽约时报》报道：组装工程和混凝土路面浇筑工程由美国公司完成，但是桥面预制板工程和建材由中国公司承担。官方表示，启用中国公司，加州政府节省了数亿美元。

若接受联邦资金，就必须购买高价的美国产钢材和预制件。

ABC报道的结尾说，"这就是为什么'购买美国货'的法规落空了，但是如果各州都能绕过它，美国货就永远回不来了。"

该报道还提到纽约市亚历山大·汉密尔顿大桥维修项目，造价4亿美元，但没有提供更多细节。

《纽约时报》对该大桥的承包商中建美国分公司做了简短报道，这家中国国有建筑企业新泽西分公司的标志"在纽约市市政工程工地上随处可见"；报道还说，该公司在美国的雇员达到500人，而且，纽约市的工地只雇佣来自行业工会的工人。但是，报道没有提到是否涉及联邦资金。

第三个项目位于阿拉斯加，造价1.9亿美元。据ABC网站的报道，需要进口数千万美元的建筑材料和预制构件，而且，根据我们的调查，涉及联邦资金……

分析：

首先，译者需要确定译文的文本功能、目标读者及其信息需求。从文本内容来看，这篇调查报告旨在回答媒体和公众对于美国工程被外国公司承包、美国人失去工作机会的质疑；同时，报告也从侧面反映了当今中国企业走出去面临的巨大挑战。因此，译文的目标读者应该是政府相关部门、国内智库的研究人员和企业的决策与管理层。译文提供的信息关联性要强。例如，中国企业如何获得项目、面对的困难和应对对策、成功的经验与失败的教训等。如果信息来自国外重要的智库报告或主流媒体的报道，应当特别标注信息来源。

第1、2段说明了调研报告的起因，应当完整翻译。

第3～9段说明了一个病毒邮件如何歪曲了ABC的报道，与目标读者的信息需求关系不大，可以略去。这说明译者应当全面深入地阅读和理解原文，但是没有必要逐字逐句地进行翻译。

第10～15段阐述了中国企业海外承包面临的挑战与障碍：美国法律规定的"购买美国货"条款，中国公司获得项目的原因之一，造价低、速度快。这里有五个问题需要具体说明：首先，第10段最后一句增译"以摆脱联邦法律'购买美国货'的限制"，这是根据第14段的内容进行增译的，旨在说明加州政府拒绝联邦资金的原因，因此，增译不是随意的。其二，为了突出主题信息，段落和句式的表述应当经济简明，略去关联性不强的文字。因此，第12段，ABC News interviewed a CalTrans official who said 可简述为："加州交通局的一位官员表示"；同样，第15段，At the end of his report, ABC News reporter Chris Cuomo says 可简述为："ABC报道的结尾说"。其三，第12段最后一句 From a story in the *New York Times* last year："这一点可以从去年的《纽约时报》看到"（或：这一点可以从去年《纽约时报》的一则报道中得以证实），调查报告用一则新闻报道来说明事实，同时，这句话的作用是承上启下。其四，第13段与第14段内容衔接紧密，为了表达上下文中清晰的逻辑关系，中文翻译可以将两段缩写成一段，而英文写作则可以根据论述的层次分段。其五，By the way, Cuomo is the son of former New York Gov. Mario Cuomo, a Democrat 与主题关联性不强，可以删略。

第16段提供了另一座桥梁维修工程信息，正是目标读者，即企业的决策与管理层需要的信息，应当翻译。

第17段阐述了中国公司获得项目的原因之二，实现本地化运作，包括企业形象宣传本地化和用人本地化。例如，打出中建新泽西分公司的标志，而不是中建总公司；在当地雇佣行业工会的会员。这些都是主题关联性很强的信息，应当全部翻译。另外，China Construction America 怎样译？如果将 China Construction 输入百度查询，可以查出是指中国建筑工程总公司，简称中建总公司。

同理，第18段提供了阿拉斯加的一座桥梁维修工程信息，也是目标读者需要的信息，要酌情进行翻译，但是，没有必要将"ABC新闻没有报道，然而，当天ABC新闻网站上有文字报道"一一译出。（…went unnamed in the ABC News broadcast. However, it was named in a longer, print version of Cuomo's report that ran on ABC News' website that same day.）也没有必要说明 The article did not say whether any federal money would be used on the Alaska project，只要译出"根据我们的调查，涉及联邦资金"即可。(However, we found that it does involve federal money…)

总之，编译的目的是为目标读者节省时间，方便读者快速获取、掌握和使用信息，这就要求译者要不断储备与丰富相关专业知识和阅历，才能对信息性质做出准确的甄别与判断，挖掘潜在的信息价值，实现语言服务的增值。同时，为了实现主题信息突出，信息的逻辑性与关联性强，经济简明策略需要贯彻在译写的整个过程之中，学习编译的过程也是学习一种工作方法。

第三章　信息查询技巧在应用文本翻译中的作用

一、引言

在翻译实践中，面对题材各异的文本信息和众多知识点，怎样准确理解和通顺传达信息，对译者是一个挑战，涉及译者的资料查询和筛选能力、获取专业知识的能力以及翻译策略等诸多方面。所谓获取专业知识的能力，是指在阅读原文的过程中，译者在脑海中要逐步建立起与文本内容相关的专业知识的基本概念和发展脉络，并运用这些专业知识进行思辨，这样才能沿着原文作者的知识体系、逻辑推理和论证思辨进行翻译，特别是在翻译专业性较强的文本时更是如此，译者只有渗入相关专业领域，才能寻找到专业的表达方式，查找和筛选准确的信息。而且，对译者来说，找到专业知识的切入点对建构相关专业知识的基本概念和发展脉络，理解和掌握各个知识点，从而产生贴近原文的译文至关重要。

"第24届韩素音青年翻译竞赛"英译汉就是一个典型例证，该文本涉及社会科学、建筑、城市设计与规划等方面的专业知识和术语，是对译者的阅读理解能力、资料查询和筛选能力、获取专业知识的能力和综合运用能力的全面考验。同时，该文本又具有相当的学术性，译者需要找到对应的学术语言进行转换，努力使译文对读者产生的效果与原文相同。

二、从语境中获取专业信息

竞赛原文语言精练，涉及专业知识广泛，为译者准确理解原文带来相当大的困难。因此，译者在阅读原文的过程中，首先要找到与文本内容相关的专业知识的切入点，逐步建构专业知识的基本概念，弄清发展脉络，并以此为基点向专业领域渗透，才能准确把握信息，以专业的视角进行分析与判断，使译文沿着原作的逻辑思维脉络展开。

对于没有建筑专业知识的译者来说，通读原文可以帮助译者初步了解原作旨意，但还不足以找到与文本内容相关的专业知识的切入点。那么，逐段阅读，仔细读完前 4 段，并将 1~4 段作为一个整体来探究，原作的思路渐渐清晰。

例 1

1 We tend to view architecture <u>as permanent</u>, <u>as aspiring to the status of monuments</u>. And that kind of architecture has its place. But so does architecture of a different sort.

2 For most of the first decade of the 2000s, <u>architecture was about the statement building</u>. Whether it was a controversial memorial or an impossibly luxurious condo tower, <u>architecture's raison d'être was to make a lasting impression</u>. Architecture has always been synonymous with permanence, but should it be?

3 In the last few years, the opposite may be true. Architectural billings are at an all-time low. Major commissions are few and far between. The architecture that's been making news is fast and fleeting: pop-up shops, food carts, marketplaces, performance spaces. And while many manifestations of the genre have jumped the shark (i.e., a Toys R Us pop-up shop), there is undeniable opportunity in the temporary: it is an apt response to a civilization in flux. And like many prevailing trends — collaborative consumption (a.k.a., "sharing"), community gardens, barter and trade — "temporary" is so retro that it's become radical.

4 In November, I had the pleasure of moderating Motopia, a panel at University of Southern California's School of Architecture, with Robert Kronenburg, an architect, professor at University of Liverpool and <u>portable/ temporary/mobile</u> guru. Author of a shelf full of books on the topic, including *Flexible*: *Architecture that Responds to Change*, *Portable Architecture*: *Design and Technology* and *Houses in Motion*: *The Genesis*, Kronenburg is a man obsessed.

分析：

从原文可以看出，作者将建筑分为两大类——永久性建筑（permanent）和临时性建筑（temporary），用对比的手法凸显两者的特征与差异，这正是专业知识的切入点，弄清这两类建筑的基本特征和相互关系，才能沿着作者的思路译写。

作者认为，永久性建筑像纪念碑一样持久永恒，（as permanent, as

aspiring to the status of monuments 第 1 段），这类建筑的存在是为了制造持久的影响力（architecture's raison d'être was to make a lasting impression 第 2 段），因此，这样的建筑就是彰显自我之建构体（architecture was about the statement building 第 2 段）；临时性建筑具有移动和便携的特征，处于动态的变化之中（portable, mobile, in motion 第 4 段）。

下面逐段进行分析：

We tend to view architecture **as permanent, as aspiring to the status of monuments**. And that kind of architecture has its place. But so does architecture of a different sort.

译文 1：

我们往往会认为建筑物就该是永久性的，甚至希望达到与纪念碑相提并论的地位。此类建筑固然占有一席之地，但另一类建筑同样有其存在的价值。

分析：

对照原文，这段译文与原文很贴切。但是如果不读原文，只读译文的话，就会感觉意思不够明确。而且，译文的语言风格不够简练。

本段，作者用精练的语言对建筑类型进行了划分，同理，译文也尽可能贴近原作的语言风格。作者将永久性建筑比作纪念碑（as…as…），而纪念碑的意义在于"持久永恒""崇高伟大"和"具有纪念意义"，这类建筑有其存在的必然性（that kind of architecture has its place）。

第 1 句中的 aspiring to 意为 hoping, desiring，希望达到某种目标或境界。直译：希望建筑物达到纪念碑一样的境地，也就是像纪念碑那样持久永恒。因此可以改译成如下译文。

译文 2：

我们希望建筑像纪念碑一样持久永恒，这类建筑出自必然，但是另一类建筑也是如此。

For most of the first decade of the 2000s, **architecture was about the statement building**. Whether it was a controversial memorial or an impossibly luxurious condo tower, **architecture's raison d'être was to make a lasting impression**. Architecture has always been synonymous with permanence, but should it be?

译文 1：

在 21 世纪头 10 年的大部分时间里，建筑艺术就是要使建筑物起到某种昭示作用。无论是颇具争议的纪念碑，还是奢华程度令人难以想象的公寓大厦，建筑存在的理由就是要给人留下难以磨灭的印象。建筑从来就是"永久性"的同义词。但是，它果真应该是如此吗？

分析：

怎样理解 architecture was about the statement building？这里的 architecture 和 it 同指像 memorial 和 condo tower 那样的永久性建筑。statement building 直译是"宣言书式的建筑"，但是宣言什么？"昭示"什么？考虑到下一句 architecture's raison d'être was to make a lasting impression，意为这类建筑的存在是为了制造持久的影响力。因此，这句话可以直译为"建筑就是彰显自我之建构体"。建筑只有表现自我，也就是建筑的投资人或建筑师通过建筑表现自己的愿望、理想和设计天赋，展示财富和权威，如庄严雄伟、经典高雅、时代精神、鹤立鸡群、高技术派、独具风格、具有纪念意义等，才能给人留下深刻的印象，制造持久的影响力。因此可以改译成如下译文。

译文2：

21世纪前10年的大部分时间里，建筑的目的就是彰显自我，无论是颇具争议的纪念碑，还是极尽奢华的高层公寓，建筑的存在就是为了制造持久的影响力，建筑一直以来就是"永久"的同义词。但是建筑就应当"永久"吗？

In the last few years, the opposite may be true. **Architectural billings are at an all-time low**. **Major commissions are few and far between**. The architecture that's been making news is fast and fleeting: pop-up shops, food carts, marketplaces, performance spaces. And while many <u>manifestations of the genre</u> have jumped the shark (i. e., a Toys R Us pop-up shop), there is undeniable opportunity in the temporary: it is an apt response to a civilization in flux. And like many prevailing trends — collaborative consumption (a. k. a., "sharing"), community gardens, barter and trade — "**temporary**" is so retro that it's become radical.

译文1：

在过去的几年中，实际情形也许恰恰相反。建筑业的经济效益可以说是空前的不景气，承担大型建筑项目的机会寥寥无几，而那些备受媒体瞩目的建筑也只是来去匆匆，像游击商店、食品车、市场、演出场地等。虽然许多此类风格的建筑早已成明日黄花（如"玩具反斗城"游击店），但临时性建筑的机遇是无可否认的：这是对日新月异的文明现象的恰当回应。就如同合作消费（或"分享制"）、社区田园、易物交易等许多流行的做法那样，"临时性"建筑如此趋于回归，俨然非同一般，令人刮目相看。

分析：

第3段有几个理解的重点。

（1）Architectural billings are at an all-time low 与 Major commissions are few and far between 互为因果关系，bill 的字典释义是 send a bill to，给……开账单。建筑业的账单就意味着建筑业的投资，而"大型建筑项目委托寥寥无几"既是建筑投资低迷的原因，也是其结果，正因为如此，造价低廉的临时性建筑才有了发展空间。

（2）manifestation 的字典释义是 the act of showing or making clear，表明、显示；genre 的字典释义是 form, style 此处是指前面提到的 pop-up shops, food carts, marketplaces, performance spaces 这类临时性建筑。因此，many manifestations of the genre 是指临时性建筑形式或风格的种种表现。

（3）"temporary" 在此处是指临时性建筑理念的回归。因此可以译成如下译文。

译文2：

近几年，情况可能正好相反。建筑投资一直低迷，大型建筑项目委托寥寥无几。其他跃入媒体视线的建筑形式如过眼云烟，转瞬即逝，例如，零售快闪店、流动食品车、市场、演艺场所等。尽管这类建筑的种种表现已失去吸引力——例如"玩具反斗城"，但是，临时性建筑的发展空间毋庸置疑，因为这是对处于变革之中的文明进程做出的恰如其分的反应。与当今许多流行趋势一样，例如，"合作消费"（又称之为"分享"）、"社区花园""易货市场"，"临时性"理念回归建筑已成为一种趋势。

弄清了这两种建筑（永久性建筑和临时性建筑）的基本特征和差异，文中涉及的许多专业知识和信息就比较容易查找和判断了。

例2

Mobility has an innate **potency**, Kronenburg believes. **Movable environments** are more dynamic than **static ones**, so why should architecture be so static? The idea that perhaps all buildings shouldn't aspire to permanence represents a huge shift for architecture. Without that **burden**, architects, designers, builders and developers can take advantage of and implement current technologies faster. Architecture could be reusable, recyclable and sustainable. **Recast in this way, it could better solve seemingly unsolvable problems. And still succeed in creating a sense of place.**

译文1:

克罗能伯格认为，可移动性有一种内在的生发力。既然可移动的环境要比静止的更具有活力，为什么建筑物就非得静止不动呢？或许并非所有的建筑物都应追求永恒，这一观点标志着建筑设计的巨大转变。摆脱了传统的束缚，建筑师、设计师、建造者和开发商就能更快地利用当前新技术之长，并付诸实施。建筑是可再利用、可循环、可持续的。以此方式重新定位和着手，一些看似解决不了的问题就可以迎刃而解，这样的建筑物仍能给人们带来身临其境的感觉。

分析：

本段有几个理解的重点。

(1) potency 的词典释义是 the power to influence, the strength of the effect of something，在此可以理解成动力、效力、活力。

(2) mobility（移动性）创造 movable environments（动态环境），那么，static ones 就是静态环境。

(3) the idea 是指 perhaps all buildings shouldn't aspire to permanence 的建筑理念。

那么 burden 就是求恒逐稳的传统设计理念。

(4) architects, designers, builders and developers，这里的 builders 直译为建设者，是指施工单位，可译为承建商、承包商。

(5) 由于建筑可以重复循环利用和可持续发展（Architecture could be reusable, recyclable and sustainable），因此 recast in this way 意指重塑建筑理念。

(6) 作者认为，移动性建筑创造动态环境；反之，永久性建筑创造静态环境，有场地感（sense of place）。但是，动态环境比静态环境更具活力（Movable environments are more dynamic than static ones, so why should architecture be so static?），而且同样能创造建筑的场地感。此处，将 creating a sense of place 译为"给人们带来身临实地的感觉"与实际语境不符。

译文2：

克罗能伯格认为，移动性本身蕴含内在的动力。既然动态环境比静态环境更具活力，建筑为什么非得静止不动呢？或许并非所有建筑都应该追求永恒。这种观点标志着建筑理念发生了重大转变，摆脱了传统设计理念的束缚，建筑师、设计师、承建商和开发商就能够更快地利用与实施新技术，从而使建筑可以重复利用、再循环和可持续发展。若能如此重塑建筑理念，看似无法解决的问题便可迎刃而解，并且同样能创造建筑的"场地感"。

三、如何查找和筛选信息

面对众多的信息来源，如何查找和筛选信息对译者也是一个挑战，译者只有对相关专业知识有更深入的了解，对信息筛选才能更有把握，提供准确信息。另外，查询信息需要选择与输入准确的关键词，对于陌生的事物，译者还可以借助图像（image）或 DV 作参考，这对于还未能走出国门的译者了解外部世界很有帮助，体现了一种探究式的翻译方式和学习过程。

例3

再来分析一下第 3 段中的 pop-up shops。

分析：

pop-up shops 又称为 pop-up store, pop-up retail, flash retailing, guerrilla store，网上的相关介绍很多。仅从 Wikipedia, the free encyclopedia 就能查到很多信息，需要译者加以整理。

Pop-up retail, also known as pop-up store (pop-up shop in the UK and Australia) or flash retailing, is a trend of opening short-term sales spaces in Canada, the United States, the United Kingdom and Australia.

A pop-up retail space is a venue that is temporary —involving "popping-up" one day, then disappearing anywhere from one day to several weeks later. They are often used by marketers for seasonal items such as Halloween costumes, decorations, or Christmas gifts and etc.

There are different benefits to Popups, marketing, testing products, locations, or markets, and as a low cost way to start a business. Some are seasonal, others go on to sign long term leases, and some use it as creative engagement.

还可以在 Yahoo 上查找图像，借助图像帮助译者理解掌握，从而产生贴近原文的译文。

译文：

零售/时尚商品格子间（商场或购物中心中按照尺寸租赁的产品展示与销售场地或空间，如图1所示）、时尚潮店、零售/品牌商品游击店、快闪店、品牌/线下体验店（如图2—图4所示）。

图1　Samsung Galaxy S III launches here in the UK　　图2　H&M Beach pop-up store

图3　pop-up store bus concept　　图4　Adidas pop-up store looks like a giant shoebox

例4

In November, I had the pleasure of moderating **Motopia**, a panel at University of Southern California's School of Architecture, with Robert Kronenburg, an architect, professor at University of Liverpool and **portable/temporary/mobile** guru. Author of a shelf full of books on the topic, including *Flexible: Architecture that Responds to Change*, *Portable Architecture: Design and Technology* and *Houses **in Motion**: The Genesis*, Kronenburg is a man obsessed.

Motopia——移动乌托邦

分析：

Motopia 看似与 Utopia 相关，但是，何为"移动乌托邦"？由于本文的主题是移动式建筑（portable/temporary/mobile），在此语境下的 Motopia 的含义需要进一步查证。在 Yahoo 上输入关键词：Motopia, a panel at University of Southern California's School of Architecture，获得的信息与原文正好相互印证。

<u>Motopia: A New Age of Modular Construction</u>, an event put on by USC's <u>School of Architecture</u>, will bring together today's most creative designers of mobile architecture and examine solutions to current economic, social and environmental concerns in the housing industry; identify emerging technologies and trends; and synthesize recent advancements in design, manufacturing, materials and systems. ——Archidaily 06 Sep. 2011

从这条信息我们可以看出，模块化结构或建构技术（<u>Modular Construction</u>）是实现移动式和便携式建筑的手段，为了传达确切信息，在翻译中可以对 Motopia 作注释性增译。

译文：

本人有幸在 11 月份与利物浦大学教授、建筑师罗伯特·克罗能伯格共同主持了一个主题为"Motopia——模块化结构新时代"的研讨会。他在便携式、临时性、移动型建筑方面的研究成果卓著，包括《灵活性：应对变化的建筑》《便携式建筑：设计与技术》《移动型住宅的起源》，可谓沉迷其中。

例 5

In his presentation, Kronenburg offered examples of how portable, temporary architecture has been used in every aspect of human activity, including health care (from **Florence Nightingale's redesigned hospitals** to the **Airstream trailers** used as mobile medical clinics during the Kennedy Administration), housing (from yurts to tents to architect **Shigeru Ban's post-earthquake paper houses**), culture and commerce (stage sets and **Great Exhibition** buildings, **centuries-old Bouquinistes** along the Seine, **mobile food**, art and music venues offering everything from the recording of stories to tasty crème brulees).

这一段里有几个信息点需要查询。

（1）Florence Nightingale's redesigned hospitals

译文1：

南丁格尔重新设计的医院。

分析：

我们知道，南丁格尔是现代护理学的创始人，但是，关于南丁格尔设计医院却鲜有听说，而且原文使用了 hospitals，那就是说她设计的医院不止一家。为了信息准确，需要查询网络资源。

首先在 Yahoo 上输入 Florence Nightingale，得到一则信息，但是单靠一个信息源还不足以说明问题：

…that she came to understand that most of the soldiers at the hospital were killed by poor sanitary living conditions. This experience influenced her later career, when she advocated sanitary living conditions as a priority for hospitals. Through her advocacy and attention to the sanitary design of hospitals, she reduced deaths in the army during peacetime. —Wikipedia, the free encyclopedia

需要再搜索一个信息源相互佐证，接着输入关键词 Florence Nightingale's redesigned hospitals，得到另一则信息：

In the post-war period, Nightingale began studying new designs for modern hospitals all over Europe, in order to help the army reform its health and sanitary systems. In Paris she found a revolutionary design in which separate units, or pavilions, made up one large hospital. By making each pavilion a light and airy self-contained unit, the hospital minimized the spread of infections. She later succeeded in promoting this design in England. —Historynet. com

从这两则信息中我们可以判断，为了改善医院卫生条件，阻断病菌传播，南丁格尔倡导推广一种由采光通风良好的独立单元构成的大型医院（separate units, or pavilions, made up one large hospital; making each pavilion a light and airy self-contained unit）。

译文2：

南丁格尔倡导的新型医院。

（2）airstream trailers

从百度或 Yahoo 上可以查到，airstream trailers 意为"清风房车"（如图所示）。

第三章　信息查询技巧在应用文本翻译中的作用

图5　airsream trailers

图6　cardboard house

（3）Shigeru Ban's post-earthquake paper houses

译文：

坂茂设计的震后纸板/筒房。如图6、图7所示。

分析：

只要将 Shigeru Ban's post-earthquake paper houses 输入 Yahoo 就能得到图文并茂的信息。

Shigeru Ban is a Japanese architect, known for his innovative work with paper, particularly recycled cardboard tubes used to quickly and efficiently house disaster victims.

图7　paper tube church

图8　crystal palace

（4）Great Exhibition

译文：

国际博览会。

分析：

从百度、谷歌和 Yahoo 上可以查到，Great Exhibition 特指1851年在伦敦举办的第一届万国工业博览会，从文字描述和图片上可以看出，Great Exhibition building 是一座巨大的单体建筑/展馆，称之为"水晶宫"（Crystal Palace，如图8所示）。而此处 Great Exhibition buildings 用了复数，

49

应当泛指国际博览会展馆。我们知道，大多数世博会展馆都是临时性建筑。

(5) bouqinistes along the Seine

译文：

塞纳河沿岸的流动旧书摊。（如图9所示）

分析：

从Yahoo可以查到相关文字与图片资料。

The Bouquinistes of Paris, France, are booksellers of used and antiquarian books who ply their trade along large sections of the banks of the Seine. The tradition of the second-hand booksellers began around the 16th century. The Seine is thus described as "the only river in the world that runs between two bookshelves." ——Wikipedia, the free encyclopedia

图9　塞纳河沿岸的流动旧书摊

(6) mobile food

分析：

从Yahoo图片查询可以看出，mobile food 和 food carts（第3段）同指流动饮食摊点，前者可译为"流动食品摊点"，后者可译为"流动食品车"。如图10所示。

图10　流动食品车

译文：

克罗能伯格在演讲中列举了便携式、移动型建筑用于人类活动方方面面的实例，包括医疗（从弗罗伦斯·南丁格尔倡导的新型医院，到肯尼迪执政时期用作流动医疗诊所的"清风房车"）、居住（从蒙古包到帐篷，再到建筑师坂茂设计的震后纸板/筒房），以及文化与商业设施（如各种舞台布景、国际博览会展馆、塞纳河沿岸具有百年历史传统的流动旧书摊、流动食品摊点、出售各种商品的艺术与音乐场所，从录音故事到美味的焦糖奶油布丁，应有尽有）。

例 6

This is as true for development and city planning as it is for architecture. City-making may have happened all at once at the desk of master planners like <u>Daniel Burnham or Robert Moses</u>, but that's really not the way things happen today. No single master plan can anticipate the evolving and varied needs of an increasingly diverse population or achieve the resiliency, responsiveness and flexibility that <u>shorter-term, experimental endeavors</u> can. Which is not to say long-term planning doesn't have its place. The two work well hand in hand. Mike Lydon, founding principal of <u>The Street Plans Collaborative</u>, argues for injecting spontaneity into urban development, and sees these temporary interventions (what he calls "tactical urbanism") as short-term actions to effect long-term change.

译文：

建筑尚且如此，城市开发与规划更不用说。从前，城市建设蓝图可能在丹尼尔·伯纳姆或罗伯特·摩西那样的规划大师的案台上一气呵成，但如今的情形已全然不同了。面对人口构成的日益多元化，需求也在不断变化，没有一个总体规划可以预测种种不同需求，做到应变自如，灵活应对，这些短期规划与探索实验都能做到。这并不是说长远规划没有立足之地，而是两者相辅相成。SPC 公司创始人麦克·莱登主张将自发性注入城市开发，认为这些临时介入（他称之为"策略性城市主义"）作为短期行为，足以引发长远的变化。

分析：

（1）Daniel Burnham or Robert Moses

通过信息搜索可知，丹尼尔·伯纳姆和罗伯特·摩西都是 20 世纪美国的建筑与规划大师，因此，City-making may have happened all at once at the desk of master planners 意指从前、过去的规划。

Daniel Hudson Burnham (September 4, 1846—June 1, 1912) was an American architect and urban designer. He was the Director of Works for the World's Columbian Exposition in Chicago.

Robert Moses (December 18, 1888 – July 29, 1981) was a public official who worked mainly in the New York metropolitan area, known as the "master builder" of mid-20th century New York City.

(2) shorter-term, experimental endeavors 意指"近期/短期规划与探索尝试,与 master plan 或 long-term planning 对应。

(3) The Street Plans Collaborative

译文 1：
街道规划协会。

译文 2：
SPC 公司。

分析：
根据网上查询的以下两则信息,The Street Plans Collaborative 是一家兼具研究功能的设计规划公司,在迈阿密、纽约和旧金山都有事务所。

Mike Lydon is a Principal of The Street Plans Collaborative, an award-winning planning, design, and research-advocacy firm based in Miami, New York City, and San Francisco.

Mike Lydon is a Principal with Street Plans and leads the firm's New York City office. Mike is an internationally recognized planner, writer, speaker, and advocate for livable cities.

例 7

Though there's been tremendous media attention given to quick and cheap projects like **San Francisco's Pavement to Parks** and New York's "gutter cafes," **Lydon sees something bigger than fodder for the style section**. "A lot of these things were not just fun and cool," he says. "It was not just a bottom-up effort. It's not D.I.Y. urbanism. It's a continuum of ideas, techniques and tactics being employed at all different scales."

这一段里有个信息点和难点需要解决。

(1) San Francisco's Pavement to Parks

译文：
旧金山的"路边景观空间项目"。（如图 11 所示）
分析：
从 Yahoo 查找到如下文字和图片信息。

San Francisco's Pavement to Parks Program facilitates the conversion of utilitarian and often underused spaces in the street into publicly accessible open spaces available for all to enjoy. The Parklet Program provides a path for merchants, community organizations, business owners, and residents to take individual actions in the development and beautification of the City's public realm.

A parklet repurposes part of the street into a space for people. Parklets are intended as aesthetic enhancements to the streetscape, providing an economical solution to the need for increased public open space. They provide amenities like seating, planting, bike parking, and art. —Pavement to Parks：Plazas & Public Space, sfpavementtoparks. sfplanning. org/parklets. html

图 11　不同形式的路边公共景观空间

（2）Lydon sees something bigger than fodder for the style section.
译文 1：
但莱登所看到的不仅仅是那些满足时尚栏目的东西。
分析：
fodder 的字典释义是 things or people used for supplying a continuous demand of the stated kind, 源源不断的供应物（供应者），在此处特指那些不起眼的建筑，如前一句提到的快速便捷、造价低廉的项目（quick and cheap projects like San Francisco's Pavement to Parks and New York's "gutter cafes"），它们可以是临时性建筑。紧接着，作者又说，"许多这样的建筑

不只是为了好玩和耍酷（A lot of these things were not just fun and cool），而是多种理念、技术和谋略相互融合的统一体（It's a continuum of ideas, techniques and tactics being employed at all different scales）。因此，这句话可译为：但莱登所看到的不仅仅是那些表现风格与时尚的建筑小品。

译文2：

尽管媒体对快速便捷、造价低廉的项目给予了极大关注，例如旧金山的"路边景观空间项目"和纽约的"路边咖啡馆"，但莱登所看到的不仅仅是那些表现风格与时尚的建筑小品。他说："许多这样的建筑不只是为了好玩和耍酷，不只是发自社会基层的尝试，也不是自助型（D.I.Y）的城市主义，而是多种理念、技术和谋略在各种不同规模建筑项目中相互融合的统一体。"

小结

综上所述，翻译的过程是译者探寻原作思维脉络的过程，译者只有不断提高获取专业知识的能力，才能理清原作所涉及的专业知识的发展脉络，沿着原作的思路，产生贴近原文的译文。虽然在这篇译文中，有些细节的翻译是否准确无伤大雅，但是译者应当具备这样的信息搜索能力和探究知识的能力。

第四章 技术写作对应用文本翻译的借鉴作用

一、引言

全球化、信息化时代，各种媒介、各类信息纷至沓来，读者不得不在各种媒介、各类信息之间不断进行选择，以便用最短时间、以最小代价、最大限度地获取所需信息。这对应用文本的翻译，特别是外宣文本英译是一个极大的挑战：要实现文本功能，译文要能引发读者的阅读意愿，适应读者的思维和阅读习惯，符合读者的认知能力，满足读者的信息需求。

然而，我国传统的外宣英译注重准确传递文本所包含的各种信息，注重语言转换技巧，但是对译文是否易被读者接受，文本目标是否实现考虑不多，视乎语言转换完成了，信息就自然传递了，译者对译文的文本功能和宣传目标缺乏整体把握。因而，译文的信息传递效果是未知的，不为译者所重视。

在欧美国家，为了应对社会多元化的信息需求，多种写作技术应运而生，如创造性写作（creative writing）、技术写作（technical writing）或职业写作（professional writing）等，这些写作技术通过加强写作的目的性和针对性，提高文本的被接受程度，旨在提高信息传递的有效性。

二、技术写作

根据 Wikipedia 的定义：Technical Writing, also known as Professional Writing, involves the use of clear language to convey information in a way that is easily understood by the intended audience.

根据美国密歇根州立大学职业/技术写作专业简介（*Profile of Professional / Technical Writing at Michigan State University*），技术写作是专业化的高级写作，包括数字媒体环境下的写作、以学科或文化内容为依托的写作、以编辑和出版为目的的写作等。技术写作的核心是信息传播，内容包括所有应用文本、科技文本以及网页文案等，例如备忘录、建议书、项目策划、可行性报告、各种广告与招商宣传、产品与企业宣传、技术手册和科技文献等。

技术写作与传统写作的不同之处在于,技术写作针对特定读者群,具有明确的目的性。技术写作是用准确清楚的语言表达,易为读者接受的方式正确传递信息,确保读者能够快速准确地掌握和运用所传递的信息。

为了达到上述目的,技术写作的培养目标是:

(1) Understanding how different contexts—related, for instance, to delivery mode, document type and genre, audience, and purpose—shape a writing-related task. 理解不同的信息传播环境会产生不同的写作任务——传播方式、文本格式、文本类型、目标读者和写作目的。

(2) Writing to and for various audiences—cultural, professional, organizational—in effective and persuasive ways. 针对不同读者的专业写作——不同文化或职业背景、不同机构组织的读者,注重信息传递效果。

(3) Writing creatively, with panache and flair; informatively, with clarity, conciseness, and comprehensibility; persuasively, with detail, description, and supporting evidence. 创造性地写作,不同文本,风格各异,内容详实,清晰准确,易于理解;描述翔尽,论证充分,说服力强。

(4) Conveying complex information in informative, understandable ways with both words and images. 运用文字与图像将纷繁复杂的信息内容转换成易于理解掌握的信息文本。

可见,技术写作具有很强的针对性和适应性,而且,其适应性是多方位的,要求文本与信息传播方式相适应,与读者的文化背景和认知能力相适应,与读者的信息需求相适应。而且,技术写作要求语言表达准确清楚,内容翔实充分,易于理解掌握,版面设计易于信息查询。设定这些目标是为了提高写作的有效性和信息传递效率。因此,技术写作对以传递信息为主要目标的应用文本翻译具有实际的借鉴作用。

三、技术写作对外宣文本翻译的借鉴作用

外宣文本英译的本质是传递信息,要提高信息传递的有效性,译者对译文的文本功能要有整体把握,根据文本目标、文本形式和信息传播方式进行译写,实现文本功能。为使文本易于理解掌握,译文要符合读者的认

知能力，贴近读者的思维方式和语言表达习惯，满足读者的信息需求。

（一）明确目标读者，贴近读者的认知能力

外宣文本的目标读者不是英汉双语兼通的少数国内外读者，而是普通国外读者，译文要适应读者的认知能力，便于读者快速理解掌握。

例 1

曼哈顿的梦想几乎让整个中国的大城市为之迷醉。

但是，中国究竟需要多少曼哈顿？又应该怎样建设曼哈顿？上海的陆家嘴、北京的朝阳、深圳的福田，是经验还是教训？

理性与务实的 CBD 规划价值观，从这个意义上说，长沙 CBD 规划或将成为未来中国大城市 CBD 规划的先行者。而在巨大历史机遇期上的天津滨海新区 CBD 是否选择了正确的建设模式？

原译：

1　The dream of Manhattan almost made all metropolises in China crazy.

2　But, how many Manhattans does China need? How to build Manhattan? Lujiazui in Shanghai, Chaoyang in Beijing, Futian in Shenzhen, are these experience or lessons?

3　The criterion of CBD planning should to be rational and practical, by this mean: planning of Changsha CBD may become a forerunner of urban planning in China. However, the Tianjin Sea Coast New Area's CBD, which facing a great opportunity, does it choose the correct construction pattern?

分析：

原文看似简单，但是如果忽视国外读者的认知能力和阅读习惯，译文将不知所云。

第 1 段，从英语的逻辑思维和表达习惯上看，我们可以 make sb. crazy，但不可能 make sth. crazy，因此，建设曼哈顿的梦想不能让 metropolises crazy，可译为 appeal to metropolises。

第 2 段，"上海的陆家嘴、北京的朝阳、深圳的福田"是中国著名的中央商务区，但是国外读者不一定了解，因此需要具体译写为 the construction of CBD in the districts of Lujiazui (Shanghai), Chaoyang (Beijing) and Futian (Shenzhen)。

第 3 段，何为"在巨大历史机遇期上的天津滨海新区 CBD"？仔细阅读原文发现，这个历史机遇就是原文提出的："将天津滨海新区建设成北方的浦东，对环渤海区域经济起重要作用"，因此，可以理解成"由历史机遇引发的天津滨海新区 CBD 的建设"，这句话可译为 the development of the CBD in Tianjin Binhai New Area, initiated by the great historic opportunity。这些信息，译者可以通过网络查实。同时，译者需要理清第 3 段语句之间存在的因果和转折关系，使译文表达逻辑清晰，易于理解掌握，避免"死译硬译"。最后，"而在巨大历史机遇期上的天津滨海新区 CBD 是否选择了正确的建设模式"是作者对天津滨海新区开发提出的问题，不是向读者发问，可以转化为肯定句 it is doubtful whether。

改译：

1 The dream of building Manhattan has been appealing to metropolises in China.

2 However, how many CBD does the country need? How to build Manhattan in China? Does the construction of CBD in the districts of Lujiazui (Shanghai), Chaoyang (Beijing) and Futian (Shenzhen) serve as examples or lessons to learn?

3 Based on the conception of rational and practical CBD planning, the CBD planning in Changsha may set a precedent for the future CBD planning in metropolises of the country. Nevertheless, it is doubtful whether the development of the CBD in Tianjin Binhai New Area, initiated by the great historic opportunity, has adopted the appropriate construction mode.

（二）明确文本功能，贴近读者的信息需求

外宣英译要注重提供实质性信息，删减或改写中国文化语境中特有的表达，使译文更加贴近英语读者的信息需求，提高译文的被接受程度，引发读者的阅读意愿，实现文本功能。在我国翻译界，许多学者认识到，翻译的标准并非只有"信""达""雅"，"忠实"与"通顺"，译者可以根据不同的文本类型、不同的目标读者、不同的翻译目的，调整翻译标准，选择相应的翻译策略，对不完全适合译入语表达或欣赏习惯的文字进行必要的删节或改写。由此，有学者将汉译英定义为有条件的英文写作；翻译实际上也是用另一种文字对原作进行改写和重写（转引自王银泉，2009：46）。这种以传递信息为目的的翻译理念与国外技术写作理念有着异曲同工之处。但是在实践中，真正做到根据文本功能和读者需求对译文进行必要的调整和改写还是有限的。

例2

梅园新村位于长江路东端,是一组欧式建筑,尽管经历了岁月的风雨,但依然保持着当年的风采。这里就是中国共产党代表团办公原址。从1946年5月到1947年3月,周恩来同志率领中共代表团在这里与国民党政府进行了十个多月的和平谈判,写下了历史上光辉的一页。1961年在这里建成中共代表团梅园新村纪念馆;1990年兴建了"国共南京谈判史料陈列馆",同年7月1日周恩来全身铜像落成。

译文1:

Situated at the east end of Changjiang Road in Nanjing, Meiyuan New Village, a cluster of buildings of European style, is the former address of the CPC delegation. From May, 1946 to March, 1947, Comrade Zhou Enlai led the delegation in a successful 10-month-odd peace negotiation with KMT government, thus leaving a splendid page in history. In 1961, the Memorial Hall to the CPC Delegation was set up on the basis of the Village. In 1990, it saw the establishment of the Exhibition of Historical Data on the CPC-KMT Negotiation. On July 1 of that year, a full-length copper statue of Zhou Enlai was erected there. The Village, though exposed to the elements for decades, still retains the elegance of the early years. (袁晓宁)

分析:

考虑到国外读者对中国近现代史知之甚少,译文的文本功能是介绍旅游景点和观赏内容,不是进行中国近现代史教育。通过网络查询得知:"中国共产党代表团梅园新村纪念馆,由中共代表团办事处旧址、国共南京谈判史料陈列馆、周恩来铜像、周恩来图书馆等组成。"因此,根据英语读者的文化背景和思维习惯,略去对历史事件的评价,可以提高读者对译文的接受程度。此外,原文中的年代标注代表了国人在不同历史时期对历史人物和事件的态度所发生的变化,对中国人来说很有意义,但是对外国读者却不然,因此可以酌情从略。

译文2:

Situated at the east end of Changjiang Road in Nanjing, Meiyuan New Village, a cluster of buildings in European style, is the former address of the CPC delegation, where Zhou Enlai led the delegation in a series of peace negotiation with KMT government in 1940s. The Village is now turned into the Memorial Hall to the CPC Delegation, with a full-length copper statue of Zhou

Enlai and the Exhibition of Historical Data on the CPC-KMT Negotiation established there.

例3

"南京1912"是集文化、餐饮、娱乐休闲观光为一体的时尚休闲商业区及知名品牌展示地。"南京1912"紧邻总统府西侧,呈 L 型环绕总统府,占地3万平方米,总建筑面积3万平方米,由20余栋民国府衙式建筑及太平、博爱、共和、新世纪四大广场组成。"昔日总统府邸,今日城市客厅",东西方时尚在这里交融汇聚,古典与现代也在这里前后传承。"南京1912"文化休闲街区,提供了在保护城市记忆和文化遗产的前提下挖掘城市文化资源的成功模式。

译文1:

Bordering the Presidential Palace on the west, Nanjing 1912 is a popular, L-shaped street block with a cluster of tourist shops, bars, restaurants, teahouses, cafes, as well as up-market shops. With an area of 30,000 square meters and equally large floorage, the block boasts more than 20 mansions in distinctive architectural style of the Republic of China, and four squares known respectively as Taiping (Peace), Boai (Fraternity), Gonghe (Republic) and Xinshiji (New Century). It is about 1000 meters from the Xinjiekou commercial circle, the city's largest shopping center. Nanjing 1912, so to speak, is where vogues of the East and the West blend, and classic and contemporary cultures mingle. (袁晓宁)

分析:

(1) 通过比较原文和译文可以看出,译者针对外国读者的信息需求,增译了"It is about 1000 meters from the Xinjiekou commercial circle, the city's largest shopping center.",为读者提供实用信息。

(2) 仔细研究原文可以看出,"南京1912"是一个历史文化遗产保护与商业开发项目(通过网络查询得以证实)。但是,这类城市广场和历史街区保护与改造项目在西方国家比比皆是,人们已经习以为常,因此,可以略去评价性信息("昔日总统府邸,今日城市客厅",东西方时尚在这里交融汇聚,古典与现代也在这里前后传承),其历史与文化价值让游客自己判定,只要译出项目的性质和内容,方便游客自己选择即可。但是,该项目的目的"保护城市记忆和文化遗产"可以保留。

译文2：

Bordering the Presidential Palace on the west, Nanjing 1912 is a popular, L-shaped street block with a cluster of tourist shops, bars, restaurants, teahouses, cafes, as well as up-market shops. Occupying a land area of 30,000 square meters, with a floor space of the same size, the block boasts 20-odd mansions in distinctive architectural style of Republic China as well as four squares, namely Taiping, Boai, Gonghe and Xinshiji. Nanjing 1912 project is meant to preserve and present the historical and cultural heritage of the city. It is about 1,000 meters from the Xinjiekou commercial circle, the city's largest shopping center.

（三）贴近读者的思维和表达习惯，提高文本的可读性和被接受程度

翻译的过程实际上是译者促成跨文化交际活动的过程，在此，译者起着主导作用，最终产生什么样的语篇，取决于译者对语篇内容及其语域的把握，以及译者根据译文读者的思维和阅读习惯，对译语语篇的构建能力（袁晓宁，2010：61）。为了准确快速地传播信息，减少读者的理解负担，译文要贴近国外读者的思维和表达习惯，注重两种语言在思维和表达方面的差异，借鉴相关平行文本，通过平行文本获得准确可靠的译法，提高译文的可读性，使译文的信息传递效果与原文基本相同。

例4

南京市境内，东郊有中山陵、明孝陵、灵谷寺，城南有夫子庙、中华门、雨花台，城西有莫愁湖、朝天宫，城东有梅园新村、总统府旧址，城北有玄武湖、鸡鸣寺。这些众多的旅游景点，形成了以历史古迹为核心的南京独特的旅游观光胜地。

分析：

英汉民族有着不同的文化背景、思维方式和价值观，因而两种语言在表达方式和语篇结构上不尽相同。具体地说，汉语语篇通常喜欢从空泛的信息入手，由远及近，在结尾时点题；而英语语篇开宗明义，直奔主题。英语的语篇结构特征常常是先总提，后分提；而汉语则相反，往往是先分提，后总提。通过分析原文可以看出，结尾句"这些众多的旅游景点，形成了以历史古迹为核心的南京独特的旅游观光胜地"是该段落的主题句，因此，在英译时应该根据英文的语篇构成习惯，将主题句放在段

落之首，然后再对主题句进行一一阐释，层次清楚，符合英文的表达习惯。

译文：

The plentiful travel destinations in Nanjing form her unique tourist resorts featuring cultural relics of historic interest. Situated on the eastern outskirts of the city are Dr. Sun Yat-sen's Mausoleum, Xiaoling Mausoleum of the Ming Dynasty, and the Spirit Valley; in the southern part of the city lie the Confucius Temple, Zhonghua City Gate, the Rain Flower Terrace (Yuhuatai); in the western part Mochou Lake, and Chao Tien Temple; in the eastern part Meiyuan New Village, and Presidential Palace; in the northern part Xuanwu lake, and Jiming Temple. （袁晓宁）

例 5

具有三千多年建城史的北京，是中华传统文化的典型代表，奥运会如在这里举行，将使东西方文化在世界人口五分之一的国度交融。一个在改革开放进程中蓬勃发展的新北京，将以古典与现代合璧的姿态，把自己悠远深厚的文化底蕴，兼容并蓄的宽广胸怀，谦和礼貌的功德素养，奋发有为的进取精神展现给全世界，为世界奉献一届与众不同的新奥运，为奥林匹克运动在新世纪的发展带来新的动力，促使这一运动真正成为跨文化、跨民族、跨国度的世界性文化体系。

译文：

Beijing, with more than 3,000 years of history as a city, is a model of traditional Chinese culture. If the Olympiad is held here, the eastern and western cultures will have a chance to integrate. Beijing will present the world with a unique Olympiad so that the event can truly become a global culture transcending national characteristics. （引自《对外宣传翻译理论与实践》）

分析：

对照汉英文本可以看出，英文漏译很多。但是，如果将中文文本中惯用的套话与表达全部译入目的语，将会使英文的行文臃肿，内容空泛，大大降低文本的可读性，外宣目的无从实现。因此，需要根据译文读者的思维习惯来译写，删减没有实质内容的套话。

（四）根据信息传播方式进行译写

信息传播方式不同，译文的语言表达形式和风格会不同，文本的简约或详细程度也会不同。

例 6

You'll notice how kind new Sanara is to your hair. See it. Feel it. Sanara's naturally derived formulations bring out the shine and smoothness in your hair, leaving it manageable and healthy. You won't actually see how kind Sanara is to the environment, but it's nice to know that the whole range is biodegradable, so it doesn't pollute water or soil. And naturally, the packaging is recyclable.

译文 1：

包装说明书（书面体）：

眼见为实，感觉为真。新品莎拉娜由天然配方制成，能使头发光泽、柔顺、健康，易于护理。莎拉娜系列具有生物降解特性，包装可回收利用，对水土、环境不会造成污染。

译文 2：

电视媒体（口语体）：

新品莎拉娜对您的秀发有亲和力，视觉靓、感觉好，令您的秀发光泽、柔顺、健康。莎拉娜，护理简易，天然配方，生物降解，包装再生利用，不伤水土，保护自然。（方梦之）

（五）小结

就外宣文本英译而言，完成语言转换并不意味着信息传递成功，因为，信息传递的有效性与读者的阅读意愿和对文本的接受程度密切相关。外宣英译要达到最佳信息传递效果，译者对译文的文本功能要有整体把握，考虑目标读者的潜在需求，根据文本类型与功能，选择相应的翻译策略。因为，译文的可读性与忠实原文同等重要。

将技术写作引入外宣文本英译的意义，在于采用表达准确清楚的语言，易为读者接受的方式传递信息，提高译文的被接受程度，确保信息传递的准确性和有效性，实现译文的文本功能。

第五章　外宣翻译的目的与策略原则

一、概述

外宣翻译是将有关中国的各种信息译成外文，通过图书、期刊、报纸、广播、电视、网络等媒体以及国际会议进行对外发表和传播，内容包括我国政治经济和文化教育等发展状况、各级政府的信息通报、投资指南、旅游指南、城市/企业事业机构的宣传介绍、各种大型国际性活动宣传等。外宣翻译的成效与国家和区域形象的塑造宣传、企业品牌推广、中国文化的国际传播密切相关。

就中文宣传文本的翻译而言，有三个显著特征：一是信息特征强，二是注重宣传效应，三是许多中文外宣文本自身存在诸多不足。目前，这类文本翻译的社会需求很大，但在中译外的翻译实践中存在的问题也最多。

外宣文本英译的现状

外宣翻译的目的是为了使译文读者能够准确无误、方便快捷地理解和获得译文所传递的信息，在此过程中，译者不仅要设法化解英汉两种语言在表达方式、逻辑关系、语体风格和文化等方面的差异而引起的理解上的困难，而且要满足译文的文本功能，适应目标读者的阅读和表达习惯，从而取得最佳的宣传效果。

因此，外宣翻译的实质是信息传播与文化交流，但是，这种信息传播和文化交流不是单向的一厢情愿，需要考虑和尊重彼此的欣赏习惯，沟通和抵达彼此的情感意境。为了实现外宣翻译的目的，需要使用在国际语境中被广泛理解接受的方式、习惯与话语来阐释与叙事。

然而，在外宣英译实践中，译文让读者费解，甚至误解的现象比比皆是。具体表现为，译文带有严重的"死译硬译"痕迹，许多中文里的套话空话和中国文化语境中特有的表达被机械地翻译成英文，虽然在形式上汉语转换成了英语，但是在句子结构、语篇结构、语言风格、信息传递等层面上依然保留了汉语的典型特征，即所谓的中式英语，不符合译文读者的阅读和表达习惯，因而不能引发读者的阅读兴趣，无法达到外宣英译的最终目的。

究其原因主要有三：首先，译者对中文文本的实际内容缺乏深入了解，只满足于寻求两种语言之间的对应转换；其次，对英汉两种语言在表达方式、逻辑关系、语体风格和文化等方面的差异重视不够，译文在语篇结构、语言风格、信息传递等方面依然保留了汉语的典型特征；最后，长期以来，我们的翻译标准强调信、达、雅，译者也一直以忠实原作为己任，注重探索两种语言之间的转换技巧和策略，努力寻找有关中国式思维模式最贴切的英文转换，但是对译文读者的文化背景、思维方式、认知能力和信息需求关注不够，视乎语言转换完成了，信息就自然传递了，译者对译文的可读性和适用性考虑不多，对译文的文本功能和宣传目标缺乏整体把握，因而，译文的信息传递效果是未知的，不为译者所重视。

例1

北京中轴线的"中国气质"在于横亘千年的历史，从元朝大都到08奥运，从皇城到市井，城市设计该如何回答？

原译：

Due to thousands years of history, Beijing's axis has its peculiarity. It was named Dadu in Yuan Dynasty and will hold Olympic Games in 2008. Urban design should settle the questions from Forbidden City to civil community.

分析：

这段原文包含了丰富的中国历史文化内容，译者首先需要弄懂原文的含义。但是，译文的语句之间却没有什么联系，令人费解。原因在于译者没有把中文原文的内容读懂，只是一一对应地进行了翻译。在后面的段落中，原文作者写道："明清时代留下的北京城市轴线，主要是遵循了元大都的形制，是国家的无价之宝，中轴线在古代以皇城为核心，一半体现皇权一半融入市井，现在城市轴线向北延伸出奥运公园，向南延伸出城市的南大门，长度增至原来的3倍，迫切需要城市规划，中国城市将这个问题抛给了规划界：我们究竟需要怎样的城市轴线？"

因此，原文旨在说明：北京的城市中轴线体现了这座城市千年的历史与文化的传承和变迁，从元朝的都城发展成为现代的奥运会举办城市，中轴线将古代的皇城与市井联系在一起，并且延伸至奥林匹克公园。城市中轴线代表了城市在时间和空间上的延续与拓展，中轴线是中国历史城市的主要特征，随着城市的不断扩展延伸，城市设计者应当怎样规划设计城市的中轴线呢(如下图所示)?

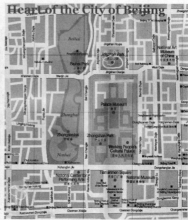

图 北京城市中轴线不断延伸,意味着城市在不断扩大

改译:

The central axis in Beijing represents the development of Chinese history of a thousand years, from the establishment of Dadu, the capital in Yuan Dynasty (1272AD), to the construction of the venue for the 2008 Olympic Games, connecting the Forbidden City to business streets. However, it is arguable how urban design will approach the central axis in the process of large scale urban development.

所以,在翻译的过程中,译者首先需要对语篇内容有整体把握,而不是逐句进行语言转换。其次,译者需要有很强的文化意识,将语言转换放在文化中进行,使翻译成为一种跨文化的实践活动。因此,这一段采用了增译和释译的方式:from the establishment of Dadu, the capital in Yuan Dynasty (1272AD), to the construction of the venue for the 2008 Olympic Games; how urban design will approach the central axis in the process of large scale urban development。另外,"市井"意为中国古代城市中的"街市"或"市场",也就是今天的"商业区",因此不能译成 civil community,可译为 business streets 或 commercial area。

二、对外宣传翻译的目的论原则

（一）外宣翻译的目的论原则

目的论认为翻译是一种跨文化的交际行为，任何行为都有其相应的目的性。例如，旅游宣传通过满足游客对旅游项目的特色性、观赏性、知识性等方面的需求，达到吸引游客参与旅游项目的目的。又如，招商宣传的目的是为了唤起外商潜在的投资兴趣，吸引外商前去商洽投资开发项目，以期获得开发资金和专项技术。

翻译行为所要达到的目的决定了翻译关注的重点不是译文与原文之间是否对等，而是在分析原文的基础上，以实现译文功能为目的，选择最佳的翻译策略和方法。为了达到文本目的，译者在翻译过程中应从译语读者的认知能力、思维方式和信息需求出发，选择相应的翻译策略和方法。因此，翻译的标准不是单一的，而是多元化的。

外宣翻译中，译者往往会采用"变译"的手段实现翻译的目的。所谓"变译"是相对于"全译"而言的，"全译"是将原文没有遗漏地进行翻译，主要应用于文学作品的翻译。而"变译"则是对原文信息采用扩充、取舍、浓缩、补充等方法，以传达信息的中心内容或部分内容的翻译方法，包括编译、译写、改译、摘译、缩译等。

编译是译者根据译文读者获取和理解信息的实际需求对原作经过加工整理后再翻译，通过调整篇章结构，删减一些次要信息，对文字进行加工处理，使译文更加条理化，更具有针对性，更能为译文读者所接受。

有学者认为，翻译就是改写的一种方式（Lefevere，1992）。外宣翻译中改写的主要目的是通过对不适宜对外宣传的内容进行过滤，弱化"宣传口吻"，使之易于被读者接受，实现外宣文本的目标。

因此，<u>外宣翻译传递的信息往往是有选择的</u>，或综合地或概要地或部分地传递，也就是说，<u>无论是在翻译方法还是在译文的文本形式上，翻译的可变性很大</u>。

以目的论为指导，外宣翻译需要寻找合适的切入点，即便是同一个主题也可以采用不同的视角和叙事方式陈述。例如，2010 上海世博会以色列馆，其宣传策略直抵人心。展览的第一部分表达了犹太民族对中国上海在"二战"期间拯救 3 万犹太难民的感激之情，拉近了不同种族间的情感距离；第二部分展示了爱因斯坦的《相对论》手稿，展现了犹太民族为人类科学发展做出的卓越贡献；随后推介以色列高科技产业、生态农业和旅游项目，此情此景令人难忘。

例 2

横琴居国之东南，南海之滨，珠江之西，港澳之邻，方圆 106.46 平方公里，为珠海最大之岛屿。横琴与澳门一河之隔，咫尺相望，桥隧相连；港距 34 海里，港珠澳大桥跨海而至，为举国唯一与港澳路桥相通之枢纽要地。<u>横琴拥山面海，山舞清韵，河脉纵横，水漾碧波</u>。

开发横琴乃国之战略。2009 年，习近平总书记亲启横琴开发，国务院颁布横琴总体发展规划，横琴以粤港澳深度合作示范区之名，<u>横空出世，琴鸣天下</u>。2012 年 12 月，习总书记再临横琴，寄予："蓝图已经绘就，工作扎实起步，前景可期。" 2014 年 12 月，国务院批复设立中国（广东）自由贸易试验区，横琴为三大片区之一。<u>自踏上逐梦征程</u>，横琴携手港澳促合作，<u>谋共赢</u>，构建全新开放格局；<u>锐意改革谋发展、创新篇</u>，开创国内"十大率先"；沧海桑田大开发、聚产业，城市建设日新月异。一座现代化未来之城，<u>正以风华正茂之态</u>，于濠江之畔拔地而起。

未来，横琴将成为连通港澳、区域共建之"开放岛"，经济繁荣、宜居宜业之"活力岛"，知识密集、信息发达之"智能岛"，资源节约、环境友好之"生态岛"，<u>干部清正、政府清廉之"廉洁岛"，以卓然之姿</u>，屹立于南中国，成为世界观中国之窗口，中国出世界之门户，中华民族之理想家园。

译文 1：

1　Hengqin Island is located in Southeast China, west of Pearl River, close to the coast of the South China Sea and adjacent to Hong Kong and Macao. With a size of 106.46 km², it is the largest island in Zhuhai. Hengqin and Macao are separated by a river and connected by bridges and channels. Responsible for the fame of Hengqin, at a distance of 34 nautical miles from Hong Kong, the Hong Kong – Zhuhai – Macao Bridge is a unique key hub in China which provides access to both Hong Kong and Macao. Hengqin is also embraced by green mountains and blue sea and rivers.

2　The development of Hengqin is a national strategy. Since General Secretary of the CPC Central Committee Xi Jinping directly instructed the development of Hengqin, and the State Council Issued the General Plan for the Development of Hengqin in 2009, the island has become the national demonstration area for close cooperation between Guangdong Province, Hong Kong and Macao. On his second visit to Hengqin in December 2012, General Secretary Xi said, "The blueprint of development has been accomplished and a bright prospect is foreseeable with steady progress in the start-up stage". In December 2014, the State Council approved the application to establish the China (Guangdong) Pilot Free Trade Zone, wherein Hengqin is defined as one of the three major areas of the Zone. Since it embarked on the long journey towards pursuing its dreams, Hengqin has collaborated with Hong Kong and Macao to facilitate multilateral cooperation and mutual benefits, and to construct a new pattern of opening-up. Its resolute determination in reformation and the pursuit of new development takes a leading position in initiating ten innovations around the country. The urban construction and industrial development of Hengqin is progressing with speed and scale. A modern city of the future is rising up beside Haojiang River with prime energy and vigor.

3 In the future, Hengqin will become an "open island" connecting Hong Kong and Macao, a main force for regional development, a vital island with a prosperous economy and an pleasant living and business environment, and knowledge-intensive smart island with advanced information technology, a resource-saving and environmentally friendly ecological island, and an honest island with fair and incorrupt leadership and government, standing majestically in Southern China as a window through which the world may get to know China, a gateway for China to the world, and a dreamland of the Chinese people.

分析：

这篇横琴岛发展规划宣传语言优美精练，但是如果依照原文逐一译出，不能达到主题信息突出的宣传效果。

第1段，将押韵的四字并列句转化为实意的信息内容；结尾的"横琴拥山面海，山舞清韵，河脉纵横，水漾碧波"是要展现横琴拥有多种类型的地貌与景观特征，而 Hengqin is also embraced by green mountains and blue sea and rivers 是不言而喻的。

第2段，原文通过列述国家领导人的视察和国务院的批复凸显横琴开发的重要战略地位和影响力，这在中文语篇中很常见，是信息传播的重点，但是如果直接译成英文，语句之间的逻辑关系和主题的关联性会削弱；另外，为了贯彻主题信息突出原则，需要删除没有实际内容的空话、套话和口号式语言表达。这部分的叙事方式需要调整。

第3段,"开放岛""活力岛""智能岛""生态岛""廉洁岛",三字并列与重复产生韵律与美感,但出现在英文中则不然,会显得臃肿累赘,应当简化。况且,清正廉洁本是政府的职责,不应作为特色与优势去宣扬。

译文2:

Hengqin Island is located in Southeast China, west of Pearl River, facing the South China Sea. With a distance of 34 nautical miles from Hong Kong, the island serves as the key transportation hub, with a direct access to Hong Kong by the Hong Kong – Zhuhai – Macao Bridge over the sea, and to Macao by bridge and channel over a river. As the largest island (106.46 km^2) in Zhuhai, it boasts a unique landscape of blue sea, green hills and glimmering rivers and streams running through.

The development of Hengqin is a national strategy, which was initiated by General Secretary of the CPC Central Committee Xi Jinping in 2009. Established as a national demonstration area for close cooperation between Guangdong Province, Hong Kong and Macao, the General Plan of the Development of Hengqin has been issued by the State Council. "The blueprint of the development is articulated and a bright prospect is foreseeable with the project kicked off", as stated by Xi Jinping on his second visit in Dec. 2012. In December 2014, the State Council approved the establishment of the China (Guangdong) Pilot Free Trade Zone, wherein Hengqin is included/defined as one of the three major areas of the Zone. Since then, it has embarked on the collaboration with Hong Kong and Macao, innovating the opening-up form. Establishing ten initiatives (innovations) and industry clusters, a dynamic future city is emerging at the Haojiang River.

In the future, Hengqin will be operating as a main force for regional development involving Hong Kong and Macao, featuring top-notch information technology, knowledge-intensive industry, resource-conserving society, and ecological environment. It will stand out in South China as a window for the world to witness the progress in China, a gateway for China to go global and an ideal land for Chinese to realize their dreams.

(二)外宣翻译的辅助性原则

除了翻译目的论外,对外宣翻译具有指导作用的还有"主题信息突出"与"经济简明"的策略原则,在此原则之下辅以若干其他原则。

(1) 文本信息的传递应准确简明,便于受众在相对短的时间内获得更多信息。

(2) 文本信息的传递应考虑受众的需求。

(3) 文本信息的传递应考虑受众的认知能力和思维习惯。

(4) 文本信息的传递应考虑不同信息性质的价值度以及文本自身的不足。

(5) 文本信息的传递应考虑不同文本的语言与文化差异。

(6) 文本信息的传递应考虑信息传播的方式(如广告、包装袋、宣传册、新闻发布会等)。

例3

近年来,宣武区以国际传媒大道、马连道采购中心区、大栅栏传统商业区、琉璃厂文化创意产业园区、牛街民族特色街和天桥民俗特色街为重点,<u>加快推进功能街区建设,经济持续发展,城市面貌日新月异</u>;以保护古都风貌、弘扬宣南文化为重点,加快推进文化创意产业发展和文化事业建设,人民群众的精神文化生活日益丰富;以创建和谐社区为重点,加快推进社会建设,社会安定祥和,人民生活品质明显提高。今天的宣武,大道通衢,路桥飞架;碧水蓝天,绿荫掩映;民风淳朴,社会和谐。随着现代、人文、和谐<u>宣武建设的全面推进</u>,一个古老而现代的首都新城区正快速崛起在宣南大地。

译文:

Capitalizing on Beijing's historical and cultural legacy, Xuanwu District will continue to thrive for many years to come. Its old streets and stores have been renovated; the living standard here is rapidly improving; safe and harmonious residential communities have been built up. The extraordinary new International Media Boulevard, Maliandao Purchasing Central Area, Dashilan Business Street, Liulichang Cultural Street, Niujie Ethnic Cuture Street and Tianqiao Folk Culture Street, all these features support a district combing the best of tradition and modernity. (引自《对外宣传翻译理论与实践》)

分析:

原文结构是中文典型的归纳式语篇,首先举例描述了宣武区的经济发展和文化建设,最后点出主题——一个古老而现代的首都新城区正快速崛起。而英文译文在语篇组织上,根据英语语篇特征对原文进行了语篇重构，调整了语句顺序，将中心信息置于句首，开篇直奔主题，进而举例具体描述。

另外，对不符合英语读者思维方式和信息需求的表达，对中文工整对仗、整齐划一的渲染与修饰语进行压缩与删减，对画线部分用 Its old streets and stores have been renovated; the living standard here is rapidly improving; safe and harmonious residential communities have been built up 加以概括，减少官话套话，弱化"宣传味"。

三、"外宣三贴近"原则

中国文化"走出去"，翻译是一个重要环节和条件。完整、系统、准确、深入地向世界说明中国，真正实现中国文化与世界文化的汇通与融合，是"外宣翻译"的责任和历史使命。因此，"外宣翻译"要遵循"外宣三贴近"原则，即贴近中国发展的实际，贴近国外受众对中国信息的需求，贴近国外受众的思维习惯（黄友义，2004：24）。而且，最好的外宣英译不是按照中文原文一一对应地进行语言转换，而是在充分理解原文意旨的基础上，对原文进行适当加工，包括对原文内容与文字的增删和重组，甚至重写，按照国外受众的思维习惯去把握翻译，从而取得最佳的宣传效果。

"外宣三贴近"原则与技术写作的互补性

传统的应用翻译注重准确传递文本包含的各种信息，但对译文是否适合读者阅读，是否能发挥其功能与用途考虑不多。而"外宣三贴近"原则不仅注重信息传递的完整性和准确性，同时还强调译文的可读性，要求译文贴近读者的信息需求和思维习惯。在这方面，"外宣三贴近"原则与技术写作具有相当的共性，二者都注重信息传递的完整性、准确性和文本的可读性。但是相对而言，技术写作更强调文本的针对性、适用性和信息传递的有效性，也就是针对目标读者的信息需求和认知能力而写作，为了实现文本的功能与用途而写作，同时注重提高信息传递的效率，要求文字表达简明清晰，方便查找信息。因此，"外宣三贴近"原则与技术写作对外宣文本译英具有很强的借鉴作用。

四、实例分析

（一）将中文常见的华丽或形象的描述转换为朴素的语言，删减过多的比喻和修饰

中英文行文与遣词方面存在巨大差异。汉语表达主观色彩浓厚，擅长抒发情感；而英语则讲究逻辑理性。因此，在翻译的过程中必然会涉及对原文的重组、重写以及由此引起的文字与内容的增删，避免"死译""硬译"。同时，将中文文本中概念化或抽象的描述转化为实意的或具体的表达。

例4

……诞生于上世纪八十年代末的虎豹集团，<u>信守孜孜、永不言退</u>的发展理念，在市场经济的大潮中，<u>任凭浊浪排空，惊涛拍岸，独有胜似闲庭信步</u>的自信，<u>处变不惊，运筹帷幄。尽握无限商机于掌间，渐显王者之气于天地</u>。虎豹人以其特有的灵气，<u>极目一流，精益求精</u>，集世界顶尖服装生产技术装备之大成。<u>裁天上彩虹，绣人间缤纷</u>，开设计之先河，臻质量之高峰，领导服装潮流，<u>尽显领袖风采</u>。……（浙江虎豹集团宣传资料）

分析：

这篇企业宣传，言辞夸张，过度渲染，在中文宣传文本中很常见，但是如果一一对应地译成英语，一大堆华而不实的渲染会降低文本的可读性，影响实质性信息的传递。而且，译文的目标读者主要是国外同行和合作者。

上述文字中能让国外读者关注或体现企业特色的内容主要有四项：①成立时间；②汇集世界顶尖生产技术装备；③领导服装潮流；④产品质量高。其他画线部分的文字都是华而不实之词，没有信息价值。在翻译过程中，译者应根据文本内容，预测目标读者最可能关注的信息内容，突出主题信息，对原文中的描述性文字给予淡化或简化。根据上述四项相关信息内容重组语句。

译文：

Founded in the late 1980s and striving for ceaseless development, the Hubao Group has achieved great successes in the fashion-manufacturing sector. It is outstanding for being well-equipped with the world's most advanced technologies and is renowned for its maintenance of a high-standard quality system. It is now taking the lead in fashion designs and enjoys a good market share with quality products. The Hubao people have been keeping updating their products with their diligence and intelligence. (曾利沙)

(二) 删去不利于对外宣传的语句

翻译是思想与文化的交流，在对外宣传翻译中，对于可有可无或关联性不强的信息，或者对宣传不利的语言表达应当略去，<u>对外宣传要注意内外有别</u>，突出主要信息。

例 5

中国市场动态：需要测试仪器

中国涤纶长丝的生产，将不再扩展生产能力而着重开发新产品和提高质量。为此需要进口相当数量的各类测试仪器和油剂等辅料。<u>据了解，由于前两年盲目引进设备，目前已有的和即将投产的涤纶长丝的生产能力已达 29 万吨/年，远超过每年 18 万吨的社会总需求量。</u>

译文：

China Market: Testing Instruments Needed

For less but better and newer dacron fiber products, China needs advanced testing instruments, dyestuff, oils and other subsidiaries. The country is drastically cutting down its annual dacronfiber productivity of 290 000 tons, as its home need is 180 000 tons.

(三) 灵活处理一些概念性的翻译

汉译英时，必须充分考虑到双方文化背景和社会环境的差异，这种差异往往会导致理解困难。译者需要养成换位思考的习惯，从外国人的角度考虑所传递的信息是否能够被理解和接受，可以用增补或注释的方法为读者提供更多信息，以弥补文化差异。例如，在翻译"要扶持大龄下岗人员再就业"时，如何翻译"大龄"，需要进行适当的补充，可译为"give assistance to laid-off persons who have difficulties finding reemployment because of their disadvantaged age"。又如，如果翻译"三高农业"，如果直译成"three high agricultures"令人费解，这时需要采取释译，可译为"high-yield, cost-efficient and high-tech farming"。

例 6

复旦大学积极响应上海市委、市府"聚焦张江"的战略决策,响应市府关于在张江园区建设"以研究和应用为主,面向产业,相对集中,资源共享"的高等教育大学校区的要求,和张江(集团)共同建设复旦大学张江校区。

译文 1:

Zhangjiang Campus is being jointly constructed by Fudan University and Zhangjiang Group, in line with Shanghai Municipal Government's "Focusing On Zhangjiang" strategy. According to this strategy, the development of higher education in Zhangjiang area in Pudong New District should be geared to the following three demands: the twin emphases on research and application, catering for the industrial needs, and relative concentration and sharing resources together.

分析:

什么是"聚焦张江"的战略决策("Focusing On Zhangjiang" strategy)?这个表达太抽象,英语读者很难理解,需要使之具体化(to develop higher education in Zhangjiang area),删去概念化的表达。

译文 2:

Zhangjiang Campus is being jointly constructed by Fudan University and Zhangjiang Group, in line with Shanghai Municipal Government's strategy to develop higher education in Zhangjiang area, Pudong New District. The development is geared to the following three demands: the twin emphases on research and application, catering for the industrial needs, and relative concentration and sharing resources together.

例 7

做好"家电下乡""农机下乡""汽车、摩托车下乡"等工作,把中央财政的400亿元补贴资金用活,使企业增加销售、农民得到实惠。

分析:

家电、农机、汽车"三下乡"的概念需要具体译出,便于读者理解。同时,原作用了三个"下乡",符合汉语工整对仗、朗朗上口的行文特点,但是英语的特点是避免重复,因此没有必要将三个"下乡"全部译出,只要译出一个"下乡"就行了。

译文:

We will implement the programs for bringing to the countryside home appliances, agricultural machinery, and automobiles and motorbikes, and we will make effective use of the 40 billion Yuan in central government subsidies provided to enable enterprises to increase their sales and farmers to enjoy real benefits.

(四) 有些形容词和副词从汉语表达方式上看,能够增强语气,但转化成英文未必起到同样效果,最好删去

汉语经常用很强的副词修饰动词和形容词,用形容词修饰名词,以加重语气,但英译时不能一一对应地照译,否则译文就会显得臃肿累赘。例如,"毫无根据的捏造""不幸的悲剧""不切合实际的幻想""共同合作""完全征服"不能译成 groundless lies, unfortunate tragedy, impractical illusion, common cooperation, completely conquer 应该把冗余信息 groundless, unfortunate, impractical, common, completely 去掉,避免过多使用修饰词。

例8

为了进一步提升品牌的认可度,我们将参加更多的海外展会,同时我们已经扩大了广告宣传力度,特别是在香港。

译文:

To improve public recognition of our brand, we are attending more exhibitions overseas. Meanwhile, we have spent more on advertising, especially in Hong Kong. (引自《商务汉英翻译》)

分析:

汉语中经常使用一些强化语气的表达方式,译成英语时需要用朴实的词语替换。

(五) 经济简明,主题信息突出

下面是一则香港法国文化年的展览宣传,语言表达经济简明,主题信息突出,话题直奔展览主题,没有空话套话和过度夸张渲染的表达,注重事实性信息的传递。除了第一段煽情外,其他段落主要围绕展览内容展开,最后一段强调展览意义。只是有些中文表达受英文影响,而且,香港的中英文外宣文本与内地外宣文本在语言表达上有一定差异。

例9

Louis Vuitton: A Passion for Creation
路易威登：创意情感

Creativity is the vitality of a modern city; passion is the origin of artistic inspiration. Le Frence May 2009 exhibition, "Louis Vuitton: A Passion for Creation" witnesses the fruits of infinite creativity triggered by unrestrained expression of artistic creation.

译文1：
创意是现代都市的活力，情感是艺术灵感的源泉。作为2009年法国五月节重点项目的"路易威登：创意情感"展览，正印证了情感全然投入艺术创作而触发无限创意的成果。

译文2：
2009年法国五月节的展览项目"路易威登：创意情感"，见证了情感全然投入艺术创作而触发无限创意的成果。

The composition of this exhibition demonstrates different concepts and practices of contemporary and avant-garde art. The display commences with antique trunks and suitcases of Louis Vuitton which have evolved as a symbol of "art traveling". Artists and designers, amongst them Takashi Murakami, Stephen Sprouse and Richard Prince, share a close partnership with Louis Vuitton, and have been invited to display their work of painting, installations, fashion and sculpture exclusively for this exhibition. By artfully incorporating the Louis Vuitton monogram into their work, commercial elements merge with art and design to reflect the high adaptability and evolution of contemporary art.

译文1：
这次展览的构成，展示了当代及前卫艺术的各种理念和实践结果。展览首部分展示了作为"艺术旅游"表徵的路易威登皮具、箱子外，也别具心思地邀请了与其有密切合作关系的艺术家和设计家特别为展览而创作的绘画、装置、时装、雕塑作品。这些作品巧妙融入了路易威登的标志、品牌图像等，将艺术、设计与商业元素共冶一炉，反映了当代艺术兼容并包、推陈出新的创新精神。

译文2：
这次展览的多元化组合，展示了当代及前卫艺术的各种理念和实践成果。展览的第一部分展示了象征"艺术旅游"的路易威登经典皮具和箱子,也别出心裁地邀请了与其有密切合作关系的艺术家和设计家特别为本次展览创作的绘画、装置、时装和雕塑等作品参展。这些作品巧妙地融入了路易威登的品牌标志图案,(monogram: a symbol of identity, usu. one's initials) 将艺术、设计与商业元素融为一体。

The second section of the exhibition features a selection from the contemporary art collection of the Foundation Louis Vuitton, including works by renowned Chinese, European and American artists. These works express the artists' feelings, questioning and interpretations of modern city life, culture and humanity.

译文1:

展览另一构成部分精选自路易威登基金会的当代艺术收藏,包括来自中国、欧洲、美国等当代艺术家以不同媒介,包括绘画、录像、摄影、装置来演绎其对当代城市、生活、文化、人文的感思、质疑和诠释的精作。

译文2:

展览的第二部分选自路易威登基金会的当代艺术精品收藏,包括来自中国、欧洲、美国等当代艺术家以不同媒介,例如绘画、录像、摄影、装置等精作,演绎其对当代城市、生活、文化、人文的思考、质疑和诠释。

分析:

(1) 译文1定语太长,可以拆分。

(2) 这里的"绘画、录像、摄影、装置等精作"是增译,虽然第2段已经列述展览内容,第3段再次提醒读者展品种类,这是专门针对中文读者而增译。因为西方已有1000多年的展览传统,而华人世界则不然,特别是在中国大陆,展览在近十多年才开始流行,而且,西方的艺术教育也非常普及。

Included in the exhibition is a three dimensional model and brief introduction to the forthcoming Foundation Louis Vuitton Museum in France, designed by iconic architect Frank Gehry, which will be inaugurated in 2012. This new museum is an incorporation of technology, architecture and aesthetic. Its naturalistic curving contours and forms are innovative and representative of the architect's signature style, and will act as an enlightened inspiration to cultural facilities in the future. In addition, American master Richard Prince is to wrap the facade of the Hong Kong Museum of Art with his work *Hong Kong after Dark* series, presenting a new landscape of art to the landmark in the panoramic Victoria Harbor of Hong Kong. The piece provokes our reflection by revealing the mystique of nightlife, and the desire that lies between fantasy and reality.

译文1：

除了这两部分的展品外，路易威登更特别展出由国际知名美国建筑大师 Frank Gehry 设计、将于2012年落成的路易威登创意基金会美术馆的建筑模型及相关资料。这幢将科技、建筑与美学结合完美无间的新美术馆，轮廓线条和造型有若行云流水，富于前瞻性，体现了这位建筑大师的一贯风格，也会为未来的新文化艺术建设带来启发。此外，美国艺术大师 Richard Prince 以其作品 *Hong Kong after Dark* 覆盖艺术馆外墙，呈现这幢艺术地标新景观，在五光十色的维港之滨，<u>展现了夜生活迷离、憧憬和现实交错的迷情欲望，令人深思</u>。

译文2：

第三部分特别展出了由国际知名的美国建筑大师 Frank Gehry 设计的路易威登基金会博物馆模型及相关资料，新馆将于2012年落成。这幢将科技、建筑与美学完美结合，轮廓线条与造型有若行云流水，富于前瞻性，体现了这位建筑大师的一贯风格，将为未来的文化设施建设带来启发。此外，美国艺术大师 Richard Prince 以其作品 *Hong Kong after Dark*（《夜幕中的香港》）覆盖艺术馆外墙，让这幢艺术地标呈现新景观，在五光十色的维港之滨，<u>展现夜生活的梦幻迷离、憧憬与现实交错，令人遐想万千</u>。

分析：

The piece provokes our reflection by revealing the mystique of nightlife, and the desire that lies between fantasy and reality. 将这句话译成"展现了夜生活迷离、憧憬和现实交错的迷情欲望，令人深思"好像是到了酒吧一条街，而不是艺术馆。故将其译成"展现夜生活的梦幻迷离、憧憬与现实交错，令人遐想万千"比较中性与贴切。

To tie in with the Hong Kong context, and in extension of its principle of nurturing creative talents, the Foundation has invited a curator and commissioned seven Hong Kong artists to participate in this exhibition. Although working in different media and styles, their work originates from their thoughts and passion for the unique urban life, social affairs, cultural heritage and psychology of Hong Kong, and is a mirror to the creative expression and characteristic of Hong Kong contemporary art.

译文1：

为与香港建立更密切关系，秉持其培育创意人才的宗旨和令展览更具香港特色，路易威登创意基金会委任的策展人，邀请和委约七位香港艺术家创作作品，同场展出。这七位艺术家以不同媒介和风格手法演绎的作品，源于其对香港城市生活、社会事件、文化生态、心理反应的思虑和情感，正反映了当代香港艺术的创意情感和特质。

分析：

To tie in with the Hong Kong context, tie in 意为 to have a close connection to, context 意为 surrounding condition，所以，这里需要增词，意思才能表达完整。译为：建立更密切关系，令展览更具香港特色。

译文2：

路易威登基金会委任了策展人，并邀约七位香港艺术家共同参展。

This exhibition marks a first collaboration between the Hong Kong Museum of Art and Louis Vuitton, a leading world brand name. Most of the exhibits have never been shown outside Paris and the exhibition has been organized exclusively for Hong Kong. Audiences are afforded an opportunity to view a valuable collection of Louis Vuitton and its commission works and a selection of the collection of the Foundation Louis Vuitton, the masterpiece by a contemporary architect and achievements of local young artists. The partnership between public and private sectors to organize a large-scale art exhibition also provides more opportunities for the people in Hong Kong to appreciate contemporary and avant-garde art. It also acts as an extension to the close link between the Hong Kong government and the Consulate General of France in Hong Kong and Macau.

译文1：

这次展览是艺术馆与世界品牌路易威登首次合作，而展览是为香港特别筹划，大部分展品也是首度在巴黎以外展出。展览令香港市民得以目睹路易威登和路易威登创意基金会的珍藏和特别委约作品，当代建筑大师的心血结晶和本地年轻艺术家的创意成就，实属难能可贵。今次的合作模式，也反映了公共机构和商业品牌的忠诚合作，合办纯粹艺术性的大展，令本港市民对当代和前卫艺术有更深入认识和欣赏机会。展览亦延展了香港政府与法国驻香港及澳门总领事馆一直以来的紧密文化交流，体现了中法两国良好的合作关系。

译文2：

这次展览是博物馆与世界品牌路易威登的首次合作，展览专为香港特别筹划，大部分展品首次在巴黎以外展出，令香港市民得以观赏路易威登和路易威登基金会的珍藏和特别委约作品，包括当代建筑大师的心血结晶和本地年轻艺术家的创意成就。这次由公共机构与商业品牌合作举办纯粹的艺术大展，为本港市民提供了深入认识与欣赏当代和前卫艺术的机会，也延伸了香港政府与法国驻香港及澳门总领事馆的密切联系。

（六）考虑受众的思维习惯以及信息传播方式

例10

涡阳苔干，名优特产，驰名中外，声震古今，翠绿、鲜嫩、青脆、可口，有"天然海蜇"和"健康食品"之称；清乾隆年间奉献皇宫，故又名"贡菜"。本品含蛋白质等十余种矿物质，有清热降压……诸功效；畅销国内，远销日本、港澳等地，为下厨及馈赠佳品。

译文：

GuoyangTaigan, a time-honored specialty enjoying great popularity, is jade green *in color* and delicious *in taste*. It is also named "Plant Jellyfish" or "Health Food", and was particularly chosen as one of the vegetarian offerings to the Palace of the Qing Dynasty. The main nutritive substances of Taigan are protein…etc. Taigan has been believed to be able to produce certain medical effects, namely, to allay internal heat and fever, … It sells well both in mainland China and Hong Kong, Macao and Japan. …

分析：

这是"苔干"包装袋上的英文介绍，"苔干"，即干菜，但是译文给英语读者的印象好像不是菜，而是有若干疗效（produce certain medical effects）的药用食品（medical diet）。虽然中国传统文化有食疗之说，但是理性的西方读者不会相信，这种夸张的文字应略去。译文中列出的营养元素应当是能被科学验证，至于这些营养物质有何"疗效"，让读者自己去判断。

产品说明的翻译还应考虑信息传播方式，也就是译文所出现的特殊环境（如杂志、广告牌、包装袋等），这篇译文出现在"苔干"的包装袋上，空间非常有限，应当力求简明；此外，译文 green *in color* and delicious *in taste* 画线部分属于冗余文字，予以删去。

第六章　旅游文本翻译

一、概述

随着全球化进程的加快与深化，跨国旅游已经成为人们丰富精神生活的重要组成部分。旅游有助于人们开阔眼界，丰富人生阅历，深入认识世界，亲身体验不同国家的地理风貌、文化传统和社会生活的方方面面。

旅游业是一个巨大的产业，不仅带来旅游景点的门票收入，更是带动了交通、餐饮、会议、酒店、购物体验、文化体育等相关产业的发展。会展旅游业已经成为推动我国经济发展的重要支柱产业之一，各地政府和企业不断投入巨资，打造或创新会展旅游产业，以便拓展更大的旅游发展空间。

旅游是文化的形和体，文化是旅游的根和魂，旅游宣传是文化沟通与交流的手段。实践证明，国际文化和文化产品的交流与合作远比国家和政府之间的交往更为现实有效。实现中国文化"走出去"战略的一个重要途径就是吸引海外旅游者体验中国文化，用互动方式展示中国，为我国蓬勃发展的文化创意产业吸引高端客源。因此，旅游文本翻译在旅游推广、发展经济和丰富人们精神生活方面发挥着重要作用。

旅游文本包括自然景观、人文景观、博物馆、酒店、餐饮等的宣传介绍。

旅游文本的目的在于提供旅游信息，吸引和呼唤读者去行动、去体验。旅游文本翻译属于对外宣传范畴，其目的是吸引更多海外游客体验中国。因此，旅游文本翻译强调可读性，满足读者的信息需求，以求达到信息传递的最佳效果。

旅游文本翻译从体裁上讲，属于功能翻译学派所界定的"信息型"（informative）+"呼唤型"（vocative）功能文本，它主要有两个功能，一是传递信息，二是唤起行动。

二、旅游指南的主题信息性质与分类

(一) 旅游产业发展的主题化特征

在一个全球旅游和信息互通的时代,游客对旅游项目或活动的品位和特色要求越来越高。我国旅游业为吸引更多海内外游客,对旅游项目的开发设计和宣传也越来越主题化(theme-oriented),即所谓"特色游"(feature tour),以满足不同层次和不同兴趣的游客需要。例如,"活力广东"(Guangdong of Vitality);清远——粤北后花园(the Backyard of Northern Guangdong);江西"红色"旅游(Red Tourism in Jiangxi / Revolutionary Site Tourism in Jiangxi)。这种主题化旅游的特点是突出旅游地或项目的特色性、观赏性、怡情性、知识性等。因此,旅游指南的写作和翻译也应突出这种主题化特色,根据旅游者对旅游项目的主题性、特色性、观赏性、怡情性、知识性等需求进行翻译。此外,译者还要对中文旅游文本的语言文字特征有明晰的认识,选择相应的翻译策略,以便有效地指导翻译实践。

(二) 旅游指南信息性质分类

旅游指南的文字信息主要分为八大类型。

1. **事实性信息 (Factive Information)**

信息性质:基本信息。信息功能:向游客介绍有关旅游地及其主题项目的特色、条件与环境等信息。信息特征:具有客观性。信息传达度:相对最强;译者应对信息价值做出判断,决定翻译传递的信息量。

2. **描述性信息 (Descriptive Information)**

信息性质:兼具基本信息和附加信息——对旅游地及其主题特色项目特征的描述性信息。信息功能:描述旅游地及其主题特色项目的性质与特征。信息特征:兼具客观性和主观性,可能有夸张的倾向。信息传达度:适中;译者应对中文原文过度渲染夸张的文字信息进行删减。

3. **评价性信息 (Evaluative /Appraisal Information)**

信息性质:附加信息——对旅游地及其主题项目的评价等。信息功能:加深游客对有关主题项目的认识。信息特征:具有暗示或诱导性,这类文字会带有原作者的个人表达风格,主观性强。信息传达度:适中;译者应对中文原文过度渲染夸张或累赘的文字进行删减。

4. 文化信息（Cultural Information）

信息性质：兼具基本信息与附加信息——旅游地及其主题特色项目具有的民族文化特色。信息功能：加深游客对中华文化的了解，增进文化交流。信息特征：有文化内容过载现象，有些中文文本包含的信息过于宽泛，且内容太深，非常专业化，像是教科书，一般游客难以理解掌握。信息传达度：相对较强，但具较大的灵活性；译者应把握海外游客对相关文化内容的需求和接受能力。

5. 召唤性信息（Vocative Information）

信息性质：附加信息——就主题项目向游客发出的召唤性信息。信息功能：唤起游客潜在的热情或兴趣。信息特征：带有汉民族特有的思维和表达方式。信息传达度：相对较强；译者应注意把握海外游客的心理需求与接受能力。

6. 美学信息（Aesthetic Information）

信息性质：附加信息——运用修辞形式、意象形态、结构形式与节奏等语言文字形式。信息功能：具有汉民族语言文字审美感，以增强文本的感染力。信息特征：带有汉民族语言文化思维特征，但一般难以在另一种语言中体现。信息传达度：相对较弱；译者应注意两种语言的差异。

7. 风格信息（Stylistic Information）

信息性质：附加信息——主要指个人文字风格。信息功能：增强或影响基本信息的接受效果。信息特征：具有原作者个性特征，如文字运用或简练明快，或冗长繁复。信息传达度：较弱。

8. 提示性信息（Information of Tips）

信息性质：基本信息兼具附加信息——依附于二三级主题信息之后的有关注意事项。信息功能：向游客提供项目开放时间、交通乘车、购物须知及民俗禁忌等。信息传达度：强。

（引自《应用翻译讲义》，有所删改）

通过以下实例观察不同性质的信息在旅游宣传和翻译中的作用。

例1

原文：

杭州——人间天堂

1 意大利著名旅行家马可·波罗曾经这样叙述他印象中的杭州：

"这是世界上最美妙迷人的城市,它使人觉得自己是在天堂。"在中国,也流传着这样的话:"上有天堂,下有苏杭。"杭州的名气主要在于风景如画的西湖。西湖一年四季都美不胜收,宋代著名诗人苏东坡用"淡妆浓抹总相宜"的诗句来赞誉西湖。在杭州,您可以饱览西湖的秀色,也不妨漫步街头闹市,品尝一下杭州的名菜名点,还可购上几样名特土产。

2 苏堤和白堤把西湖一分为二,仿佛两条绿色的缎带,飘逸于绿波之上,湖中心有三个小岛:阮公墩、湖心亭和小瀛洲。湖水泛着涟漪,四周山林茂密,点缀着楼台亭阁,是我国最有名的旅游景点之一。

3 杭州人观看西湖有个说法:"晴湖不如雨湖,雨湖不如夜湖。"您在杭州,一定要去领略一下西湖的风韵,看看此说是否有道理。

4 杭州是中国著名的六大古都之一,已有两千多年的历史。杭州不仅以自然美景闻名于世,而且有着传统文化的魅力;不仅有历史文人墨客的题咏,而且有美味佳肴和漂亮的工艺品。

5 杭州是中国的"丝绸之府",丝绸产品品种繁多,其中以织锦尤为引人注目。杭州还生产黑纸扇和檀香扇。其他特产有西湖绸伞和中国十大名茶之一的西湖龙井。

6 杭州有许多有名的餐馆,供应各邦菜点,还有一百多家旅馆酒店,为游客提供舒适的住宿。

7 一般来说,游览西湖及周围景点花上两天时间较为合适。到杭州旅游,既令人愉快,又能得到文化享受。(引自《实用旅游英语翻译教程》)

译文:

Hangzhou—Paradise on Earth

1 The famous Italian traveler Marco Polo was so impressed by the beauty of Hangzhou that he described it as "the most fascinating city in the world where one feels that one is in paradise." Similarly, in China a century-old popular saying goes like "Suzhou and Hangzhou, paradises on earth". As Hangzhou's beauty lies mainly in its picturesque West Lake all the year round, you will not only find the lake a perfect delight to the eye but also find it a joy to stroll along the busy streets, taste delicious Hangzhou dishes and buy some special local products.

2 The West Lake is bisected by the Su Causeway and the Bai Causeway which look like two green ribbons floating gracefully on the blue waters. The

lake, with three isles in the center and thickly-wooded hills dotted by exquisite pavilions on its four sides, is one of China's best known scenic spots.

3　Hangzhou residents have their way of enjoying the beauty of the Lake, "The West Lake looks delightful on rainy days than on clear days, and is at its best when darkness falls".

4　One of China's six ancient capital cities, Hangzhou has a history of more than 2,000 years. It is famous not only for its natural beauty but also for its cultural traditions. Apart from a large number of poems and inscriptions in its praise left behind by scholars and men of letters through the centuries, it also boasts delicious food and pretty handicrafts.

5　Hangzhou is the home of silk in China. Its silk products come in a great variety, among which its brocade is especially attractive. Hangzhou also specializes in making black paper fans and sandalwood fans. Other specialties include silk parasols and West Lake Longjing Tea, which is among the top ten produced in China.

6　Hangzhou boasts many fine restaurants, serving a wide range of cuisines. The city also offers comfortable accommodation with a great choice of hotels.

7　It is advisable for a tourist to have a two-day tour of the West Lake and scenic spots around it. And you will find the trip to Hangzhou both pleasant and culturally rewarding.

分析：

第1段，借用名人之言以及东西方对杭州的赞美之词，概括和突出杭州旅游之魅力与主题，属于评价性信息和召唤性信息，恰如其分地推广杭州旅游："What to do"，"What to see"，"How to enjoy"。信息价值度强。但是，"宋代著名诗人苏东坡用'淡妆浓抹总相宜'的诗句来赞誉西湖"（The West Lake was compared by Su Dongpo, a celebrated poet of the Song Dynasty, to a beauty "who is always charming in either light or heavy makeup."），对中文读者来说有很强的历史文化价值，普通英语读者不一定能领会，可以从略。

第2段，具体描述西湖风景，属于描述性信息和美学信息，信息价值度较强。

第3段用评价性信息"晴湖不如雨湖，雨湖不如夜湖"介绍如何观赏西湖，但是，"您在杭州，一定要去领略一下西湖的风韵，看看此说是否有道理"信息价值度低，为了不阻断信息的连续性，可以略去。

第4段，介绍杭州的历史文化遗产，属于事实性信息和文化信息，信息价值度强。

第5段，介绍杭州特产，属于事实性信息，信息价值度较强。

第6段，介绍杭州的食宿条件，属于事实性信息，信息价值度较强。

第7段，提示性信息（对旅游时间安排的建议）和召唤性信息，信息价值度较强。

（三）旅游指南主题分级与特点

下面以香港旅游发展局2001年推出的中英文对照《香港旅游锦囊》（*Visitor's Kit*）为例。这本旅游指南，主题信息突出，图文并茂，译文有简有繁，主题结构层次分明，可以根据其性质与功能划分为一级主题（first-level theme）、二级主题（secondary-level theme）和三级主题（third-level theme）。

一级主题是指南首页的概括性介绍，包括两部分内容：首先简要介绍旅游地的历史、地理、文化特征；其次介绍旅游城市或旅游地重点推出的特色主题项目，如民俗文化、自然景观、人文景观等。一级主题的译介要求简洁扼要、主题信息突出。如《香港旅游锦囊》首页的"动感之都：就是香港"就是一级主题，英语译文突出的就是体现"动感"这一主题所包含的系列旅游项目及盛事的概览性介绍，弱化和虚化了原文一些关联性不大的描述和评价性文字。

二级主题是指对一级主题概览中列出的重点或品牌旅游项目或景观的介绍。这类主题项目特色突出，信息的译介倾向于具体化，描述性和评价性文字比较突出，目的是给游客提供感性认识，以唤起他们潜在的兴趣。

三级主题是指当地其他一些小型的特定旅游项目，包括购物、美食、建筑风格、工艺品展示、茶道表演等。这类信息译介倾向于具体细节描写，让海外游客了解中华文化、风土人情或有关活动的具体特色等。

三、主题关联信息突出策略原则及其可操作性

随着旅游产业向主题化特色化发展，旅游指南译介必然要反映这一发展趋势。由于中西语言文化方面的差异以及不同的接受心理和信息需求度，旅游指南的译介不能完全按照中文文本一一对译，需要译者给予必要的动态调节，但这种调节并非是主观随意的，应从"主题信息突出"策

略原则出发予以把握。在具体实践中,译者可以根据不同主题,对突出什么、弱化或虚化什么做出判断。

下面主要以《香港旅游锦囊》的中、英对照文本为例,讨论一、二、三级主题信息突出策略原则及其相关准则的应用。

(一) 主题关联信息突出策略原则在一级主题翻译中的应用

在对一级主题信息内容的翻译中,译者在策略原则上应突出主题事实的关联性信息,弱化、简化或虚化与主题关联性不大的、冗长繁杂的描述或评价性文字。

例2

动感之都:就是香港!

1 香港地方虽小,却多彩多姿。她那与众不同的气质,是多么独一无二……

2 中国人的传统,西方的文化,加上百多年的殖民历史,香港俨如是一个多元文化的万花筒,眼见耳闻,千姿百态,难怪号称"动感之都"。

3 世界级的建筑、全年不绝的盛事、时尚的生活方式,造就了香港的典雅风华,令人目眩心醉。另一方面,她也可令人疯狂,精致美食和潮流精品,最为旅客津津乐道,超过一万家餐厅和无数商店,正等待着您去发掘。

4 由现在至2003年,"动感之都:就是香港!"大型旅游推广项目带来一连串缤纷热闹的盛事。焦点是五个主要大型活动,打响头炮的是2001年12月至2002年2月的"全城动感灯辉",接踵而来的有"国泰航空国际会演贺新禧""花城荟萃大展""新世纪劲买"以及2003年的"动感热舞嘉年华"。如您能适逢其会,参与其中,您的香港之旅必定会留下更多美好的回忆。

译文:

City of Life: Hong Kong Is It!

1 Hong Kong City of Life is a small place that lives large. A living fusion of East and West, it presents visitors with an ever-changing kaleidoscope of color and culture.

2 Combining around 150 yeas of colonial influence and 5,000 years of Chinese tradition, Hong Kong has its own special brand of magic and mystique.

3 From now until 2003, Hong Kong is featuring its "City of Life: Hong Kong Is It!" campaign, with 5 major events including "Hong Kong Lights Up" in December 2001 to February 2002, the Cathay Pacific International Chinese New Year Parade, the Hong Kong Flower Extravaganza, as well as the Mega Hong Kong Sale in 2002 and the City of Life Street Carnival in 2003. If you can include these events in your itinerary, your trip to Hong Kong will be all the more memorable.

Fusion—meeting together

Mystique—mysterious and attractive image

Extravaganza—a spectacular event

Carnival—a celebration with singing, dancing, and usu. a parade

Itinerary—a travel plan

分析：

一级主题的翻译体现了鲜明的主题信息突出特征：从文字信息性质看，第1段中的描述性信息"多彩多姿"及评价性信息"她那与众不同的气质，是多么独一无二"在译介中被弱化了。第2段中还有类似的描述被略去。译者选用 a small place that lives large 表现香港"小中见大"的生活气息，简洁新颖。但若将该语句单独作为一段则有点简短空洞，还需要相应的内容与之呼应，故译者将原文段第2段后面部分能反映"小中见大"和"动感"的文字提至第1段来表达，略去描述性文字"眼见耳闻""千姿百态"和评价性文字"难怪号称'动感之都'"，在译文中突出 large 的内涵，即"多元文化"特征和"万花筒"（蕴含"千姿百态"）的语义信息，并且还刻意突出中西文化交融和体现"动感"的信息，如…living fusion of East and West，…. ever-changing kaleidoscope of color and culture，译文简洁达意，表现力强，体现了整体把握调节译文内容，达到主题信息突出之目的。

第2段以简练的文字概括了香港的历史文化特征，译文增译具体数字 around 150 yeas … and 5,000 years，客观地突出了对当今香港具有深远影响的事实性信息，同时还增加了评价性信息…has its own special brand（独特品牌）of magic and mystique（魔力和神秘性），这是译者的创造性处理：用旅游品牌及其"魔力和神秘"诱导游客的猎奇心理，主观与客观表达相结合，增加了文本的美学效果。

第 3 段原文信息在译文中略去，可能出于以下考虑：

这篇文字的主题信息是"动感之都"，突出宣传香港旅游发展局策划推出的一系列阶段性（2001—2003）旅游盛事，而原文第 3 段中的事实性信息，诸如建筑、美食和精品以及上万家餐厅等均与一级主题内容关联性不大，属于《香港旅游锦囊》后面三级主题信息部分的内容，在此处的信息功能与价值度很小，应当略去。

第 4 段突出宣传了"动感之都"的主题信息，这是香港推出的跨越三年的一系列旅游文化盛事，这段文字信息基本上全部译出。《香港旅游锦囊》首页英译文体现了旅游指南一级主题信息突出的策略原则。

（引自《应用翻译讲义》）

（二）主题信息突出策略原则在二级主题翻译中的应用

例 3

九龙寨公园（九龙城区）

昔日的九龙城寨是一个"三不管"的地方，可以说是龙蛇混杂之地。其后，城寨全面清拆，并于 1995 年于原址建成今日的九龙寨公园。九龙寨公园曾获荣誉奖状，它具有江南园林风格，并刻意保留了现今难得一见的南中国"衙门"建筑，以及历史遗迹如南门古迹、石匾、大炮、柱基、清朝官府的碑铭等。

原译：

Kowloon Walled City Park (Kowloon City District)

The former Koloon Walled City, once a semi-lawless, high-rise slum, has been transformed into an award-winning park featuring a Qing Dynasty almshouse, the Old South Gate, pavilions, sculptures, flower garden and a playground.

分析：

这是《香港旅游锦囊》中所包含的二级主题信息。"九龙寨公园"的译介应突出其两大特色：江南园林艺术和历史遗迹，以唤起海外游客的兴趣。

但英译文不仅略去了"江南园林风格""现今难得一见的衙门建筑""石匾、大炮、柱基、清朝官府的碑铭""城寨全面清拆"等文化信息，取而代之的是 pavilions, sculptures, flower garden and a playground（亭、雕塑、花园和运动场）等没有历史文物特征的信息内容，尤其是译文用 almshouse "济贫院" 取代了 "衙门"（"衙门" 已收入英语词典，释义为 the offices and residence of a mandarin）。此外，第1句中的 "一个'三不管'的地方，可以说是龙蛇混杂之地"，旨在说明这里发生的巨大变化，但这不是游客关注的信息。可见译者对这条二级主题信息的翻译有很大的随意性，没能将主题信息突出策略原则贯彻到整个指南的翻译中，失去了文本风格的整体感。

改译：

The Kowloon Walled City, with its former walls removed, was transformed into the present Park in 1995, which has been honored awards for its fascinating scenes featuring South China gardening art as well as relics characteristic of yamen architecture of the Qing Dynasty, the Old South Gate, stone plaques, cannons, plinths, feudal official inscriptions, etc.（曾利沙）

（三）主题信息突出策略原则在三级主题翻译中的应用

例 4

鲤鱼门海鲜美食村

鲤鱼门以海鲜美食驰名，最适宜三五知己晚饭共聚。在这里，顾客可到海鲜摊子亲自挑选鲜活的海产，然后亲自交给菜馆炮制，客人更可指定烹调的方式。当然，在点菜前宜先查询价钱。

译文：

Lei Yue Mun Seafood Bazaar

This fishing village is popular for its seafood and ideal for a night out with friends. You can choose your own fresh fish (so fresh it's still swimming in a tank!) and decide how you'd like it prepared. Make sure you ask the price before ordering.（曾利沙）

分析：

这条有关 "美食" 的三级主题信息，译者突出了海鲜美食的 "鲜活" 和 "自主烹调方式"，也译出了为游客着想的 "在点菜前宜先查询价钱" 的提示性信息。为了突出 "鲜活" 这一主题关联信息，译者增译了 so fresh it's still swimming in a tank！（但是这句话的增译可能不适合欧美国家的游客）。此外，原文"最适宜三五知己"是泛说，可删略；原文"亲自交给菜馆炮制"被"客人更可指定烹调的方式"所蕴含，故可删略。这条三级主题信息的译介体现了主题信息突出策略原则。

例5

长沙湾道时装街及鸭寮街跳蚤市场

介于钦州街至黄竹街之间的一段长沙湾道，时装批发店铺林立，女士们可以低廉的价格购买到时尚的服饰。鸭寮街跳蚤市场，主要售卖电器用品、电子零件等，亦有摊贩出售古老时钟、钱币及各式各样的收藏品，如果细心找寻，可能发现超值的稀有古物也说不定。

原译：

Cheung Sha Wan Road fashion street and
Ap Liu Street（Sham Shui Po District）

Cheung Sha Wan Road, Sham Shui Po, is a great place to pick up trendy fashions at wholesale prices. Most of the shops can be found between Yen Chow Street and Wong Chuk Street. <u>And at Ap Liu Street's flee market you might unearth a collectible souvenir.</u>

分析：

这条以"购物"为主的三级主题信息介绍，涉及时装街和跳蚤市场。在对前者的操作中，译者增译了评价性信息 a great place，译出相应的事实信息 trendy fashions at wholesale prices。但在对后者的操作中，却对最能唤起游客潜在兴趣的事实信息"古老时钟、钱币、各式收藏品"和带有诱导信息的"可能发现超值的稀有古物"作了删略处理，将其概括性地译为 you might unearth a collectible souvenir，从而将鸭寮街跳蚤市场的特色和吸引力弱化了。因为，souvenir 意为 thing taken, brought as a gift; and kept to remind one of a person, a place or an event，纪念品到处有售，不一定具有收藏价值，不能与"收藏品"和"稀有古物"相提并论。可见此三级主题信息翻译也存在随意性。

改译：

And at Ap Liu Street's flea market you may find a variety of collections for sale such as coins and old-fashioned clocks. With a keen eye, you may accidentally unearth rare antiques！（曾利沙）

例 6

以下是 2011 年纽约旅游宣传中的一则购物指南，属于三级主题信息，这种灵活多变和煽情的表达方式值得学习借鉴。

Shop NYC: Great Gifts for Mother's Day

1 If you're looking for a gift for May 8, you've come to the right place: the shopping capital of the world. Here are some excellent ideas from a variety of stores.

2 Has Mom seen every episode of Sex and the City, The Sopranos…? Then drop by The HBO Shop located in midtown Manhattan, home to a variety of T-shirts featuring your favorite characters from Sex and the City…The HBO Shop also offers a wide range of Sex and the City merchandise, including… You'll also find full line of The Sopranos memorabilia…

3 For seemingly limitless gift ideas, one of the best places to start is the iconic department store, Macy's, the 11-floor flagship store located in Herald Square—just south of Times Square and a hop, skip, and a jump from the Empire State Building and Penn Station—is home to an enormous selection of fashion items, the hottest new items, products for family and home, great sales, and much more. Broadway at 34th St.

分析：

第 1 段煽情，诱发购物愿望；第 2 段介绍特色或主题化商品；第 3 段介绍著名的梅西百货和便利的交通方式。这些都是实用的适时性信息，具有很强的针对性。

四、英汉旅游文体特色及其风格差异

旅游文本属于大众通俗读物，旨在传播旅游信息，唤起旅游热情。因此，旅游文本翻译不是文学翻译，旅游活动不是文学欣赏和文化调研。由于中西方语言文化上的差异，读者在各自特定的语言文化环境熏陶下，养成了一种固有的思维方式和审美习惯。因此，应用翻译中出现的"英译汉化"现象，其根源在于译者忽略了汉、英语言文化上的差异，忽略了译文读者的文化心理和审美习惯，一味将汉语的思维模式和审美要求强加于英译文之上，与英语读者产生审美意识上的错位。（贾文波，2008）

同时,由于不同的文化背景和语言表达习惯,中西方读者对同一旅游主题的信息需求会有很大差异。而且,旅游文本的写作具有多样性,旅游文本的翻译也是多元化的,译者通过对文本种类与文本特色的判断,选择相应的翻译策略与方法。

(一) 文本特征

不同的文化背景和语言表达习惯,形成了英汉各自不同的写作风格和审美标准,而且对同一主题文本的信息需求也有很大差别。

1. 中文旅游文本特征

(1) 中文旅游文本涉及的内容广泛,喜欢追溯历史,像是一本教科书。

下面这段武汉市旅游宣传涉及的内容很多:历史人物、古建筑、古代史和近现代史等等,包罗万象。但是,要想理解掌握这些信息内容,游客需要一定的相关历史文化背景知识,才能体验到这座位于湖滨的历史文化名城的魅力。武汉是位于我国中部河流湖泊密布的大都市,以此与具有相似地理和战略地位的芝加哥做一对比。

例7

武汉市自然风光绚丽多姿,人文景观璀璨夺目。屈原曾在这里行吟;李白曾在这里漫游;商代盘龙城遗址,是长江流域发现的第一座商代古城;龟山脚下的古琴台流传着俞伯牙和钟子期知音相会的千年佳话;黄鹤楼名闻天下,晴川阁古色古香。市内有辛亥首义红楼、农民运动讲习所、八七会议遗址等52所革命纪念地。

(2) 语言表达华丽,用词丰富,运用多种修辞手段营造美景,给读者带来身临其境的感觉,从而达到吸引游客的目的。

例8

原文:
这儿的峡谷又是另一番景象:谷中急水奔流,穿峡而过,两岸树木葱茏,鲜花繁茂,碧草萋萋,活脱脱一幅春意盎然的天然风景画。各种奇峰异岭,令人感受各异,遐想万千。

分析:
这段中文旅游宣传文本,用了多个四字和六字结构词组,具有节奏韵律之美。但是,这种语言文字结构的美感在英语中难以表达出来,因为中文有些词是重复使用的叠词,如"萋萋、脱脱";有的是语义重复,纯属出于结构平衡之需,如"奇峰、异岭"。若按中文词句翻译,译文会显得文字累赘,故英译时需要按照英语的句式结构习惯予以处理。

译文:

It is another gorge through which a rapid stream flows. Trees, flowers and grass thrive on both banks, showing a picture of natural vitality. The weird peaks arouse disparate thoughts. (方梦之)

2. 英语旅游文本特征

英语旅游文本注重介绍景点的事实性信息和特色,文体大多风格简约,结构严谨而不复杂,表达直观通俗,注重信息传递的准确性和语言表达的吸引力,易于各种不同文化层次的读者阅读与接受。

下面是两个旅游网站上的芝加哥旅游宣传,介绍了芝加哥多彩的文化艺术和丰富的城市生活元素,语言表达平实易懂,富有表现力,使得这座城市的卖点突出(画线部分),很有感召力,易于游客理解掌握,马上付诸行动:What to see, What to do 和 How to enjoy。

例9

Chicago

Chicago is located in the Midwest. It is the third largest city in the United States. Chicago is a huge vibrant city and sprawling metropolitan area. <u>It is the home of the blues and the truth of jazz</u>, the heart of comedy and the first builder of the skyscraper. Here, the age of railroads found its center, and airplanes followed. It is one of the world's great cities, and yet the metropolitan <u>luxuries of theater, shopping, and fine dining have barely put a dent in real Midwestern friendliness</u>. It's a city with a swagger, but without the surliness or even the fake smiles that can be found in other cities.

As the hub of the Midwest, Chicago is easy to find —<u>its picturesque skyline calls across the waters of huge Lake Michigan, a first impression that soon reveals world-class museums of art and science, miles of sandy beaches, huge parks and public art, and perhaps the finest downtown collection of architecture in the world.</u>

With a wealth of iconic sights and neighborhoods to explore, there's enough to fill a visit of weeks or even months without ever seeing the end. Prepare to cover a lot of ground: the meaning of Chicago is only found in movement, through its subways and archaic elevated tracks, and eyes raised to the sky.

Chicago Wikitravel——http://wikitravel.org/en/Chicago

例 10

Plan Your Chicago Vacation

Chicago is a city with an appetite—<u>for food, of course, but also for design, history, and culture. Come here to marvel at the cutting-edge architecture or take in the gorgeous views of Lake Michigan</u>; <u>to spend a day cheering with baseball fans and a night laughing at a comedy show</u>; <u>to shop, to visit renowned institutions like the Field Museum and the Adler Planetarium</u>, and to experience the legendary blues scene. To do all this, you'll need nourishment: <u>taste deep-dish pizza, piled-high hot dogs, Italian beef sandwiches</u>, and more.

Chicago Travel Guide——http://www.fodors.com/world/north-america/usa/illinois/chicago/

例 11

If you want to discover the <u>dazzling beauty</u> of the Alps, you'll soon realize that a trip to Gornergrat at 3,089 m is a "<u>must-see</u>" <u>excursion</u>. For more than 100 years the Gornergrat Bahn has been making the ascent to the <u>panoramic mountain</u> a truly unique and wonderful experience. From Zermatt, the popular Gornergrat Bahn, Europe's highest open-air cogwheel railway departs daily every 24 minutes, climbing to the Gornergrat 9.339 km away. The train crosses impressive bridges, <u>galleries</u> and tunnels in the midst of idyllic forests and alpine meadows, past rocky gorges and tarns. (Accompanied by the majestic mountains, first and foremost by the Matterborn.) The Gornergrat's sunny viewing platform, accessible all year, makes the Gornergrat ridge a top destination, and not just because of its altitude. Surrounded by 29 peaks rising to above 4,000 m / 13,000 ft and by Swizerland's greatest mountain and second longest glacier in the Alps, it offers a <u>spectacular mountain panorama</u> <u>second to none</u>.

分析：

这篇英文自然风光旅游宣传对观光项目的悠久历史、景区特色和交通方式等事实性信息都做了详尽描述，用词准确生动，语言表达富有感染力。

译文：

要想探索美丽的阿尔卑斯山，登上海拔 3089 米的戈尔内格拉特是"必游之旅"。100 多年来，戈尔内格拉特铁路公司已将这趟登山之旅变换成一场全时空景观的绝佳体验。戈尔内格拉特铁路公司运营的欧洲海拔最高的开敞式齿轨列车每 24 分钟从采儿马特发车，驶向 9.339 公里外的戈尔内格拉特。列车在壮丽的桥梁与景观隧道中穿梭，沿途经过原生态丛林、阿尔卑斯牧场、奇山异石的峡谷和点缀其间的湖泊，一路有宏伟的山峰相伴，其中最壮丽的当属马特宏峰。戈尔内格拉特观景平台沐浴在灿烂的阳光下，全年开放。由此，戈尔内格拉特山脊成为最热门的观光目的地，但其吸引力不仅仅是其海拔高度。置身于 29 座海拔 4000 多米高的雄伟山峰以及瑞士最高峰和阿尔卑斯山第二长冰川的环抱中，游客可以尽享峰峦环绕的无敌景观。

（引自《实用旅游英语翻译教程》）

（二）多积累、研究和模仿

译者要译出语言和风格都地道的旅游篇章，需要积累大量的英语平行文本，研究英语作者在类似的场景中频繁使用的句型和词语，并进行模仿。

旅游文本必须以读者为中心才能实现文本功能，即实现译文与原文的功能对应。为了有效传递信息，感染受众，译者必须顾及译文读者的欣赏习惯和心理感受，在译文中尽量使用他们所熟悉的语言表达方式，这样才能尽可能使译文获得近似原文的读者效应。

例 12

这篇洛克菲勒大厦旅游观光宣传文本介绍了登上大厦之巅的观景特色以及该中心的几个观光项目组合，提供了非常实用的信息，对广州塔的旅游宣传很有借鉴作用。

原文：

New York offers many venues that feature different skyline views—but few come close to Top of the Rock. High-tech sky shuttle elevators will take you up to the 67th floor and the Grand Viewing Room, a wrap-around space that has northern and southern views. The 70th floor—a mere 20 feet wide and 200 feet long—crowns the building with a 360-degree panoramic view of the city. Top of the Rock offers many ticketing options that combine admission to neighboring attractions at a reduced price. These include the Rock Pass, which also grants admission the NBC Studio Tour, and is available at the box offices for both venues; the Art & Observation Tour, which includes a tour of the exquisite art and architecture of Rockefeller Center, and the Rock MoMA (Museum of Modern Art) combination ticket. Another intriguing option is the Sunrise Sunset ticket, which allows you to visit twice in one day—during the daylight and in the evening. Tickets are available for purchase by calling 877-NYC-ROCK or by visiting…

The Grand Viewing Room on the 67th floor, a wrap-around space that has northern and southern views. （借助图片帮助理解和翻译）

分析：

第一句属于评价性信息和召唤性信息，非常煽情。其后的语句都属于事实性信息，最后以提示性信息收尾，直截了当，直奔主题。

译文：

纽约拥有众多的观景点，展现了不同的城市景观，但都无法与站在洛克菲勒大厦之巅观景媲美。高科技空中巴士电梯带您登上67层的环绕式观景大厅，在那里可以观赏南北景观，登上70层的观景台（长200英尺，宽20英尺）可以观赏到360度的环绕景观。洛克菲勒中心提供多个景点的折扣/优惠套票：洛克菲勒中心门票，包括NBC（National Broadcasting Company美国全国广播公司）摄影棚之旅；艺术与观赏之旅，包括观赏洛克菲勒中心的精美艺术品与建筑，以及洛克菲勒现代艺术博物馆；另一个诱人的选择是观日出赏日落，这款门票可以让您在一天之内两次进入洛克菲勒中心。

例13

原文：

1 广州塔是一座集旅游、餐饮、文化娱乐和环保科普教育等多功能于一体，具有丰富文化内涵的大型景观建筑，她集合了当代工程设计和施工最新技术，承接了广州这座历史古城2000多年的文化，向世人展示了腾飞的广州挑战自我、面向世界的视野和气魄。

2 广州塔矗立在广州市新中轴线与珠江景观的交汇处，与海心沙岛市民广场和珠江新城隔江相望，和北岸双塔"三足鼎立"，与广州歌剧院、广东省博物馆、广州图书馆、广州第二少年宫四大文化建筑遥相呼应，是广州新的制高点。她在鳞次栉比的中国超高建筑中独占魁首，其塔体高约450米，天线桅杆高150米，以总高度600米占据世界第一高电视塔的地位。

3 新高度、新视野，广州塔令您体验全新广州城貌。

原译：

1 Canton Tower, the new landmark building of Guangzhou is a must-go scenic spot for tourists. 600 meters above sea level, Canton Tower, which is the highest TV tower of the world, tops the city skyline. In the tourist hall at the top of the tower, you can get a panoramic view of the spectacular city landscape.

2 You may marvel at the unique and beautiful structure and mind-numbing height of Canton Tower. The tower is cordially called by Guangzhou citizens as "small waistline". Once you step into the elevators in the 7.2-meter-high tower bottom, you begin your remarkable tour of the tower. High-

speed double-deck elevators fly from the tower bottom to the top at ten-minute intervals. At a speed of five meters per second, the elevator will take you to the top at 433 meters within less than one and a half minutes. <u>As the elevator rises, you can appreciate the shrinking view of city landscape through the elevator's transparent glass door.</u>

3 The thrilling moment comes once you step into the tourist hall at the top. Standing at the highest point of the city, you feel as if the sky and clouds are at your fingertips. Through the 360° circular ground glass, <u>you will be shocked at the breathtaking view of the city</u>. If you have the "audacity", you can step into the transparent viewing corridor. <u>Through the transparent glass floor under your feet, you may feel your heart beating and pulse racing when you look all the way down to the tower bottom.</u>

分析：

通过比较中英文本，可以看出这两个文本有明显差异，说明译者已经注意到了中外读者在信息需求和审美习惯上的差异，但是两个文本都没有提供充足的实质性信息。

中文原文中的画线部分属于评价性信息，与广州塔的特色和吸引力关联性不大，信息价值度低。况且，电视观光塔在国内外大城市中已经相当普及，对外国游客来说算不上什么工程奇迹。

译文存在如下问题：

（1）译文省略了"广州塔矗立在广州市新中轴线与珠江景观的交汇处，与海心沙岛市民广场和珠江新城隔江相望，广州歌剧院、广东省博物馆、广州图书馆……"等重要信息（如下图所示）。首先，城市中轴线（中轴对称）是中国历史上城市布局的重要特色，只有通过鸟瞰的方式才能得以展现，需要特别介绍；其次，海心沙、广州歌剧院、广东省博物馆、广州图书馆是广州新的文化地标景观，它们是建筑大师的设计创意，将这些重要信息略去，那么登高远眺看什么。

（2）The tower is cordially called by Guangzhou citizens as "small waistline"，广州塔被称为"小蛮腰"，这是从中国人的审美视角描述，不一定符合外国游客的审美习惯。

（3）译文第2段和第3段属于描述性信息和评价性信息，缺乏事实性信息。

（4）译文中其他画线部分属于一般性常识，没有太大的信息价值。

广州市新中轴线起始点鸟瞰，近景：海心沙广场；中景：歌剧院（左）、博物馆和图书馆（右）

因此，译者在翻译中应该对译文的语篇结构等方面进行调整，以适应译文读者的思维方式和信息需求。为了突出广州塔的特色，需要对原文提供的信息进行筛选和重组，第 1 段介绍广州塔的位置、设施配置和周边景观；第 2 段介绍如何登塔，如何观景。参照例 12 对原译做如下修改。

改译：

1 Canton Tower, the new landmark structure in Guangzhou is a must-go sightseeing spot, offering an array of facilities like restaurants, leisure activities and education. Being the highest of its kind in the world, the TV tower, 600 meter in height, tops the city skyline. Situated at a joint point where the new city axis meets the Pear River, <u>the top of the tower offers a panoramic view of the spectacular city landscape</u>, especially the new attractions <u>with their signature designs</u>, such as Guangzhou Opera House, Guangdong Museum, Guangzhou New Library and Haixinsha Square where the opening ceremony of the 2010 Guangzhou Asian Games was staged.

2 High-speed double-deck sky shuttle elevators will take you to the top at 433 meters, at ten-minute intervals. If you are not content with enjoying the view inside the viewing hall, you can step into the transparent viewing corridor.

Standing on the transparent glass floor, you will feel like hanging in the air, with your heart beating loudly and pulse racing when your look all the way down.

（三）译前精简内容，弱化宣传语气

翻译自然及人文景观前，先进行译前处理，直接压缩观点性的想象、修饰成分，精简原引的诗词警句，弱化僵硬呆板的宣传语气。

旅游景点曾经是文人墨客的云游之地，留下了千古名言诗句，极大地丰富了旅游地的自然景观和历史文化内涵，中文旅游文本往往会引用名言诗句来突出景点的历史价值和美学价值，那些诗词典故对中文读者无疑是美的享受。但是，国外游客对中国历史文化知之甚少，如果将诗词和朝代毫无保留地翻译成英文，会增加读者的理解负担，降低译文的可读性。因为旅游文本是大众通俗读物，旨在传播旅游信息，引发旅游热情。因此，译者应当打破汉语原文的构篇模式，依据英语习惯的规范重新谋篇。

对于同一类中国山水风光的旅游宣传，中外写手的视角和表达方式截然不同。

例 14

Emei Shan

On the boat, tourists can enjoy the landscape on the both sides of the river, which is beautifully described by the great poet Li Bai in his line, "The crescent moon shines bright like autumn's golden brow" … For the landscape of Leshan, the famous poet Zhang Wentao from the Qing Dynasty praised in one of his poems, …

分析：

这段指南没有摆脱汉语修辞的束缚，原文的诗句毫无遗漏，没有考虑英语读者的审美习惯、接受能力和信息需求。

例 15

Tai Shan

Tai Shan is 1545m above sea level, with a climbing distance of 7.5km from base to summit on the central route…

The tourist season peaks from May to October... The summit can be very cold, windy and wet; army coats are available there for rental and you can buy waterproof coats from one of the ubiquitous vendors. (from *China*, *Lonely Planet*)

分析：

这段指南出自英语作者之手，全文紧紧围绕登山的难度和天气展开，提供了登山所需的实用信息。

例 16

原文：

飞水潭

飞水潭是鼎湖山空气含负离子最高的地方之一，飞瀑、绿树、幽潭组成了一个清凉世界。这里常有女子弹古筝，端正的面庞、悠扬的乐曲与溪流声交相辉映，就是一幅绝美的图画。（瀑布从40多米高的崖顶深处狂奔而来，忽而形成千尺飞流，如白练悬空；忽而溅作满天雨花……）（引自《肇庆旅游指南》）

原译：

Flying Water Pond is one of the places with the highest density of negative ions in the air in the Dinghu Mountain. The flying waterfall, green trees, and the deep pond constitute a picturesque world. Here often a beautiful lady plays zheng, a Chinese zither with 25 strings. Her angelical face, melodious music and the stream flow sound match harmoniously. What a beautiful scene it is!

分析：

第1句是对景点的描述，属于事实性信息；第2句"这里常有女子弹古筝，端正的面庞、悠扬的乐曲与溪流声交相辉映"不是景点中自然景观的组成部分，而是作者的主观遐想，而且，由于中西文化的差异，西方读者很难将高山流水与中国的丝竹乐联想在一起，因此可作适当处理。

改译：

The Splashing Water Pool is well-known for its higher density of negative ions in the Dinghu Mountain area, where the splashing waterfall, the deep pool and surrounding green trees present to you a picturesque scene. （曾利沙）

（四）旅游译本的功能是宣传特色，吸引游客

译者要考虑英语读者的接受能力，压缩频繁出现的历史专有名词，为难理解的关键信息提供背景知识，提高传达的效果。

例 17

Founded in the first year of Yongkang of Eastern Jin Dynasty (300 A. D), it got its name as Tongtai Temple in the first year of Datong of Liang Dynasty (527 A. D) …In Southern Tang Dynasty, it was renamed as Jing Ju Temple, and then as Yuan Ji Temple…Since the 20th year of Honggu of Ming Dynasty (1387 A. D), it was called as Ji Ming Temple. (from *The Ancient Ji Ming Temple*)

分析：

在旅游宣传中，没有必要引用诗词和事无巨细地列举各朝代名称，否则会阻断文章的连贯性，大大降低阅读理解效果。

五、酒店文宣的文体特点

酒店文宣的目的是推广酒店形象，吸引潜在的顾客。酒店文宣翻译的成效在于"译文对译语读者产生的效果应与原文对原文读者产生的效果一致"，这应成为酒店文宣翻译遵循的策略。由于英汉酒店文宣在文本结构和语言风格上存在一定的差异，译者应把重点放在传达原文的信息上，尽量使译文符合目标语的文本和文化规范，而不是拘泥于原文的形式和结构，以形害义，影响目标语读者对译文的接受。

酒店文宣的基本结构顺序是：介绍酒店的总体形象，详细介绍酒店的各种设施和特色，号召游客入住（作为最后的总结）。

例 18

Welcome to Best Western River North Hotel Chicago

1　BEST WESTERN River North is an award-winning hotel offering full-service amenities, exceptional value, and a spectacular location whether you're coming on business or to take the trip of a lifetime.

2　For a memorable and unbeatable experience and the friendliest service in the Windy City, join us for a few days of extraordinary hospitality! Experience for yourself why *National Geographic Traveler Magazine* named us "One of the best hotels in Chicago" and the Travel Channel calls us the "Best moderate hotel in Chicago."

3 Please join our email list and receive occasional special offers from BEST WESTERN River North, including Seasonal giveaways, contests, specials and discounts at the hotel, highlights of Chicago attractions, and much more!

分析:

第 1 段介绍酒店的总体形象、设施、服务与环境: award-winning hotel, full-service amenities, exceptional value, a spectacular location。

第 2 段通过宣传酒店在业界获得的赞誉, 推介酒店为游客提供的非凡体验与服务。

第 3 段介绍酒店特色 occasional special offers: Seasonal giveaways, contests, specials and discounts at the hotel, highlights of Chicago attractions, 强调游客在此能做什么、体验什么、享受什么, 增强说服力和感染力, 号召游客入住。

例 19

杭州之江饭店矗立于杭城中心地段, 邻市政中心及京杭大运河, 距西湖 2.5 公里、萧山国际机场 30 公里, 交通便捷, 地理位置优越。

杭州之江饭店规模宏大, 占地 50 亩, 建筑面积 5.8 万平方米, 总投资约 2 亿元人民币。其拥有的客房、餐位、会席及泊位数居全省单体酒店之冠, 是浙江省内最负盛名、规模最大的四星级旅游涉外饭店和省级会议中心。

"常饮江南水, 不尽之江情", 之江人热忱恭迎您的光临, 努力为您营造一种理想的生活体验。

分析:

这篇酒店文宣介绍了酒店优越的地理位置、投资规模和设施, 但这些都不是游客最为关心的内容。游客最想知道的信息, 例如酒店特色、能提供什么样的体验与服务等却只字未提。

(一) 中文酒店文宣的文体特点

1. 开头 "公式化"

中文酒店文宣的开头比较单一, 套用一种类似新闻报道式的第三人称客观描述的手法，鲜有情感的渗入，显得"公式化"；句子结构严谨，力图在一个长句子中尽量详细介绍有关信息。

"×××酒店位于（开头以酒店名称引导）……，是一所……酒店，位于……城市的中心地带/黄金/繁华地段，距……有×米之遥"（所处位置或所在城市的特色）。

例20

广东迎宾馆是一家地处繁华市中心的四星级宾馆，著名的北京路商业步行街信步可达，毗邻最大的地铁站公园前站，与交易会、火车站仅数里之隔。

2. 文本顺序形式

中文酒店文宣的顺序形式大同小异，采用"话题性顺序形式"，而且"酒店"一词被反复使用；在语言表达上以平铺直叙为主，鲜用各种修辞手法，酒店特色不鲜明。

例21

三亚银泰度假酒店矗立于著名旅游度假胜地三亚市大东海之滨……三亚银泰度假酒店以7公里海岸线的海景坐落在海南岛南端著名的大东海海滨度假区的中心位置。酒店集令人陶醉的海景……酒店拥有2万平方米的热带园林和3个各具风格的室外游泳池。酒店共计拥有420间热带时尚风情的客房和套房。另外，酒店每天晚上7：00至10：00推出特色池畔木排海鲜烧烤晚宴……

3. 结尾

突出酒店特色（如优质的服务或便利的位置等），表达欢迎和号召客人光临的口号性用语。

例22

我们坚持"一点一滴，尽心尽力"的服务宗旨，为您带来至诚温馨的享受。东莞之行，入住银城酒店是您理想的选择。

例23

让每一位客人体验殷勤待客之道，感受非凡礼遇，是我们始终如一的服务宗旨。

(二) 英文酒店文宣的文体特点

1. 开头多样化,没有固定形式

相比之下,英文酒店文宣的开头没有固定形式,呈现多样化,侧重点因酒店的具体情况不同而有所不同。

运用大量"广告语言":①具有韵律节奏的简练语言风格,大部分为简单句,少部分为复合句;②以读者的视角介入,用 You 引导句子,拉近与读者之间的距离;③大量运用广告英语中常用的修辞手法,如比喻、形容词的最高级形式,语言表述富有变化,语气热烈,具有鼓动性。

例 24

You can't get closer to London!

Just step out of the hotel's door and you're right in the liveliest part of London: Piccadilly Circus. The most famous theatres, restaurants and shops are all within a few minutes walk of the hotel. The choice of entertainment within a few hundred yards is absolutely unbeatable—you'll feel the pulse of Piccadilly from the Regent Palace: it's right at the heart of London. (The Regent Palace Hotel, London 强调酒店优越的地理位置,尽享都市风华)

例 25

Imagine a 5-star Georgian retreat in the city center of Scotland's Capital City. Consistently classified as one of the AA's Top 200 Hotels in Britain and Ireland and recently awarded a Scottish Boutique Hotel Special Commendation from the Scottish Hotel of the Year Awards 2007. (Howard Hotel Edinburgh, Scotland 强调酒店在旅游界所获得的荣誉)

例 26

There's one thing that guests at the Royal Lancaster Hotel always seem to agree on—the views are breathtaking. With Hyde Park, the largest of the Royal Parks, directly to the south, and vistas east to the City of London, we have arguably the best views in London. Whether looking down from the hotel's deluxe bedrooms—416 in total—or enjoying the view from the hotel restaurants, it's as if the heart of this great city is within your reach—and indeed it is! (Royal Lancaster Hotel 强调酒店所处位置的风景优美)

例 27

WELCOME TO THE RITZ LONDON. The Ritz: The world's greatest hotel, as conceived by the world's greatest hotelier. For over a century The Ritz has been the benchmark by which other hotels are measured. A London landmark at 150 Piccadilly, The Ritz has been home to the great and the good, the intelligentsia, the glitterati and thousands of discerning guests since 1906. (THE RITZ LONDON 宣传酒店的悠久历史和高端客户群)

2. 文本顺序形式

"话题性顺序形式",但是避免重复,通过"求雅替换"的方式实现衔接,避免行文单调。

例 28

Where nothing is overlooked except Hyde Park.

Everything about **Mandarin Oriental Hyde Park** has style. With the world class shopping of Knightsbridge as its doorstep and leafy Hyde Park at the rear, **the address** is one of the most prestigious in London, England, enjoying wonderful views of the Household Cavalry as they proceed to Buckingham Palace. **The hotel rooms** and luxury suites are opulent. **The bar** is chic. **The restaurants** superb. **Our service**? It has a style of its own. (用 the address, the hotel rooms, the bar, the restaurants 和 our service 替换 Mandarin Oriental Hyde Park)

3. 结尾

像中文酒店文宣一样,口号型的结尾在英文酒店文宣中也很常见。例如:"Whether you are staying for one day or six months, for business or for pleasure, the Hyde Park Hotel is a very practical and ideal base." "Enjoy a warm welcome at the Sheraton Heathrow Hotel."

此外,英文酒店文宣还有以下两种结尾方式,在中文酒店文宣中很少见到。①引语性结尾(citatory conclusion)。借用旅客和报纸杂志对酒店的评价结尾。②指引性结尾(instructive conclusion)。指示读者寻求更详尽的酒店信息结尾。

例 29

"Service is impeccable" —The Times(One Aldwych Hotel of London)

例 30

In order to get a better idea of where the hotel is situated please load this illustrated map or this street map or this London underground map. (The hotel is just north of Hyde Park) (The Orchard Hotel)

总结：

译文在表述原文内容时按照目标语的文本习惯表述，从而达到类似于原文预期的交际目的。

例 31

原文：

享受地利之便的北京红墙饭店与故宫博物院、景山、北海公园、北京最繁华的商业区王府井步行街仅几步之遥；周边的北大红楼（五四新文化运动发祥地）、老黄城根、四合院民居、老北京胡同环绕四周，宾客可以乘坐饭店具有北京特色的三轮车前往游览和亲身感受普通北京居民的传统生活。入住本饭店的客人可以在晨间上皇家公园跑步，也可在夜幕时分驻足观赏皇城御河宫灯倒影。忙碌一天，情侣朋友相约在饭店附近的什刹海酒吧一条街，把酒品茗，享受这份承载皇族生活历史风韵下的宁静以及现代文明碰撞交汇的繁华。……北京红墙饭店秉承个性化的温馨服务理念，拥有严格专业的管理团队，饭店所有员工以热情诚挚的服务殷切期待您的光临！

原译：

Redwall Hotel is located in a very favorable area. The Palace, Jinshan and Beihai Royal Park, the most famous shopping center of Beijing-Wangfujing Street are all within a few minutes walk. Red Building of Beijing University (The place where the May Fourth New Culture Movement initiated), relics of the imperial city, traditional Chinese folk house and Hutong surround the hotel. You may experience the life of Beijing people by the tricycle offered by the hotel. The guest in our hotel may jog in the imperial park in the morning and may watch the shadow of palace lantern in the palace canal. After a busy day, with friends drink wine at Shichahai Bar Street near the hotel and enjoy the serenity and the prosperity that mixes ancient history and modern culture of China. ...Beijing Redwall Hotel always obeys the personalization and warmth service idea, has strict and professional management group. The staffs of Redwall Hotel welcome your coming by passionate and cordial hearts.

分析:

问题：主语不一致，无主句，并列结构连接不当，汉化式的表达；更重要的是，译文没有考虑酒店文宣的文本和文体特点。

改译:

Just around the corner from the hustle and bustle of Beijing's shopping center—Wangfujing Street, you will find a haven of peace and comfort: Redwall Hotel. This excellently located hotel is ideally suited for travelers in the capital, with the imperial Palace, the relics of the Imperial City and the former Royal Parks of Jingshan and Beihai only several minutes away. Staying at the Redwall turns a holiday into sheer delight. Whether touring typical Beijing hutungs by tricycle, watching the colorful reflections of lanterns on the Imperial Palace Canal at night or savoring refreshing drinks at Shichahai Bar Street, at the Redwall hotel you will discover the essence of gracious living...With Redwall's signature hospitality, the staff at our Beijing hotel look forward to welcoming you! （李德超，王克非）

分析:

对酒店所处的优越的地理位置和便利条件分类陈述，第1句强调酒店位于商业中心但是闹中取静的特点，第2句突出酒店位于历史街区被名胜古迹所环绕的优势，第3句和第4句介绍如何"享受这份承载皇族生活历史风韵下的宁静以及现代文明"，第5句以"Redwall's signature hospitality"红墙饭店所特有的待客之道这一召唤性语句结束。

第七章　企业外宣文本翻译

一、企业外宣的目的

企业宣传文本（Corporate Promotional Text）属于"信息文本"（informative text）和"呼唤文本"（vocative text），旨在宣传企业产品和服务，展示企业良好形象，吸引潜在顾客，扩大企业间的交流合作，开拓国际市场。

二、英汉企业外宣特点

企业宣传文本与其他应用文本一样，具有相对固定的、带有本民族文化特色的语言表达和结构形式。因此，英汉企业宣传文本在内容、语言表达和行文结构上表现出巨大差异。

（一）文本内容

1. 中文文本

从文本内容看，中文文本往往长篇大论，大量使用概念性或空洞夸张的套话，如"历史悠久、人杰地灵"等，并且习惯罗列权威机构认证以及在国内获得的各种奖项等。殊不知，这类认证和奖项并不为西方公众所认知，在对外宣传中意义不大。而且，行文平铺直叙，在一些枝节信息上重墨渲染。另外，在产品说明中将产品介绍与广告宣传相结合。具体表现如下：

（1）信息杂陈，面面俱到。通常包含企业性质、成立时间、历史发展、产品类别、服务项目、生产规模、研发能力、财务状况、员工人数、企业文化、获奖荣誉、辉煌成就、交流合作、社会服务、目标愿景等等。

（2）充斥意识形态浓厚的政治性内容。例如，强调企业的国有性质、政治发展方向、获得的荣誉奖项、上级领导的视察和亲笔题词等。

例1

中国移动通信集团公司（以下简称"中国移动"）于2000年4月20日成立，注册资本3,000亿元人民币，资产规模超过1.72万亿人民币，客户总数8.5亿，基站总数超300万个，是全球网络规模及客户规模最大、市值排名领先的电信运营企业。

中国移动全资拥有中国移动（香港）集团有限公司，由其控股的中国移动有限公司在国内31个省（自治区、直辖市）和香港特别行政区设立全资子公司，并在香港和纽约上市。主要经营移动语音、数据、宽带、IP电话和多媒体业务，并具有计算机互联网国际联网单位经营权和国际出入口经营权。

2016年，公司准确把握趋势，坚持创新驱动，聚焦价值提升，制定并实施了"大连接"战略，加速推进转型升级，各方面工作均取得显著成效。

面向未来，中国移动将继续贯彻"创新、协调、绿色、开放、共享"发展理念，积极投身"网络强国"建设，全力支持"互联网＋"发展，与社会各界携手，努力打造数字化生活的美好明天。

例2

中国石油化工集团公司（Sinopec Group）是1998年7月国家在原中国石油化工总公司基础上重组成立的特大型石油石化企业集团，是国家独资设立的国有公司、国家授权投资的机构和国家控股公司。公司注册资本2316亿元，总部设在北京。

公司对其全资企业、控股企业、参股企业的有关国有资产行使资产受益、重大决策和选择管理者等出资人的权力，对国有资产依法进行经营、管理和监督，并相应承担保值增值责任。公司控股的中国石油化工股份有限公司先后于2000年10月和2001年8月在境外、境内发行H股和A股，并分别在香港、纽约、伦敦和上海上市。

公司主营业务范围包括实业投资及投资管理，石油、天然气的勘探、开采……

中国石油化工集团公司在2015年《财富》世界500强企业中排名第2位。

<u>分析：</u>

以上是中国移动和中石化官网上的公司概况。文本的目标读者应该是

谁？他们的信息需求是什么？他们从中可以获得什么实用的行业信息？

2. 英文文本

英语企业宣传注重突出公司形象及产品，充分传达实质性信息，用事实和数据说话。具体表现如下：

（1）企业概况比较简短，通常包含企业性质、成立时间、业务范围、产品类别、员工人数、目标愿景等等。

（2）叙述平实客观，不渲染不夸饰，不带政治色彩，都是读者最为关心、最想了解的实质信息，贴近读者需求。例如：Who we are（公司概况），What we do（主营业务），How we do it（业务流程），Our people（公司员工），Our clients（主要客户），Our culture and mission（公司宗旨与文化），Our goal and commitment（奋斗目标）。

例3

ConocoPhillips

Who We Are

Across our 30 countries of operations, over 17,000 men and women work in a truly integrated way to find and produce oil and natural gas. Our technical capabilities, asset quality and scale, and financial strength are unmatched among independent exploration and production companies and uniquely position us to compete around the world.

ConocoPhillips is committed to the efficient and effective exploration and production of oil and natural gas. Producing oil and natural gas and getting them to market takes ingenuity, technology and investment. Our innovative, collaborative efforts yield products that improve quality of life globally while producing economic benefits with far-reaching influence.

What We Do
* Exploring for Energy
* Producing Energy
* Getting Energy to Market
* Creating Innovative Solutions
* Doing Business with Us
* Power in Cooperation

Sustainable Development

Sustainable Development is about conducting our business to promote economic growth, a healthy environment and vibrant communities, now and into the future.

In Communities

We do more than create jobs and pay taxes in the communities where we operate. We listen. Our dedication as a community partner is evidenced in the local events we sponsor. It is also apparent in the conversations held between our local community liaisons and stakeholders.

分析：

这是美国能源巨头 ConocoPhillips 公司网页上的公司概况，各类信息分项说明，一目了然。

例 4

General Motors Company, one of the world's largest automakers, traces its roots back to 1908. With its global headquarters in Detroit, GM employs 209,000 people in every major region of the world and does business in more than 120 countries. GM and its strategic partners produce cars and trucks in 31 countries, and sell and service these vehicles through the following brands: Buick, Cadilac, Chevrolet, GMC. Daewoo, Holden, Isuzu, Jiefang, Opel, Vauxhall and Wuling. GM's largest national market is China, followed by the United States, Brazil, the United Kingdom, Germany, Canada and Russia. GM's OnStar subsidiary is the industry leader in vehicle safety, security and information services.

分析：

这篇公司概况用很简短的文字介绍了企业规模、全球化战略（生产、经营与雇员全球化）、品牌产品以及全球市场份额等重要信息。

（二）修饰风格

1. 中文文本

（1）通常采用第三人称，平铺直叙，措辞正式，语气庄重，如同新闻报道。

（2）辞藻华丽，工整对仗，空话套话。

例 5

1912年2月,经孙中山先生批准,中国银行正式成立。从1912年至1949年,中国银行先后行使中央银行、国际汇兑银行和国际贸易专业银行职能,坚持以服务社会民众、振兴民族金融为己任,历经磨难,艰苦奋斗,在民族金融业中长期处于领先地位,并在国际金融界占有一席之地。1949年以后,中国银行长期作为国家外汇外贸专业银行,统一经营管理国家外汇,开展国际贸易结算、侨汇和其他非贸易外汇业务,大力支持外贸发展和经济建设。改革开放以来,中国银行牢牢抓住国家利用国外资金和先进技术加快经济建设的历史机遇,充分发挥长期经营外汇业务的独特优势,成为国家利用外资的主渠道。1994年,中国银行改为国有独资商业银行。2004年8月,中国银行股份有限公司挂牌成立。2006年6月、7月,中国银行先后在香港联交所和上海证券交易所成功挂牌上市,成为国内首家"A+H"发行上市的中国商业银行。2016年,中国银行再次入选全球系统重要性银行,成为新兴市场经济体中唯一连续6年入选的金融机构。

2. 英文文本

(1) 在语言表达和行文结构上,使用通俗易懂、富于表现力的日常口语和富有鼓动性的语言,产品及服务描述简要准确。

(2) 大多采用第一人称we (our) 的叙述视角,语气亲切,易于拉近与客户的距离,用our customers 和 you (称呼顾客),体现"顾客至上"的企业文化。

例 6

At AT&T, we're bringing it all together. We deliver advanced mobile services, next-generation TV, high-speed internet and smart solutions for people and businesses. That's why we're investing to be a global leader in the Telecommunications, Media and Technology industry.

Fast, highly secure and mobile connectivity—to everything on the internet, everywhere, at every moment and on every device—is what drives us. It's reflected in our mission:

Connect people with their world, everywhere they live, work and play… and do it better than anyone else. So our customers can stay connected from nearly anywhere. It doesn't matter if they're driving home from work or traveling across the country or beyond.

Customers want to enjoy their favorite movies, TV shows, music and sports on any screen. We're the largest provider of pay TV in the United States. So, we're setting the standard for delivering video when, where and how customers want it.

In the United States, we offer TV and wireless nationwide, plus a large high-speed internet footprint. We offer a wide choice of internet speeds to meet customers' needs. With our 100% fiber network, customers in 52 markets can download a 90-minute HD movie in less than 36 seconds, a 30-minute TV episode in 3 seconds and 25 songs in 1 second. We plan to expand these speeds to at least 23 more metro areas, at least 75 metros in total. We also offer pay TV in 11 Latin American countries.

We offer solutions that help businesses in every industry serve their customers better. We deliver advanced services to nearly 3.5 million businesses on 6 continents. That includes nearly all of the Fortune 1000 as well as neighborhood businesses across the United States.

Our high-speed mobile internet network covers more than 400 million people and businesses across the U.S. and Mexico. We also wirelessly connect cars, machines, shipping containers and more. It's all part of our leadership in what's called the Internet of Things.

And we never stop innovating. The brightest minds in the business are in our AT&T Labs and Foundry centers developing new technologies, apps, products and services.

We envision a world where everything and everyone work together. We envision a world that works for you. (AT&T 概况)

(三) 文本对比

以第三届中以科技创新投资大会（2017）企业名录为例，RH Electronics 公司与珠海格力集团有限公司同属"工业应用"类企业。

例7

RH Electronics is Israel's leading EMS Company with over 1,000 employees, working on forwarding the world of sub-contract manufacturing. RH has been privately held for over 30 years, and is headquartered just 50 minutes outside of Tel Aviv. The company has additional sites in China, Europe and the

USA and manufacturing facilities with an area totaling more than 55,000m^2 worldwide. RH offers clients FTK solutions for the medical, industrial, aerospace and HLS markets. RH solutions embrace the newest and most advanced electronic manufacturing technologies, and the RH team supplements these with a personal approach and a unified team spirit. RH Technologies strives for greatness—from conception to perfection.

RH Electronics 是以色列领先的电子加工制造企业，员工超过1000，致力于全球化代工制造业。RH Electronics 私有化已30多年，总部距特拉维夫仅50分钟车程。公司在中国、欧洲和美国设有分部，在全球的生产设施超过55 000平方米。RH为客户提供包括医药、实业、航空、流媒体等行业的全流程解决方案。RH的解决方案包括最新最先进的电子制造技术，同时RH团队提供个性化的解决方案，致力于打造团队精神。RH Technologies 追求卓越——从理念到完善全过程。

分析：

直奔主题：企业性质与规模、业务范围、个性化服务和企业发展愿景。语言表达简练，信息量大，充分利用版面。

例8

Zhuhai Gree Group Co., Ltd. was founded in 1985, it is an independent enterprise legal person which capital is fully funded and authorized by State-owned Asset Supervision and Administration Commission of Zhuhai. The registered capital of the company is RMB 800 million. Through 32 years of development, Gree Group has become the largest and most powerful state-owned enterprise group in Zhuhai. In 2017, Gree sets off a new climax of "second start up", which makes manufacture industry as the core, and strives to build two platforms of "investment operation of state-owned capital" and "infrastructure city operation". The four pillar industry, including manufacturing industry, financial investment, industrial park operations and island tourism, will make greater contribution to Zhuhai Construction.

<u>珠海格力集团有限公司成立于1985年，是珠海市国资委全额出资并授权经营的独立企业法人</u>，公司注册资本8亿元人民币。

<u>经过32年的发展，格力集团目前已成为珠海市规模最大、实力最强的国有企业集团</u>。

2017年，格力集团掀起"二次创业"的新高潮，将以制造业为核心，着力打造"国有资本投资运营"和"基础设施城市运营"两个平台，最

终形成制造业、金融业、产业园区运营和海岛旅游四大支柱产业，<u>为珠海建设做出更大贡献</u>。

分析：

画线部分对英语读者来说没有实际意义，业务范围的描述比较空洞。冗余信息太多，没有充分利用版面进行企业宣传。

三、平行文本对企业外宣英译的启示

英汉外宣的文本特点是在不断的实践与运用过程中形成的，在各自的语境中对本民族读者具有相当的感染力和影响力。但是，一旦语境发生变化，如果将针对中国市场的中文文本原封不动地译成英文，其宣传促销目标无法实现。

因此，企业外宣英译需要借鉴英语平行文本，对中文原文进行改写与调整，使之与目标市场的文化相吻合，适应译语读者的阅读习惯。

（一）结构重组

一般而言，一篇典型的英语企业外宣文本由三个部分组成，即主旨（message）、主体（body）、结尾（closure）。主旨部分开门见山地说明目的，主体部分提供具体信息，结尾部分呼应开头、呼吁行动或邀请进一步联络等。结构大致为：

企业总体介绍——主旨
产品介绍——主体1
服务说明——主体2
合作邀请——结尾

例9

①Verizon is a global leader in delivering broadband, video and other wireless and wireline communications services to mass market, business, government and wholesale customers. ②Verizon Wireless operates America's largest and most reliable wireless voice and 3G network. ③Verizon also provides communications, information and entertainment services over America's most advanced fiber-optic network, and delivers innovative, seamless business solutions to customers around the world. ④We believe strongly that our role in connecting people, ideas and opportunities is vital to meeting the challenges of the future.

分析：
企业总体介绍——主旨①
产品（业务）介绍——主体②③
目标愿景——结尾④

例10

Company Profile

① EDS, the world's most experienced outsourcing services company, delivers superior returns to clients through its cost-effective, high-value services model. ② EDS core portfolio comprises information technology and business process outsourcing services, as well as information technology transformation services. ③ The two complementary, subsidiary businesses of EDS are A. T. Kearney, one of the world's leading high-value management consultancies, and UGS PLM Solutions, a leader in product data management, collaboration and product design software. ④ We support the world's leading companies and governments in 56 countries.

* World's No. 1 in Application Management Services
* World's second largest IT Outsourcing company
* Employees: more than 126,000
* 2006 revenues: 20.6 billion
* Ranked 95th on the Fortune 500

分析：
企业总体介绍——主旨①
产品（业务）介绍——主体②③
服务说明——主体④
用事实和数据说明——结尾

译文：

公司概况

EDS 公司是全球最富经验的外包服务公司，本公司通过低成本、高质量的服务模式，为客户提供超级回报。EDS 的核心业务由信息技术、外包服务流程以及信息技术转化服务构成。EDS 旗下的 A. T. Kearney 公司是全球领先的高级管理顾问公司之一，UGS PLM Solutions 公司是产品数据管理与合作以及产品设计软件领域的领导者。我们为世界上 56 个国家的知名大企业和政府机构提供服务。以下是公司的几组数字：

管理服务业务全球第一

世界第二大IT外包服务商

雇员：超过12万

2006年收入：206亿

《财富》500强排名：第95位

（引自《新编实用翻译教材》）

很多企业的中文简介信息结构比较散漫，结构不合理，信息不集中。

例11

①×××公司是一家拥有生产、贸易与研发的综合企业。②我们主要经营药材、食品与饲料添加剂等，产品主要出口欧洲、美国、澳大利亚、中东、非洲等国。③我们尤其擅长研制与出口维生素与抗生素的原材料。④我们的维生素以及相关产品的出口量达到1500吨，能够确保根据市场以及客户的需求来按时安排订单、运输。⑤另外，我们的市场研发中心能给客户提供信息资讯服务，告知客户国内产品与市场的现状，以便客户能够更多了解中国国情，做出更准确的判断与决策。

⑥目前最热销的有抗坏血酸系列（维生素C、包衣维生素C……）。⑦我们将以卓越的标准以及完善的服务帮助我们的客户在市场上获得最强的竞争力。⑧我们希望能够与来自国内外的新老朋友一起携手共创美好的未来。

分析：

第1段：企业总体介绍①② + 产品③ + 服务承诺④⑤

第2段：热销产品⑥ + 服务承诺⑦ + 合作邀请⑧

译文：

1　××× specializes in researching, manufacturing and marketing raw materials of pharmaceutical, food and feed additives. We mainly export to countries and regions including Europe, America, Australia, Mid-east and Africa.

2　We are especially expert in the raw materials of vitamins and antibiotics. Currently, our best-sellers are Ascorbic Acid Series (such as Vitamin C, Coated Vitamin C…)

3　We are capable of arranging prompt manufacturing and shipment for orders as big as 1500 MT vitamins and related products. Moreover, our marketing center can provide our clients with specific information on China's market so they can make more informed decisions.

4 We are convinced that our commitment to quality and service will give you more competitiveness in the marketplace. We look forward to joining hands with businesses and individuals from both China and abroad to create a brighter future. (吴建,张韵菲)

分析:
第1段:企业总体介绍
第2段:产品介绍(主打产品 + 热销产品)
第3段:服务承诺
第4段:合作邀请

(二) 逻辑重构

中文句子之间的意义衔接是隐性的。中文行文中常会出现逻辑关系不明晰、信息关联弱、信息冗余等现象,常有不同范畴的信息杂陈在一起。所以,翻译时需要对原文信息的衔接逻辑进行重构,以便简洁明晰地传递实质信息。具体策略为梳理调整,删除冗余信息,重整结构,使行文更有逻辑性。

例12

公司成立近二十年来,以科学管理创效益,以信誉服务求发展,始终把"用户完全满意"作为自己的营销理念,把"质量满意,价格满意,服务满意"作为营销基础,始终坚持用户至上、服务第一的承诺,从而赢得了越来越多用户的信赖,自1994年至今公司销售量连年递增。

译文:

Since its foundation in 1994, the company has pivoted its development on excellent service. Always "satisfying the customers in every aspect", the company has won their trust, which has in turn contributed to the ever-increasing sales over the past nearly 20 years. (吴建,张韵菲)

(三) 文化信息重构

中文外宣文本里常含有不少中国文化里特有的表达,这些表达常常无法、也不应当直接翻译成英文,因此,需要对这些特有的文化信息进行重构,主要策略是省略和具体化,介绍实质性信息,删减或改写具有浓厚意识形态色彩的内容,使译文更加贴近英语读者的需求。

例 13

×××公司在加快发展的进程中,始终坚持以科学发展观为指导,累计投入亿元资金以工哺农,加快推进社会主义新型农村建设,努力实现人与自然、人与环境的和谐统一。

分析:
画线部分与目标读者的关联性很小,内容空洞,可读性很差,译文要提供具体的实用性信息。

译文:
To achieve sustainable growth,××× Company has invested about a hundred million Yuan in agricultural programs, which has contributed to the economy of local rural areas and the environment protection as well.

(四)修辞

1. 语义重复

一般来说,中文的词义较笼统模糊,英文的词义较具体清晰,中文表达常出现语义重复的现象。

例 14

我们在最大程度上保证客户买得顺心,用得安心,修得放心。

译文:
We try our best to supply satisfactory service during the process of purchase, use and maintenance.

例 15

项目投资将用于添置关键设备,进行技术升级,使产品更能够在性能、质量、水平方面上一个档次,达到世界水平。

译文:
The funds to the project (The project investment will be used for) will be spent on acquiring / purchasing additional vital equipments and updating the techniques to qualify the products by international standards in performance and quality.

例 16

东方包装公司是一家全国性的在国内包装领域占有领先地位的包装公

司，向全国各地的各种公司，特别是食品公司和化工公司提供用于多种产品的包装机械、包装设备和包装材料以及包装。

译文：

Oriental Package Company Ltd., a leading packaging manufacturer in China, provides producers, esp. in food and chemical industries, with instruments, equipments, materials, and services for the package of their products.

2. 借鉴英语平行文本的表达方式

根据平行文本的格式、语气甚至用词对原文进行改写，尽量符合译入语读者的思维表达习惯。

例17

原译：

Bank of China has upheld the spirit of "pursuing excellence" throughout its near hundred-year history.

借鉴：

For more than a century, we have consistently provided innovative, reliable, high-quality products and services and excellent customer care.

As we continue to break new ground and deliver new solutions, we're focused on delivering the high-quality customer service that is our heritage. (AT&T)

改译：

For more than a century, we (Bank of China) have consistently provided innovative, reliable, high-quality products and services and excellent customer care that is our heritage. (卢小军)

例18

上汽集团的愿景是：为了用户满意，为了股东利益，为了社会和谐，上汽集团要建设成为品牌卓越、员工优秀，具有核心竞争能力和国际经营能力的汽车集团。

原译：

SAIC vision: For the satisfaction of our customers, for the interest of our shareholders, for the harmony of our society, we will build SAIC into an automotive company with outstanding brands, brilliant employees, core competitive competencies and international operation capabilities.

借鉴：

Our vision: "We want to satisfy all our customers' financial needs and help them succeed financially." (Wells Fargo & Company)

As a company and as individuals, we take great pride in contributing to the communities where we live and work. (Chevron)

改译：

Our vision: "We want to satisfy all our customers' needs and we take great pride in contributing to the communities where we live and work. Our people, technical expertise, financial strength, and global scope will help SAIC become a world-class automotive provider." (卢小军)

四、企业产品译介

以往，产品译介被划入科技翻译的范畴，从科技翻译的角度探讨翻译技巧与方法。随着市场竞争加剧，产品种类不断创新，技术产品与文化产品相互融合，资本运作模式变化翻新，企业产品介绍类文本的功能不再局限于介绍产品，而是兼具了广告宣传功能，产品推介也就是传播某种理念、文化和生活方式，其目的不仅是为了推介产品，诱导消费，同时还具有帮助企业吸引投资，争取基金支持的功能。因此，这类文本的文体形式和语言风格也随之发生变化，由原来的客观描述和言简意赅的说明，转变为灵活多变的生动表达。特别是，随着新媒体的出现，产品译介的语言风格也随着信息载体和信息传播方式发生变化，其目的是使产品推介直抵读者心境。因此，翻译目的也有所转变，既要传递信息，又要使译文具有等效的广告宣传功能，尽可能重现原文的语言风格，实现文本目标。

（一）网站产品推介

以可穿戴智能虚拟现实游戏产品 Oculus Rift Review（submitted in 2016）为例。

1. 注解

译介产品时，由于中外读者对产品的认知存在文化和时间方面的差异，一些在国外认知度较高的产品进入中国时需要加注解（annotation），方便读者快速理解并掌握和使用信息。

例19

It's taken several years for Oculus Rift to get from Kickstarter to consumer, ready to be reviewed and critiqued—and in that time, it has generated near rabid interest in VR.

译文：

历经多年，Oculus Rift（佩戴式游戏头显）从一个构思到赢得 Kickstarter（众筹网站平台）的支持，形成产品，然后到达用户手中，通过各种测评，已经引发了一场对虚拟世界的近乎狂热。

例 20

There's no doubt Valve has a large catalogue of games, but the release of Touch has added 53 more titles that have definitely evened the score. Despite the numbers, a lot of the games on Steam aren't quite the polished titles you'd find in the Oculus store.（在线游戏平台）

译文：

毫无疑问，维尔福软件公司（Valve Software）拥有大量的游戏产品。但是，新发布的 Touch 触摸控制器增加了 53 款游戏，使得 Oculus 的游戏产品数量与之持平。Oculus 商城的游戏不仅在数量上，而且在质量上也超过了 Steam（Valve 的在线游戏平台）上的游戏。

2. 重现原文的语言风格

为了重现原文的语言风格，需要通过词汇变通的手法来实现，如增词、减词、换词等。

例 21

The HTC Vive, PlayStation VR, Samsung Gear VR, and Google Cardboard all owe their success in part to riding on Oculus' coat tails, but as we sat around anxiously, ready to finally experience the Rift for ourselves, our expectations were perhaps too high. With the arrival of the Oculus Touch controllers, we now have the full picture of what Oculus Rift should have been all along.

译文：

无论是 HTC Vive, PlayStation VR, Samsung Gear VR 还是 Google Cardboard，其成功多半离不开 Oculus 佩戴装置。但是，当我们焦急地期盼，终于得以亲身体验时，却可能不免有些失望。现在，随着 Oculus Touch 触摸控制器的上市，我们感受到了 Oculus Rift 带来的完整画面。

分析：

通过与其他品牌的对比以及与前期产品的体验对比，推介配备了

Touch 触摸控制器的 Oculus 产品，以玩家（用户）的视角（体验）介绍产品，译文尽可能重现原文的语言风格。

称谓/视角（用户）变化：we——我们

换词：expectations were perhaps too high 可能期望过高——可能不免有些失望

减词：sat around

例 22

The rallying cry, "Step into the Rift" was at first a sad understatement, considering you weren't really doing that much stepping around while wearing Rift. In reality, there was a lot of sitting, and maybe a little bit of spinning if you were on a desk chair. The addition of the second sensor has opened up a new world of possibility for room scale, which, coupled with the Touch controllers, truly makes the Rift into an immersive VR experience.

译文：

"跨入 Rift 的虚拟世界"的口号起初并不令人振奋，因为玩家在实际佩戴时并没有多少活动余地（空间），坐的时候居多，如果是坐在转椅上，或许还可以有些转动。但如今增加了第二个感应器，并且配置了触摸控制器，便开创了新的空间尺度，戴着 Rift，玩家真正获得了身临其境的虚拟世界体验。

分析：

增词：虚拟世界

换词：a sad understatement 有些低调——并不令人振奋

desk chair——转椅

称谓/视角（用户）变化：you——玩家

例 23

If you're opting to go the controller-less route you won't need a lot of space to use Oculus Rift, but you'll want to clear away plenty of desktop space and again, a rolling chair is also useful. This all makes it easier to place the sensor and to look around in VR.

译文：

如果你选择不用触摸控制器的话，玩/使用 Oculus Rift 并不需要很大的活动空间，但仍需留出足够的桌面空间，再配一把轮椅，便于安置感应器，环视虚拟世界。

第七章 企业外宣文本翻译

分析：

换词：clear away plenty of desktop space——留出足够的桌面空间

增词：再配

（二）企业产品路演

以 2017 中国－以色列科技创新投资大会企业路演为例，每家企业只有 5 分钟路演（roadshow）时间，因此产品推介必须用词准确，经济简明，主题信息突出，文图并茂，加深印象。

例 24

Our Mission: Fundamentally change the quality of life for individuals with lower limb disability through the creation and development of market leading robotic technologies.

我们的使命：创新研发引领市场的机器人技术，从根本上改变下肢不便人士的生活质量。

The ReWalk Solution：

　　Light, wearable exoskeleton designed for all-day use

　　User-initiated walking

　　Utilizes patented tilt-sensor technology

　　Enables walking in multiple environments: ability to sit, stand, turn, climb and descend stairs

　　Supports its own weight; user does not expend unnecessary energy while walking

Rechargeable battery power

ReWalk 解决方案：

译文1：

轻便、可穿戴的日常使用外骨骼

使用者启动步行

使用荣获专利的倾斜传感器技术

多环境下行走的能力：可坐、站、转身、上下楼梯

支持其自身重量：行走时用户不消耗不必要的能量

可充式电池动力

译文2：

满足日常活动的轻便可穿戴式外置骨骼

行者自主起步

使用倾斜式传感器专利技术

多种环境下的行走能力：坐下、站立、转身、上下楼梯

承载自重：行走无须消耗非必要能量

充电电池动力

分析：

将英语介词短语 through the creation and development 变成汉语动词短语结构"创新研发引领市场的机器人技术"，通过增词，构成双数词组，押韵上口。

第八章 投资指南翻译

一、英汉投资指南的特点

投资指南（investment guide）与其他应用类语篇一样，具有较为明显、相对固定的带有本民族文化特色的语言特点和结构形式。因此，英汉投资指南在内容和语言表现形式和行文结构上均有明显差异。

从内容上看，英文投资指南，主题信息突出，注重传递实质信息，用事实和数据说话；而中文投资指南则长篇大论，喜欢渲染某些枝节信息，大量使用概念式或空洞夸大的描述性套话，如"历史悠久""战略地位突出"等，习惯罗列国家及省部级领导人的视察与重视等关联性弱的信息。

在语言表现形式和行文结构上，英文投资指南语言简练，通俗易懂，信息内容安排紧凑，结构严谨，环环相扣；中文投资指南则喜欢采用四、五、六字并列结构，讲究工整对仗，用词华丽夸张。

下面是《投资德国》（*Invest in Germany*）的简介部分

例1

Germany—A Top Location for Successful Business

1　Entrepreneurs from around the world are always welcome in Germany, a country that offers the ideal conditions for successful business transactions. Investors profit from Germany's central location in the heart of Europe, an excellent infrastructure, the country's position as leading logistics location in Europe, a qualified workforce, an excellent research landscape, and finally the large European market.

2　Germany's cosmopolitan nature is well known. Around 22,000 foreign businesses are located in the country, and the 500 largest companies in the world are represented here. All in all, foreign companies employ 2.7 million people.

3 The German market is open for business investments in practically all sectors; there are no business sectors dominated exclusively by the state. As a result of the privatization of previously state-owned companies such as the German rail company Deutsche Bahn, the postal service, or in the telecommunications sector, the government has given up the kind of state-dominated business sectors that still exist in France or the United Kingdom, for example.

4 The opening up of Eastern Europe has also created additional opportunities for companies in Germany. New markets have emerged in these countries and can be excellently entered from the center of Europe.

分析：

常规的总体介绍 + 分类介绍。

（1）概括性地介绍德国投资的总体环境。

（2）分类具体介绍德国的投资条件与优势。

《投资德国》的简介部分"德国——事业成功的首选之地"概括性地介绍了德国的投资环境、市场的国际化程度和对外开放程度，使读者对投资德国的优越性和可享受到的便利条件有一个初步认识。

第1段，采用与投资者面对面交流的方式，根据投资者最为关心的问题（Investors profit from...）来推介德国的投资环境：位于欧洲的中心，优良的基础设施，欧洲的物流中心，高素质的劳动力，优越的研究环境，巨大的欧洲市场。

第2段，宣传德国市场的国际化程度，世界500强在那里均有业务。

第3段，宣传德国市场的对外开放程度，政府不会主导任何产业，并将这一优势与英法两国作对比，凸显德国投资条件的优越。

第4段，宣传德国是进入东欧新兴市场的最佳路径。

接下来，分类介绍德国对投资者的吸引力，选取最具代表性、最为突出的优势：德国制造——享誉全球的品牌、评级最高/得分最高/最具优势的投资地、欧洲最大经济实体、科研技术转化能力等。

"Made in Germany" —a global brand

There are many reasons why international business is taking a growing interest in Germany. One is the "Made in Germany" brand, which has been standing for a mark of high quality and innovation for more than a century. With this seal of quality, Germany has been the world-leading exporter of goods for years. The innovative force of companies has since remained intact. German companies are leaders in both the development of new technologies for the environmentally friendly production of electricity and pioneering nanotechnologies. German companies are also world leaders in many other sectors, and have a leading position in the classical industries, the best example of which is the automotive industry, which has contributed much to the country's reputation all over the world.

One underlying factor for excellence in the development of new products is the leading research conducted at German universities and other institutes. Industry has also benefited from the close partnerships with the state-funded research institutes. The most recent testament to quality in research was the award of the Nobel prize to Munich physicist Theodor Hansch in 2005. With his work, the scientist has helped achieve a quantum leap in spectroscopy, which has revolutionized many products.

The universities also train excellent scientific experts, who transfer state-of-the-art development to business, and help to <u>turn sophisticated ideas into products for the global market</u> (将成熟/复杂的构想转化为国际市场需要的产品). The government makes every effort to support this and the formation of clusters, particularly in the future industries in which Germany excels, is intensively promoted.

There are good reasons why companies develop new procedures, plan intelligent products and services, and manufacture complex products in Germany: the underlying conditions are excellent, the legal system is transparent and fair, and the infrastructure is ideal. Germany is ready for the future.

Top marks for Germany as a location

There is a mood of change throughout the country as a whole. According to a survey of 155 countries by the World Bank, entitled "Doing Business in 2006", Germany was found to be one of the nations most willing to embrace reform. In a study by the American Chamber of Commerce in Germany from March 2006, German also gained "top marks" as a recognized research location.

Germany makes it easy for businesses to invest: taxes have been lowered, the labor market is flexible, bureaucracy has been further reduced, and the education sector in Germany has been expanded with an eye to the future. Germany is therefore one of the most competitive countries in the world.

Experts acknowledge the positive development. In a title story, the British magazine *Economist* sees "broad positive business trends" and highlights Germany's surprising flexibility. International business consultants Ernst & Young rate Germany as the third most attractive business location, behind the United States and China. The company surveyed 500 international managers for its rankings. Germany came out best among the European locations. （用国际知名的评估机构和专业杂志的评价做宣传）

Europe's largest economy

The German economy is characterized by small and medium-sized enterprises, which make up 85 percent of all companies. As a result, the economy is particularly flexible, varied, and competitive. Many highly-specialized companies enjoy a leading position on world markets, because research and development is particularly fostered in the SME sector. By quickly implementing innovations, companies are able to secure their leading roles in their fields.

However, Germany is also home to many large, international companies. The economy is traditionally strong in mechanical engineering, the automotive industry, aerospace, logistics, and the pharmaceutical and chemical industry. German companies also lead the field in new technologies such as the IT/ICT sector……. In the new technology sectors, Germany not only provides a good infrastructure but also offers a large network of suppliers, particularly in the various industry-specific cluster （特定产业集群） regions. The transition from an industrial society to an information society has long since been made in Germany.

Benefiting from German research

Research and development are particularly promoted by the government. All companies are treated in the same way, regardless of whether they are owned by Germans or non-Germans. Business works closely with research institutes to ensure rapid knowledge transfer from the universities to companies.

1) This is a success:

* Germany is a land of inventors. For every million residents, there are 277 patents relevant for the global market, more than anywhere else in the world. The number of German patent applications doubles every two years.

* Germany is the second-largest net exporter of technology behind the United States.

2) Germany is open to innovation and to innovative entrepreneurs. Companies are supported in their initiatives on many levels.

* The Federal Ministry of Education and Research (BMBF) supports <u>joint initiatives by small and medium-sized enterprises</u>（中小企业的联合创新）, bringing business together with public research institutes and universities, and enabling small businesses to gain access to pioneering technologies. As a result, the latest research knowledge is quickly transferred to business.

3) Numerous programs at federal and regional level promote the implementation of research results. These include for example the BMBF's "<u>patent marketing offensive</u>（专利实施战略）" at federal level, which aims to promote the setup of patent and marketing agencies for universities and research institutes. The agencies will aim to identify quickly research results that can be patented, and legally safeguard and market these.

例2

Cutting-Edge Fields: Eastern Germany's Industry Sectors of Tomorrow

1 The "Cutting-Edge Fields in Eastern Germany" study, which was commissioned, promoted and financed by the Federal Ministry of Transport, Building and Urban Affairs, has been created as a guide to help political decision-makers set Eastern Germany's economic policy agenda. But it can also guide investors. Indeed, when it comes to making investment decisions, the Eastern German industries identified as cutting-edge fields and the business sectors of tomorrow are worth taking a closer look at.

2 The study identifies two categories of potential "industry sectors of tomorrow." The first largely consists of established sectors that can count on increased demand due to major economic and social trends. These sectors are set to branch out into new, innovative fields. There are three main sectors

included here: the health care industry, cleantech and information and communication technology (a cross-application technology 复合型/跨学科应用技术).

3 The second category consists of research-intensive sectors (研究密集型产业部门) still at the beginning of the product life cycle. The activities of these sectors are found in innovative environments that can be provided for best by public research institutions. Industry and science are well-interconnected in attractive clusters. These sectors include nanotechnology/new materials, biotechnology (also as an intermediate service within the health care industry) and optical technology.

4 The industry sectors of the future are not individual industries but, rather, broad economic and technological fields (e.g., energy and environmental technology). They will become further differentiated over time, and their boundaries with other economic and technological sectors are fluid. Some industry sectors of the future are also cross-application technologies.

5 In this brochure, we introduce some of the outstanding companies and networks currently active in Eastern Germany's industry sectors of tomorrow. They are truly "living the future today".

分析：

打破了常规的总体介绍+分类介绍模式。

第1段指出，这篇东德（即前民主德国）投资指南是一个政府委托与资助的研究项目，旨在为政府决策部门提供参考，同时也可作为投资指南，显示该指南具有科学性、权威性和可行性。

第2、3段将吸引投资的领域划分成两个部分：一是已建成的原有产业领域，二是还处在产品生命周期初始阶段的研究密集型产业领域。

第4段介绍了东德未来产业之间的相互融合。最后一段逐一介绍东德的高科技产业及优秀企业。

这种语篇结构在中文投资指南中少见。

二、投资指南的汉英翻译原则

投资指南汉译英的目的是为了向海外投资者提供有关地区的投资环境、自然资源、优惠政策等方面的信息，属于外宣文本，其功能是宣传介绍，吸引外商的投资兴趣，具有信息性、诱导性和可读性强等特点。因此，投资指南的汉英翻译要充分考虑译文读者的文化背景、思维方式、认知能力、信息需求等因素。具体而言，投资指南的翻译原则应该以译文为重点，表达准确、信息突出、简明易懂。同时，应用翻译的目的性还要求译者摒弃翻译只能全译的观念，根据文本的目的和具体情况，根据委托人的要求，采用改译、编译等变译技巧。

投资指南是对外宣传的一个重要渠道，英文翻译的质量直接反映了当地人材的专业素质和政府部门的服务水平，并在一定程度上会影响海外投资者获取信息的准确性，从而影响资金、技术和项目的引入。

针对中文外宣文本自身存在的不足，例如，华而不实的修饰、为增强气势和工整对仗而使用的空话套话等特征，译者应对原文信息价值做出判断，对原文信息进行取舍、增减或重组，从而产生贴近投资者需求的译文。具体的做法是：找出原文中相关地区的投资优势和对海外投资者的主要吸引力，弄清相关地区希望在哪些领域吸引投资，推测投资者的信息需求，按照重要性的主次排列，译文的语篇构成和表达方式要便于投资者理解掌握。

（一）突出主要信息

1. 优化文本结构，突出重要的信息内容

投资指南翻译的目的是为了方便海外投资者了解当地的投资机会、投资环境以及相关的配套服务和优惠政策。因此，译文可将重要的、吸引人的信息内容置于突出位置，对文本信息内容进行重组，使之条理清晰，具有充分的说服力和感染力，不必受中文文本结构的束缚。由于英汉投资指南在内容、语言表现形式和行文结构上存在明显差异，如果将中文原文内容和文字生搬硬套进译文，其结果是费力不讨好。

例 3

前途无量的经济技术开发区

大亚湾开发区是当今中国最具发展潜力的国家经济技术开发区之一，很少有哪一个地区能够像她一样，同时拥有以下五个方面的发展优势：一是自然条件得天独厚。既可以建设世界级的大型深水良港，又拥有大面积的尚未开发的腹地，而且旅游资源和淡水资源都很丰富，单从发展临海型工业和海滨明星城市的先天条件来看，在中国沿海是不多见的。二是区位优势非常明显。紧靠香港特别行政区和深圳经济特区，可以接受它们多方面的牵引和辐射；同时，又属于珠江三角洲经济区和京九铁路线经济带的一部分，是中国和广东省要优先发展的地区之一。三是大型项目相对集中。除了举世瞩目的南海石化项目外，还有东风汽车生产基地、天然气发电厂等特大型项目以及一批与南海石化项目相关的大型项目。四是战略地位极其突出。南海石化项目作为技术领先型的原材料企业和迄今最大的中外合资项目，必将成为中国石化工业的"火车头"，并大幅度提高广东省利用外资的水平。而大亚湾作为广东省重要的基础工业基地，不仅将促进本省产业结构的优化和升级，还将直接成为广东省今后促进经济增长的主要引擎和带动区域经济发展的核心地区之一。五是投资环境十分优越。机场、铁路（国家已批准建设）、港口俱全，公路网四通八达，供水、供电、通信事业超前发展，生活环境比较舒适，高素质、低成本的劳动力资源丰富。享有相当于经济特区的优惠政策，政府部门思想解放，熟悉市场经济的国际惯例，服务意识强，办事效率高，等等。

总之，大亚湾开发区集中展现了中国沿海地区的综合优势，确实是一方不可多得的投资宝地。我们热诚欢迎国内外朋友来大亚湾开发区参观、考察和投资发展事业，并诚心诚意为投资者提供广泛的发展领域和便利条件，以及文明、优质、高效的服务，特别是对基础设施建设和高新技术项目，我们将尽可能给予政策上最大的优惠。我们愿意和广大投资者一起，共同创造大亚湾美好的明天。

分析：

《大亚湾经济技术开发区投资指南》的简介部分"前途无量的经济技术开发区"概括了五个方面的优势，其顺序排列如下：一是自然条件得天独厚，二是区位优势非常明显，三是大型项目相对集中，四是战略地位极其突出，五是投资环境十分优越。在这五个方面的优势中，投资者最关心的是自然条件和投资环境（包括机场、铁路、公路、港口等交通运输等基础设施以及通信、供水、供电、劳动力资源等），其次是区位优势和大型项目集中。

译者需要对中文文本进行译前处理，根据各要点的重要性进行重新排序，将最重要的、最有吸引力的内容前置，以便引起投资者的兴趣。因此，对原文结构作如下调整。

译前处理：

大亚湾开发区是当今中国最具发展潜力的国家经济技术开发区之一，很少有哪一个地区能够像她一样，同时拥有多方面的发展优势：

一是自然条件得天独厚，投资环境优越。机场、铁路（国家已批准建设)、港口(可以建设世界级的大型深水良港)俱全,公路网四通八达,供水、供电、通信事业超前发展;此外,这里拥有大面积的尚未开发的腹地,而且旅游资源和淡水资源都很丰富,单从发展临海型工业和海滨明星城市的先天条件来看,在中国沿海是不多见的。

二是区位优势非常明显。紧靠香港特别行政区和深圳经济特区,可以接受它们多方面的牵引和辐射;同时,又属于珠江三角洲经济区和京九铁路线经济带的一部分,是中国和广东省要优先发展的地区之一。

三是大型项目相对集中。除了举世瞩目的南海石化项目外,还有东风汽车生产基地、天然气发电厂等特大型项目以及一批与南海石化项目相关的大型项目。南海石化项目作为技术领先型的原材料企业和迄今最大的中外合资项目,必将成为中国石化工业的"火车头",并大幅度提高广东省利用外资的水平。而大亚湾作为广东省重要的基础工业基地,不仅将促进本省产业结构的优化和升级,还将直接成为广东省今后促进经济增长的主要引擎和带动区域经济发展的核心地区之一。

四是高素质、低成本的劳动力资源丰富。享有相当于经济特区的优惠政策,政府部门熟悉市场经济的国际惯例,服务意识强,办事效率高,等等。

总之,大亚湾开发区集中展现了中国沿海地区的综合优势,确实是一方不可多得的投资宝地。我们热诚欢迎国内外朋友来大亚湾开发区参观、考察和投资发展事业,并诚心诚意为投资者提供广泛的发展领域和便利条件,以及文明、优质、高效的服务,特别是对基础设施建设和高新技术项目,我们将尽可能给予政策上最大的优惠。我们愿意和广大投资者一起,共同创造大亚湾美好的明天。

译文:

Daya Bay: A Promising Economic Development Zone

Daya Bay Development Zone (DBDZ), one of the most promising national economic and technical development zones, enjoys incomparable advantages as follows:

The most remarkable one is that the Zone enjoys an excellent infrastructure, including a sound net of transportation such as airport, port (where world-rank deep-water berths can be constructed), railroad (under construction), communications, highways, and good supply of water and electricity. Apart from that, it boasts unique natural conditions not only for its vast under-developed hinterland but for its rich resources of fresh water as well as tourism. This remarkableness is rare along China's coast for developing off-shore industries or star cities.

Another outstanding advantage is its geographical position, for it is adjacent to Hong Kong and Shenzhen Special Economic Zone and the latter can exert great driving force upon it. In addition, it not only lies within the Pearl River Delta and along the Beijing-Kowloon Railway Belt but also is included among those areas enjoying priority in development offered by the provincial and state government.

Moreover, the Zone has an attractive advantage to investors for it witnesses the location of a number of large industrial projects, such as the Dongfeng automobile manufacturing base, a natural gas power plant, and the South-Sea petrochemical complex (SSPC), and a number of large auxiliary projects will be consequently set up along with it. This is strategically important for the Zone, for the SSPC, as largest joint venture and leading high-tech enterprise in raw materials, will inevitably play the role of locomotive in China's petrochemical industry, and help to make good use of foreign capital province-wide, while Daya Bay, the important provincial basic industrial base, will not only facilitate upgrading and optimizing the provincial industrial structure, but act as a main engine promoting the provincial economic development as well as one of the key districts spurring up regional economic development.

The Zone proves itself an ideal place for investment where a cheap knowledge-based labor force is available and favorable policies are authorized as to special economic zones, together with an efficient and competent administration staff who owns a good acquaintance of international practices in market economy as well as a good sense of services.

Generally, the Zone, an embodiment of the unique comprehensive advantages only seen along China's coastal areas, is indeed a bonanza for investors, who are sincerely welcomed to make survey and investment where they will be met with profitable business opportunities, conveniences and best service. And more favorable polices will be especially offered to investment in infrastructure and high-technology. We hope to enjoy good co-operation with all investors and share a prosperous tomorrow. （曾利沙）

2. 突出或增补必要信息，略去关联性弱的信息

译文的目标读者是海外投资者，因此，指南中有些对国内投资者有意义的信息对海外投资者并不重要，这些信息内容不必逐词逐句照译，而中文语句中有些对海外投资者来说语焉不详的内容则可作适当的增补。

例 4

原文：

大亚湾的开发建设一直得到中央、省、市的大力支持，1990 年以来，党和国家领导江泽民、李鹏、朱镕基、李瑞环等先后视察了大亚湾。曾来大亚湾视察工作的中央领导还有尉健行（1995 年 4 月 13 日）、杨尚昆（1991 年 1 月 31 日）、谷牧（1989 年 5 月 11 日）……

分析：

该语段的重要信息是第 1 句的内容。第 2 句列出的十余名其他中央领导的视察及具体时间对海外投资者来说并不是重要信息，可以略译。"得到……大力支持"比较抽象，需要在译文中使之具体化为 financial support and favorable policies，将空洞的大力支持转化为经济支持和政策优惠。

译文：

Financial support and favorable policies have been granted to Daya Bay (ETDZ) during its development and construction from the municipal, provincial governments as well as the State. Since 1990, it has seen a great number of leaders of the Party and the State, such as Jiang Zemin, Li Peng, Zhu Rongji, paid their visits. （曾利沙）

（二）表达准确，符合英语表达习惯

译者应准确理解及传达原文的基本内容，尽量用英语的语言表达方式进行语际转换，包括措辞达意。对原文的准确理解与表达主要应注意以下几方面。

1. 正确辨别词义的内涵，理解词的搭配意义

例 5

原文：

大亚湾经济技术开发区位于广东省惠州市南部，……属于广东省经济最发达、最活跃的珠江三角洲经济区域范围，并处在亚太经济圈的中心位置。

原译：

Daya Bay Economic and Technologic Development Zone lies in the south of Huizhou city, Guangdong Province, …The coastline is in the scope of the most advanced and active Pearl River Delta Economic Zone and lies in the center of Asia-Pacific Zone.

分析：

"开发区""经济区""经济圈"三个名词的内涵不同，不能将其统统译为"zone"。"开发区"（development zone）是指对外开放而且享有国家给予的一系列特殊政策的地区（zone 在英语中是指出于某一特殊目的而设的其特性不同于周边地区的一块相对较小的区域）；"珠江三角洲经济区"只是一种地域上的划分，相当于英语的 region，一般大于 zone；而"亚太经济圈"则是地理地缘上的划分，其区域范围更大，在英语中用 ring 表达。译者在碰到类似的情况应加以区别。

改译：

Daya Bay Economic and Technologic Development Zone lies to the south of Huizhou city, Guangdong Province, …It is included in the most advanced and dynamic Pearl River Delta Economic Region, and situated in the center of Asia-Pacific Ring as well.

例 6

原文：

由于大亚湾有着优越的地理位置，具备发展大工业的多方面的条件，……

原译：

As Daya Bay enjoys *privileged* geographic locations and is ready for developing large industries, …

分析：

"优越的地理位置"是指自然地理提供的一些"优越的"便利条件，而英语中的 privileged 是指权威部门给予的"特权"和"特许"，因此，enjoys *privileged* geographic locations 属于搭配不当。

改译：

With its outstanding geographic position, Daya Bay Development Zone possesses potential conditions for developing large-scale（or heavy）industries.（曾利沙）

（或者 has the potential for developing…）

2. 不必寻求译文的形式对应，重在符合英语表达习惯

例7

原文：

三是大型项目相对集中。除了举世瞩目的南海石化项目，还有东风汽车基地，天然气发电厂的大型项目以及一批与南海石化项目相关的项目。

原译：

A good concentration of large items *are* present here. Except for world-famous South-China Sea petrol chemical project, there are *still* Dongfeng automobile production base, natural gas power plant here and other large relative enterprises in relation with South China Sea petrol chemical projects.

分析：

"concentration"一词是指注意力的集中，一般不用于指空间物体的集中，译文中也不必用与"集中"对应的字眼。"items"主要指整体项目（project）下的一些相对小的工程项目，此处运用不当。"still"表示"尚有、至今还有"之意，用在此处与原意不符。译文不必拘泥于汉语的行文形式，而应遵循英语的行文习惯。

改译：

Thirdly, Daya Bay has a number of large-scale industrial projects located here, including the well-known South-Sea petrol-chemical complex, Dongfeng automobile manufacturing base, a natural gas power plant and some auxiliary projects to the South-Sea petrol-chemical project.

例8

原文：

同时，又属于珠江三角洲经济区和京九铁路沿线经济带的一部分，是广东省要优先发展的地区。

原译：

Meanwhile it is one of the Pearl River Delta Economic Zone and one part of the Beijing-Kowloon Railway Belt and also one of the priority development regions of Guangdong province.

分析：

原译连用三个"one (part) of"属重复使用，不符合英语表达习惯。"同时"作为语篇衔接词，在上下文中起递进作用，应译为"moreover"。

改译：

Moreover, it not only lies within the Pearl River Delta and along the Beijing-Kowloon Railway Belt but also is included among those areas enjoying priority in development in Guangdong province. （曾利沙）

3. 熟悉不同文化及其思维表达方式，把握投资者的心理

例9

原文：

"我们愿和广大投资者一起，共创大亚湾的美好明天"。

原译：

Let's put our efforts together and create a better tomorrow.

分析：

这是典型的中国式的表达方式。对于海外投资者来说，投资的主要目的不是为当地"共创美好的明天"，而是为了获得预期可观的利润，因此，将其改写为"共享明日的繁荣"。

改译：

We hope to enjoy good cooperation with investors, home and abroad, and share a prosperous tomorrow. （曾利沙）

例10

原文：

我们热诚欢迎国内外朋友来大亚湾开发区参观、考察和投资发展事业，并诚心诚意为投资者提供广泛的发展领域和便利条件，以及文明、优质、高效服务，特别是对基础设施建设和高新技术项目，我们将尽可能给予政策上最大的优惠。

原译：

We sincerely welcome you, home and abroad, to visit us for your survey and investment. We will offer you a wide development field and convenient conditions. With civilized, excellent and efficient services we will try our best to offer you most favorable policies, especially in terms of basic facilities and high-tech items.

分析：

"文明、优质、高效服务"三词并用，意在强调，是中国读者熟悉的表达方式，但是不符合英语的表达习惯，因为在西方文化里，优质高效的服务理念是理所应当的事，用"best"一词表达就足够了。

改译：

Investors, home and abroad, are expected to make survey and investment in Daya Bay Development Zone, where they will find various business opportunities together with best services, and most favorable polices will be offered to investment in infrastructure and high-technology. （曾利沙）

4. 调整语篇结构，避免重复和流水句

有些译文完整地传达了原文旨意，句子也合乎英语语法规则，但是译文受中文语篇影响，形成流水句，造成多处重复。为了使译文表达更加准确，更有逻辑性，符合英文的表达习惯，可对译文做如下修改。

例11

投资海珠（Invest in Haizhu District）

地理位置（Geographic Location）

1 海珠区是华南中心城市广州市的中心城区。广州的新城市中轴线贯穿海珠中部，长6.2公里，占新中轴线全长一半以上。

2 广州市是珠三角地区中心，也是东南亚与东北亚的几何中心，是中国的"南大门"。从广州到日本、新加坡、韩国及中国的台湾省等国家和地区均为3～4小时航程；从海珠区到港澳地区行车约需90分钟。

译文1：

Haizhu District is the core area of Guangzhou, the central city in South China. Guangzhou's new urban axis passes through the middle of Haizhu, covering a length of 6.2 kilometers, over half length of the new axis.

Guangzhou is the centre of the Pearl River Delta, the geometrical centre of Southeast Asia and Northeast Asia, and the Great Southern Gate of China. It takes about 3 to 4 hours flight from Guangzhou to Japan, Singapore, Korea and Taiwan Province respectively, and 90 minutes ride from Haizhu to Hongkong or Macao.

分析：

海珠区是广州新城区的一部分，因此，Haizhu District is the core area of Guangzhou 不准确。避免不断重复 Guangzhou 和 Haizhu。

译文 2：

Haizhu District is <u>located in the core area of Guangzhou</u>, the central city in South China. <u>The city's new axis passes through the middle of the District (or go through the District in the center), stretching 6.2 kilometers long</u>, over a half length of the new axis.

Guangzhou is both the centre of the Pearl River Delta, and the geometrical centre of Southeast Asia and Northeast Asia, <u>serving as</u> the Great Southern Gate of China.

海珠概况（General Survey）

3 海珠区为珠江广州河段前后航道环绕，是个河涌水网密布、鸟语花香的岛区，南部是素有"广州南肺"之称的万亩果林生态保护区和海珠湖湿地公园，全区总面积约 90.45 平方公里，2008 年常住人口 134.56 万。2008 年全区实现地区生产总值 487.27 亿元，同比增长 11.2%。

4 海珠区是中国古代海上"丝绸之路"的始发地，2006 年瑞典仿古商船"哥德堡号"重返海珠区东北部的黄埔古港，再次展示了"千年商埠"的历史渊源。海珠区是中国近代伟人孙中山在广州的主要活动地，"大元帅府"和伟人首创的中山大学就坐落在海珠区。

译文 1：

Haizhu is surrounded by the front and back channels of the Guangzhou reach, Pearl River. It is an island full of rivers, flowers and birds. Its southern region rests the Massive Orchard Protection Area, which is referred to as Guangzhou's "Southern Lung", and Haizhu Lake Wetland Park. The whole district covers an area of 90.45 square kilometers with a resident population of nearly 1.35 million. In 2008, the GDP in Haizhu hits 48.727 billion Yuan, an increase of 11.2% year-on-year.

Haizhu is the origin of China's ancient Maritime Silk Road. In 2006, the replica of Swedish merchant ship Gotheborg returned to the Ancient Huangpu Port, located in the northeast of Haizhu, showing the historical origin of the millenarian commercial port again. The great leader in Chinese modern history, Sun Yat-sen, conducted his activities mainly in Haizhu when he was in Guangzhou. The Generalissimo's Mansion and Sun Yat-sen University, created by the great leader, are located in Haizhu.

分析：

海珠概况这部分主要介绍海珠区所处的自然环境，拥有的历史文化资源。第3段有两处需要修改：

（1）海珠区被什么河道所环绕对海外读者并不重要，这一信息中国人也未必知道，属于与主题关联性不强的信息，根据主题信息突出原则和读者的认知能力，可略去 the front and back channels of the Guangzhou reach。

（2）充满"鸟语花香"的地方在西方国家比比皆是，因此译成"保持了良好的生态环境"更贴切。

第4段介绍海珠区的历史文化，如果按照中文语篇结构直接对译，第3段与第4段之间的语际联系较弱。而且，第4段语句之间的关联性较差，形成流水句。因此，在此处增译 It is a place of historical importance，作为这段的主题句（topic sentence），然后分两个层次分别陈述：这里是中国古代海上"丝绸之路"的始发地，这里也是中国近代伟人孙中山在广州的主要活动地。这样，语句间的逻辑关系加强，也符合英语段落发展的习惯：先点明主题，然后例举事实加以说明。

译文1：

<u>Haizhu District is surrounded by branches of Pearl River. It is an island with rivers and streams flowing through, maintaining an ideal eco-system.</u>

It is a place of historical importance. Here is the origin of China's ancient Maritime Silk Road, which started from the ancient Huangpu Port, located in the northeast of the district. In 2006, the replica of Swedish merchant ship Gotheborg returned to the port, revealing the historical origin of the millenarian commercial port. The great leader of the democratic revolution in Chinese modern history, Sun Yat-sen, conducted his activities in the District, where the Generalissimo's Mansion and Sun Yat-sen University, created by the great leader, are located.

海珠区的"四最"（The Four No.1 in the District）

5 世界最高的观光塔——广州电视观光塔就在海珠区赤岗塔附近，是广州新城市中轴线海珠段的起点，是一座以观光旅游为主，具有广播电视、文化娱乐和城市窗口功能的大型城市基础设施，配备有大型旋转餐厅、4D影院、露天观景平台等观光娱乐设施。此外，观光塔周边56万平方米范围中轴线海珠段将建成领事馆区、大型绿化广场、生态公园、广播电视中心和观景酒店等商务休闲设施。

译文1:

Guangzhou Sightseeing TV Tower, the highest sightseeing tower in the world, is located in Haizhu District, near Chigang Pagoda. It is the starting point of the Haizhu Section of Guangzhou's new urban axis, which is mainly for sightseeing. Meanwhile, it offers an array of functions as telecast, culture and recreation and city window, with large revolving restaurants, 4D cinema, open-air sightseeing platform and so forth. Furthermore, the Haizhu Section of the urban axis, a land area of 560,000 square meters around the sightseeing tower, is to be built into consulate district, recreation square, ecological park, telecast centre, sightseeing hotel and so on.

分析:

译文有多处不妥:

(1) 译文有多处重复: Guangzhou Sightseeing TV Tower, the highest sightseeing tower, which is mainly for sightseeing。

(2) 观光塔周边地段表述不准确。可译为 the area around the Tower in Haizhu Section of the axis, covering 560,000 square meters。

(3) 词的搭配不当。原译中的 the Haizhu Section of the urban axis 是地段的概念,不能 be built into consulate district; 此外,领事馆区、大型绿化广场和生态公园是片区的概念,不宜与广播电视中心和观景酒店等个体项目并列。

译文2:

Guangzhou Sightseeing TV Tower, the highest of its kind in the world, is located in Haizhu District, near Chigang Pagoda. Serving as (As a symbol of) the starting point of city's new axis in the Haizhu Section, the Tower offers an array of facilities like telecast, culture and recreation and city window, with large revolving restaurants, 4D cinema, open-air sightseeing platform and so forth. Meanwhile, the area in the Section of the axis, covering 560,000 square meters around the Tower, is to be turned into consulate district, recreation square, ecological park, and other facilities such as telecast centre, sightseeing hotel and so on.

分析:

以下原文中有几处提到展览与展馆规模在亚洲及世界的排名,多处出现重复表达的现象。为了避免重复,需要理清逻辑关系,整体考虑之后再予以翻译。通过借鉴平行文本，运用 convention venue, exhibition complex, exhibiting capacity, the venue ranks top in terms of size and aggregation of fairs, stage an event 等专业的表达方式，解决译文中的重复表达问题，使译文经济简明。

6 亚洲最大的会展中心——广州国际会展中心，展馆面积达 34 万平方米，建筑总面积超过 100 万平方米，展馆规模位居亚洲第一、世界第三。

译文1：

Guangzhou International Convention and Exhibition Center, the largest convention and exhibition center in Asia, has nearly 340,000 square meters exhibition halls, and a total construction area of over one million square meters. The scale of the exhibition halls is ranked as the No. 1 in Asia, and No. 3 in the world.

译文2：

Guangzhou International Convention and Exhibition Center boasts the largest convention venue in Asia and third in the world, with the exhibiting space reaching 340,000 square meters, and floor space one million square meters.

7 世界最大规模的展会——中国进出口商品交易会，简称"广交会"。广交会从 2008 年秋季第 104 届开始全部在琶洲举办，展览总面积达到 110 多万平方米，成为"世界第一展"。

译文1：

China Import and Export Fair, the largest fair in the world, is called Canton Fair for short. Canton Fair has been held in Pazhou since the 104th Session in the autumn of 2008. The exhibition area is more than 1.1 million square meters, which makes it the No. 1 Fair in the world.

译文2：

China Import and Export Fair, also known as Canton Fair, has been staged in Pazhou venue since the 104th Session in the autumn of 2008. With an exhibition area of more than 1.1 million square meters, it turns out to be the No. 1 Fair in the world.

8 世界最大的展馆集群——琶洲会展商务区。因展扬名的琶洲岛面积仅有 10 平方公里，建成的现代化展馆超过 60 万平方米，加上即将竣工的部分，岛上可提供的商务展览面积接近 100 万平方米，其总体规模和集聚度世界第一。

译文1：

The Pazhou International Exhibition Center is the largest exhibition center in the world. Pazhou Island, famous for its exhibitions, only has an area of 10 square kilometers. However, it is built into over 600,000 square meters modern exhibition halls and its exhibition capacity is near 1 million square meters including the section to be completed soon. Its scale and concentricity makes it the No. 1 in the world.

译文2：

The Pazhou CBD is the largest exhibition complex in the world. The 10-square-kilometer Pazhou Island, rising to fame with fairs, has been turned into a 600,000 ㎡ venue and its exhibiting capacity is reaching 1 million square meters, including the additional section to be completed. The venue ranks top in terms of size and aggregation of fairs.

商业机会（Business Opportunities）

9 海珠区经济发展方向：建立以现代服务业为重点，以会展经济、总部经济、商贸服务业、创意产业和高新技术产业为支撑的现代产业体系。

译文1：

The trend of the economic development in Haizhu District focuses on modern services, supported by convention and exhibition economy, headquarter economy, commerce and trade industry, creative industry, and high-tech industry.

译文2：

The goal of the economic development in the District is to establish a modern industry system, with focus placed on modern service, supported by convention and exhibition, headquarter economy, commerce and trade, creative industry, and high-tech industry.

10 中央政府批准的《珠江三角洲地区改革发展规划纲要（2008—2020）》把广州定位为国家中心城市和国际会展中心，广州市目前是全国第三大会展城市，而广州市的专业展馆基本都在海珠区。2008年琶洲举办展览面积近400万平方米，占全市九成以上。2008年海珠区被命名为"中国会展名区"。

译文 1：

According to the **Outline of the Plan for the Reform and Development of the Pearl River Delta**(2008 – 2020) approved by the central government, Guangzhou is defined as the National Core City and the International Convention and Exhibition Center. Guangzhou is ranked as the 3rd convention and exhibition city nationwide; meanwhile, most of the professional exhibition halls are located in Haizhu. In 2008, Pazhou had a total exhibition area of nearly 4 million square meters, taking above 90% of the exhibition area in Guangzhou. Haizhu is regarded as China's Famous Convention and Exhibition District in 2008.

译文 2：

Guangzhou is established as the National Core City and the Center of International Convention and Exhibition, according to / based on the **Plan for the Reform and Development of the Pearl River Delta**(2008 – 2020) approved by the central government. The city is ranked as the 3rd convention city in the country, with most of the professional exhibition pavilions located in the District. With the exhibiting space reaching 4 million square meters, taking over 90% of its kind in Guangzhou, Haizhu District is regarded as China's Renowned Convention and Exhibition District in 2008.

11　海珠区东北部是广州大中央商务区的重要组成部分，重点发展会展商务、国际贸易、批发零售分销、创意产业总部。瑞士龙沙制药集团已将其中国区总部设在海珠区，保利地产、广东钢铁、广新外贸等总部企业业已落户。

译文 1：

The Northeast of Haizhu is an important component of Guangzhou CBD, concentrating on the development in convention and exhibition economy, international trade, wholesale and retail, distribution, and headquarters of creative industry. Lonza Chemical, one of the world's leading suppliers to the pharmaceutical, healthcare and life science industries in Switzerland, established its China Headquarter in Haizhu. Furthermore, the headquarters of Poly Real Estate Group Co. Ltd, Guangdong Iron & Steel Group Corporation, and Guangdong Foreign Trade Group Co. Ltd. settle down in Haizhu.

译文 2：

The northeastern part is included in Guangzhou CBD, focusing on convention and exhibition, international trade, wholesale and retail, distribution, and headquarter economy of creative industry. Leading international and domestic enterprises have established their headquarters here, such as Lonza Chemical in Switzerland, Poly Real Estate Group Co. Ltd, Guangdong Iron & Steel Group Corporation, and Guangdong Foreign Trade Group Co. Ltd.

人才资源（Intellectual Resources）

广州市拥有63所高等院校、107所中等技术学校。海珠区大专院校众多，科研机构云集，有广州市"科技走廊"之称。其中，高等院校13所，约占全市的20%；科研院所25所，约占全市的1/3。广州市现有5万名博硕士研究生，68万本科生，24万名中等技术学院学生，102万专业技术工人，正为海珠区发展提供源源不断的动力。

译文1：

Guangzhou has 63 universities, and 107 vocational schools. Haizhu District is the gathering place of colleges, universities and research institutions with the title of Science Corridor in Guangzhou. This includes 13 colleges and universities, 20% of the total number in Guangzhou, and 25 research institutions, one third of the total. There are 50,000 post-graduates, 680,000 undergraduates, and 1,020,000 professional technical workers, who are the continuous power to the development of Haizhu.

译文2：

Guangzhou has 63 universities, and 107 vocational schools. Known as the Science Corridor, the District accommodates 13 colleges and universities (20% of the total), and 25 research institutions (1/3 of the total). The 50,000 post-graduates, 680,000 undergraduates, and 1,020,000 technical workers in the city are/provide a driving force for the local development.

三、相关平行文本

翻译投资指南时，需要更多地借鉴英语文本在类似场合下的表达方式（平行文本）以及多元化的宣传策略。以 *Invest in Germany* 和 *Business Guide to Germany* 为例。

(一) 政府部门的支持

1. 经济支持 (Financial Aid)

* If you start up a new business the German government will support you financially, irrespective of whether you are a German citizen or not. There are a number of options available, and depending on the size of the company a grant can cover up to 50% of the overall initial investment. Alongside the financial support you will naturally be offered practical assistance in getting your business up and running.

* Investors costs for setting up production facilities can be significantly reduced by using a number of different measures in Germany's investment incentives package. Cash incentives provided in the form of non-repayable grants make up the main components of this package.

* "Innovation program" is another source of financing for innovations. It can be used to finance personnel, travel, material, trade fair, and market launch costs, among other things. In the research and development phase, the program can cover up to 100% of the eligible costs.

2. 优先发展领域 (What Is Promoted)

* The use of new technologies and environmentally compatible, energy-saving production procedures is promoted in Germany through low-interest loans. There are also subsidies amounting to up to 50% for investments in structurally weak areas.

* The "Start-up funds" make it easier for innovative companies to obtain equity capital in the start-up and initial phase. Financing is provided for research and development costs up to the production and testing of prototypes, and investments for market launch. In some cases, the fund has a stake in the company.

* Ideas are traded on the Innovation Market. It is a market for patent holders, technology providers, young, technology-oriented companies, and investors, all of whom submit electronic adverts. If there is interest in the ideas, a subsidy can then be received for the subsequent evaluation that is usually required.

3. 服务意识 (Practical Assistance)

* The members of the Invest in Germany staff are a dedicated source of valuable information for you. They can help you to establish contacts with key decision-makers in business, administration, politics, and society, to pave the way for you and your company to do business in Germany. (Invest in Germany is the marketing agency which promotes Germany as a business location)

* Competent experts who have in-depth knowledge of the respective region and its individual opportunities put their expertise at the disposal of investors free of charge. They will answer questions concerning financial advantages, and also provide assistance in selecting a suitable site. These experts also have a network of regional and local contacts at their fingertips.

* The websites of the business development agencies also contain detailed information on who to contact, real estate offers, and available industrial sites. A visit to the federal development database is also very informative. This constantly updated database with its various search options provides detailed information on the different types of financial aid available. In many cases, the grant must be applied for by the company's bank; the application can be made by all internationally registered banks, including branches of foreign banks in Germany.

(二) 人力资源

中文文本对人力资源的描述一般比较空洞和概念化，相比之下，英语文本对人力资源的描述更务实，针对性强。

Germany has very highly qualified, motivated, and responsible specialists. The high level of knowledge and skills among the German workforce is internationally renowned. The education and training system ensures that personnel meet companies' needs.

One special feature of German education is the parallel education in a vocational school and within a company or at an inter-company training site. Depending on the profession, education and training lasts two to three years. The material taught is continuously adapted to the skills required in working life. Universities and universities of applied science produce the required experts and academics.

第九章 英语学术论文摘要译写

一、概述：学术论文摘要的一般语体结构特征

（一）摘要的一般性定义

abstract（英语摘要），释义为"brief statements of the main ideas or important points of an article or book"，意指将文章或著作的提纲和要义摘出，以便让读者预先对文章或著作的主要内容有所了解。可见，摘要是以提供文章或著作的内容梗概为目的，是文章或著作的浓缩和代表。因此，摘要写作的基本要求是简明扼要。所谓简明扼要，意指摘要所述内容必须是文章的要义或要点，有关论据或背景应当从略；同时，文字表达必须简洁明了，概括性强，让读者一目了然，迅速准确地表述文章的主旨和要义。这是摘要写作的一般性定义和要求。

例1

原文：

本书概述了建筑文化的理念与建筑文化的摄影表现，作者从游历世界20多个国家、数十座城市拍摄的城市建筑和风景园林作品中精心挑选出的170个实例，并做了图文并茂的解说，使读者了解西方建筑文化发展的梗概以及对我国城市建筑和风景园林事业的发展十分有益的信息。（《建筑文化感悟与图说》）

译文：

This book approaches the conceptions of architectural culture and the relevant photographic composition, presenting 170 selected works of architecture and landscaping from dozens of cities in 20-odd countries Mr. Zhang Zhu-gang has explored, with a view to formulating an outline of the development of western architectural culture. It caters for city planners, architects, landscape designers and photographers, with the purpose of being instrumental for the development of city, architecture and landscaping in China.

注意：图书摘要不仅要概括出主要内容，还需要指出其目的性和针对的读者群（It caters for...）。

（二）学术论文摘要的结构特征

学术研究论文（academic research papers）是指学术期刊、学术研讨会提交的论文以及大学的学位论文。学术论文的读者主要是特定学科领域的专家学者和对该学科感兴趣者。学术论文摘要的目的是让检索者迅速了解特定研究论文对自己是否具有参考价值，便于将自己正在进行的研究与他（前）人的研究题目、方法、结论等在深度和广度上进行比较，或判断自己的研究是否与他人的研究雷同，以便决定该研究题目的取舍，或调整研究方向。因此，学术论文摘要与词典对于摘要的一般性定义是不同的。特别是网络查询为检索学科领域的历史文献提供了便捷的途径，学术论文摘要对学术成果的交流与传播起着至关重要的作用。

Carole Slade（1963：38）对论文摘要的写作提出了四点要求：①陈述所要研究的问题；② 描述研究方法；③陈述研究要点及意义；④最后得出研究结论。这些要素的构成是由学术研究的传承性和交流性等因素所决定的。

从研究性质看，任何论文的写作，首先，选题都应有明确的目的性和研究价值，因而对论文研究目的或内容的表述就构成了摘要的第一要素；其次，从研究角度看，一篇论文所提出或采用的研究方法、切入角度或探讨问题的深度和广度，可能也是该研究的创新点，对读者可能更重要，这就构成了摘要的第二个要素；再次，对于有些观点比较突出、新颖、理论性较强的论文，摘要还往往需要说明论文中所阐述的要点及意义，这是构成摘要的第三个要素；最后，研究结果或结论是表明论文研究的价值所在，是论文摘要不可缺少的要素。以上分析基于学术研究的传承性和交流性，从研究者和读者的需求出发，形成学术论文摘要的四大要素：主旨、方法、要点、结论。

但是，在某些情况下，研究者需要强调研究背景，以凸显研究项目的重要性，或研究方法的不同，深度或范围的不同，或是与以往的研究形成鲜明的对比，强调本研究的创新程度或不同的视角。在这种情况下，学术论文摘要的模式便是：背景—主旨—方法—要点—结论。

也就是说，学术论文摘要需要回答下列问题：

（1）本研究的主题是什么？

（2）问题的提出，即本研究是在什么背景/情况下产生的？（可以略去）
（3）本研究采用的方法/途径是什么？
（4）本研究的要点或意义是什么？（可以略去）
（5）本研究得出的结论是什么？

通过回答上述问题，学术研究的内容、价值与创新之处充分显现，便于学术交流，加速学术成果的传播和利用。掌握学术论文摘要的结构特征对翻译很有帮助。

二、英汉论文标题和摘要的差异与翻译

从语篇类型上看，论文标题与摘要都属于"信息类"语篇。论文标题是对全文内容的高度概括，文字精练、准确、醒目。论文摘要的目的是介绍文章的主旨、论点、分析、结果、建议等，文字简练，表达客观，结构严谨，条理清晰，逻辑严密，术语正确。

（一）汉英论文标题在表达方式上的区别

1. 在表达语气上的差异

由于中国传统文化视谦虚为美德，这一传统在文章标题上也有反映，许多文章即便是很有学术见解和深度，标题也习惯用"试论""初探""浅谈""浅析"等表示谦虚的字眼，这样的表达方式在国内已经司空见惯，但是如果将其直译成英文，就不符合英语的表达习惯，不仅会削弱主题，而且会让英语读者对文章质量产生误解。

例如，"A Tentative Discussion on…"（……初探，试论……，浅谈……）；"A Few Observation on…"（对……之我见）；"A Brief Analysis of…"（浅析……）等，在此情况下，可以直接用"On…"取而代之。

例如：

（1）On Quick Response of ×××Service
×××服务的快速响应问题
更多时候，On 也可以略去。

（2）Barriers to Household Risk Management: Evidence from India
论家庭风险管理的障碍——以印度为例

2. 在句法上的差异

在句法上，汉语论文标题常用动词短语结构和字数相同的并列结构以

及无主句，英语则常用名词短语、动名词短语、介词短语等。

例如：

（1） Project Partnering: Results of Study of 280 Construction Projects

《项目合作：280建设项目案例研究》（名词短语）

（2） Training Entry-Level Engineers in Civil Engineering and Design Consulting Firm

《如何为/在土木工程和设计咨询公司培养初级工程师》（动名词短语）

（3） Towards a Methodology for Investigating Social Issues

《社会问题调研方法探究》（介词短语）

鉴于以上差异，英汉对译时，译者不仅要对全文内容有比较透彻的理解，把握文章的主题或核心内容，同时要意识到两种语言在表达和行文方式上的差异，仔细推敲上下文逻辑关系，做出相应的语用调整，避免逐字死译和汉化的表达方式。

例如：

（1）解决中国能源短缺问题的重要途径

Solutions to China's Energy Shortage

（2） An Experimental Study of Risk-Taking and Fairness

承担风险与公平原则之关系的实验性研究

（3） Implementing A Design/Build Prequalification System

实施设计和施工资格预审体系

汉语标题中常见字数齐整的并列动词结构，如果逐字译出不符合英语的表达习惯，需要根据英语表达规范，对原文进行重组，将并列动词结构改为非并列动名词短语结构或非并列名词短语结构。

例如：

（4）携手开创未来，推动合作共赢

Working Together toward a Common Future through Win-Win Cooperation

（5）坚持以就业为导向，调整高等教育结构

Career-oriented Approach towards Adjustment of Higher Education Structure

标题太长时可以用破折号或冒号隔开。

例如：

（1） Project Management Knowledge and Effects on Construction Project Outcomes: An Empirical Study

项目管理知识及其对建设项目之影响的实验性研究

(2) 普通消费增长应当成为消费政策的核心

Growth of General Public Consumption—Core of Consumer Policy

(3) 产业集群与竞争优势之因果关系及其政策影响

Industry Cluster and Competitive Edge—Their Causal Relationship and Policy Impact

(4) 转换企业经营机制必须改革人事制度

Reform of Personnel System—A Necessity for Shifting Business Management Mode

(二) 汉英论文摘要在句法和行文结构上的差异

汉英论文摘要在句法和行文结构上存在较大差异。汉语摘要比较平铺直叙，摘要结构的标识性不太强，即论文的主旨、要点、方法和结论的标识不太明显。

例2

原文：

电子商务系统安全特性分析

①商务信息安全是电子商务和网络用户进行网上交易的重要前提。②许多安全问题并不在电子商务系统上，而往往存在于执行信息传输的过程中。③本文从电子商务的理论和实践上进行较深入地分析研究，指出如何克服电子交易中的薄弱环节，并对使电子商务和网络更加安全的算法和协议进行了讨论。

译文：

On the Security of E-Commerce System

Security of business information is a major prerequisite of E-commerce and Internet transaction. Most security problems do not occur in the E-commerce system, instead, in the information transmission process. This paper analyses E-commerce from theoretical and practical perspectives, pointing out how to overcome weaknesses in transaction process, with a further discussion of algorithms and protocols for making E-commerce and network more secure.

分析:

第①、②句陈述研究背景及问题的产生,第③句陈述研究主旨与解决方案。

但是,摘要没有具体提示该研究运用了什么理论,在哪些方面进行了实践,克服了电子交易中的什么薄弱环节。因此,该摘要提供的实质性信息不够充分,其信息的查询和检索价值受到了影响。

汉语摘要常用第一人称表述作者的观点,用"本文""笔者""我们"等做主语,多用主动语态。

英文摘要通常用第三人称表达作者观点(This paper/study/investigation approaches/addresses/reveals that),较少出现"We"或"I"等,较多使用被动语态(Multimedia courseware is used in computer aided teaching)。

此外,为了节省版面空间,英文摘要常用缩写词,用大写字母拼写,替代冗长复杂的词或词组(如WTO)。但是,对于不为公众所熟知的缩写词,必须至少出现一次全称,然后再用其缩写。例如,Total Quality Management(TQM,全面质量管理);design/build prequalification system(DBPS,设计/施工资格预审体系)。

三、英语学术论文摘要解析

(一)英语学术论文摘要的语体结构特征

在实际写作中,大多数学术论文摘要的语体结构特征是按照Carole所说的结构模式或顺序进行写作的。

1. 摘要具有相对比较完整的四大结构要素,且各要素的先后顺序相对比较明晰

例3

①This paper <u>addresses</u> the issue of whether the European Monetary System has contributed to real exchange rate stability between France, Germany, and Italy. ②It <u>first approaches</u> whether bilateral PPP holds between any pair of these countries and between each of them and the United States. ③Next it <u>assesses</u> the role of relative prices and exchange rates in the adjustment process towards PPP. ④It <u>concludes</u> that PPP never holds before the EMS was created, and that PPP between France and Germany is solely due to exchange rate dynamics. (*Journal of Macroeconomics*, No. 1, 1995)

分析：

例3原文中四大结构要素顺序清楚明晰，具有典型模式特征：第①句陈述研究主旨；第②、③句说明研究内容/要点和研究方法（approach, assess）；第④句说明研究结论：在欧洲货币体系建立之前，PPP并不存在，法德之间的PPP完全取决于兑换率的动态变化。

例4

①This paper <u>estimates</u> the dynamic effects of changes in taxes in the United States. ② We <u>distinguish</u> between changes in personal and corporate income taxes and develop a new narrative account of federal tax liability changes in these two tax components. ③We <u>develop</u> an estimator which uses narratively identified tax changes as proxies for structural tax shocks and apply it to quarterly post-WWII data. ④ We <u>find</u> that short run output effects of tax shocks are large and that it is important to distinguish between different types of taxes when considering their impact on the labor market and on expenditure components. (**The Dynamic Effects of Personal and Corporate Income Tax Changes in the United States**, *American Economic Review* 2013)

分析：

例4中第①句陈述论文主旨和要点，第②句和第③句说明研究方法和要点，第④句指出研究结论。该摘要结构紧凑，层次清楚，简明扼要，使读者对该论文的主旨、研究方法、结论一目了然。

例5

①This paper describes existing guides and analytic frameworks that have been suggested for the economic evaluation of healthcare interventions. ②Using selected examples of digital health interventions, it assesses how well existing guides and frameworks align to digital health interventions. ③It shows that digital health interventions may be best characterized as complex interventions in complex systems. ④ Key features of complexity relate to intervention complexity, outcome complexity, and causal pathway complexity, with much of this driven by iterative intervention development over time and uncertainty regarding likely reach of the interventions among the relevant population.

⑤These characteristics imply that more-complex methods of economic evaluation are likely to be better able to capture fully the impact of the intervention on costs and benefits over the appropriate time horizon. ⑥This complexity includes wider measurement of costs and benefits, and a modeling framework that is able to capture dynamic interactions among the intervention, the population of interest, and the environment. ⑦The authors recommend that future research should develop and apply more-flexible modeling techniques to allow better prediction of the interdependency between interventions and important environmental influences. (**Designing and Undertaking a Health Economics Study of Digital Health Interventions**, 2016 *American Journal of Preventive Medicine*)

分析：

例5中第①、②句陈述论文主旨和研究方法，第③、④、⑤、⑥句说明研究要点，第⑦句得出研究结论。

2. 摘要结构模式和顺序并非严格一致，而是有所变化

例6

①Using data from a field experiment in Kenya, we document that providing individuals with simple informal savings technologies can substantially increase investment in preventative health and reduce vulnerability to health shocks. ②Simply providing a safe place to keep money was sufficient to increase health savings by 66 percent. ③Adding an earmarking feature was only helpful when funds were put toward emergencies, or for individuals that are frequently taxed by friends and relatives. ④Group-based savings and credit schemes had very large effects. (**Why Don't the Poor Save More? Evidence from Health Savings Experiments**, *American Economic Review* 2013)

分析：

该摘要第①句用动词的 V-ing 结构形式标识论文所采用的研究方法、分析模型，将这个短语置于表研究内容的语句之前，再陈述研究主旨、研究要点和结论（第②、③、④句）。作者如果想要突出研究方式的创新，可以用此结构。

例7

原文：

①This study examines the relationships among the PMBOK® Guide, project performance, customer satisfaction, and project success by assessing the efficacy of management techniques, tools, and skills for implementing infrastructure and building construction. ② Experienced interviewees from private engineering firms and public agencies were asked to complete a questionnaire, and the responses were analyzed by means of a structural equation model. ③ The analytical results indicate the appropriateness of prioritizing the practice of the PMBOK ® Guide in the construction industry. ④ This study contributes to the literature by providing insight into interactions among the PMBOK ® Guide and construction project outcomes in engineering practices. ⑤ Particularly, the "bidder's conference" and "procurement negotiations" are the priority techniques to minimize bidding and legal procurement problems. ⑥ Moreover, the study recommends the use of "stakeholder analysis," "communication requirements analysis," and the "communication methods" to perform effective communication management. ⑦ Although the conclusions are based on the samples collected in Taiwan, the research findings can be used by project managers and educators to tailor the PMBOK ® Guide to their unique needs and to design effective training programs for construction specialists. (**Project Management Knowledge and Effects on Construction Project Outcomes: An Empirical Study**, *Journal of Management in Engineering*, 2013)

分析：

该摘要第①句陈述研究主旨，第②句陈述研究方法，第③句陈述研究结论，第④、⑤、⑥、⑦句陈述研究意义和要点。

译文：

本研究通过评价用于基础设施和建筑工程的管理技术、工具和技巧的有效性，探讨了PMBOK指南与项目运作、客户满意度和项目成功之间的关系。通过对私营工程公司和公共机构的资深专业人士的问卷调查，运用结构公式模型分析反馈意见，分析结果显示了在建筑行业优先使用PMBOK指南的适用性。本研究对PMBOK指南与建设项目成果在工程实践中的相互作用提出自己的见解，为这方面的文献积累做出了贡献。特别是"投标会议"和"采购谈判"是优先采用的技术，用于减少投标和采购中出现的法律问题；此外，该研究建议采用"利益相关方/人分析""沟通需求分析"和"沟通方式"进行有效的沟通管理。虽然本研究的结论是基于在台湾收集的样例做出的，但本研究成果可促使项目经理和教育者调整 PMBOK 指南，使之适应其独特需求，同时用于设计高效的建筑工程人才培训项目。

例8

原文：

① This paper presents the guidelines for using the design/build prequalification system (DBPS) model in the public sector. ② The DBPS provides a framework for a public sector owner's representative to review and determine appropriate prequalification criteria for use in evaluating potential design/build project teams. ③ It allows that representative to maintain a consistent evaluation process from initial request for proposal preparation through actual prequalification selection. ④ The DBPS model is presented as an information framework. ⑤It consists of six categories of criteria for a proposed project team: economic, political, technological, corporate policy, labor/personnel, and legal. ⑥ Results of testing the model in the public sector are discussed. ⑦ Guidelines for the model's use in the public sector are provided to encourage its implementation. ⑧ A discussion of possible exceptions to the scoring system is presented. ⑨ Finally, an outline of the evaluation categories is presented and the methodology for applying this is discussed with examples.

分析：

该摘要第①句陈述研究主旨，第②、③句表明研究要点与意义，第④、⑤句阐明研究方法，第⑥、⑦、⑧、⑨句表明结论。

译文：

本文为在公共部门实施设计/施工资格预审体系（DBPS）提供了指导原则。DBPS 模型为公共部门业主的甲方代表在评估预/候选设计/施工项目团队时，审查和确定合适的资格预审标准提供了一个框架，使甲方代表从最初的招标准备阶段直至在实际的资格预审过程中都能保持稳定的评价标准。DBPS 实际上是一个信息框架，对项目团队的评价包含 6 个要素：经济、政治、技术、企业政策、员工和法律事务。本文还讨论了 DBPS 在公共部门运用的测试结果。为了促进这个体系的运用，本文提出了在公共部门使用该体系的指导原则，讨论了评分体系出现例外的情况，而且还提出了一个分类评价的框架，用实例说明使用方法。

3. 摘要也可先给出背景信息，再提出研究主题

并非所有的摘要都严格按照 Carole 所说的结构模式或顺序，有时也可以首先给出背景信息，指出研究主题是如何提出或产生的，然后再说明研究的论题或主旨。这说明，有时根据论文的内容和性质，有必要提示背景信息，但是背景信息一定要有很强的关联性。

例 9

原文：

①Partnering has generated considerable excitement in the construction industry. ② However, this enthusiasm is largely based on anecdotal evidence. ③The results of a study of 280 construction projects in which the relationship between project success and alternative approaches (including partnering) to managing the owner-contractor relationship are reported in this paper. ④The findings indicate that partnered projects achieved superior results in controlling costs, the technical performances, and in satisfying customers compared with those projects managed in an adversarial, guarded adversarial, and even informal partnering manner. ⑤Further, whether the contract was awarded on a low-bid or non-low-bid basis did not affect the relationship between partnering and project success. ⑥ Conclusions and findings pertaining to alternative management approaches are briefly addressed here. (**Project Partnering: Results of Study of 280 Construction Projects**, *Journal of Management in Engineering*, *No.* 3, 1995)

分析：

第①、②句陈述研究背景：建立合作伙伴关系在建筑业已经形成一股浪潮，然而，这种合作热情很大程度上是基于传闻轶事；第③句陈述研究主旨（the relationship between project success and alternative approaches 项目成功与不同管理方式之间的关系）和研究方式（280 construction projects 案例研究），与第①、②句形成鲜明对比，强调280个项目案例研究的科学性；第④、⑤、⑥句陈述研究要点与结论。从例9可以看出，陈述研究要点的语句中可以体现研究的结论。

译文：

建立伙伴关系在建筑业已经成为热潮，然而这种热情大都基于传闻逸事。本研究基于对280个建设项目的调研，研究项目成功与不同的管理方式之间的联系——管理业主与承包商之间的关系——（包括建立伙伴关系）。研究表明，与以对立/博弈方式或谨慎的对立/博弈方式，甚至是非正式的伙伴关系完成的项目相对比，以伙伴关系完成的项目在控制造价、技术性能和满足客户需求方面更具优势,而且,项目合同标的的高低并不影响伙伴关系的建立与项目成功之间的关系。另外,本文还简要论述了与其他管理方式相关的成果。

例10

①Why do many households remain exposed to large exogenous sources of nonsystematic income risk? ②We use a series of randomized field experiments in rural India to test the importance of price and nonprice factors in the adoption of an innovative rainfall insurance product. ③Demand is significantly price sensitive, but widespread take-up would not be achieved even if the product offered a payout ratio comparable to US insurance contracts. ④We present evidence suggesting that lack of trust, liquidity constraints, and limited salience are significant nonprice frictions that constrain demand. ⑤We suggest possible contract design improvements to mitigate these frictions. (**Barriers to Household Risk Management: Evidence from India**, *American Economic Journal: Applied Economics*, 2013)

分析:

第①句提出问题,说明该研究的重要性:为什么众多家庭面临外来因素导致的收入风险?第②句陈述研究主旨和方法:采用随机选取的一系列田野调查与试验,检验价格与非价格因素在新开发的水灾保险产品推广方面的作用。第③、④、⑤句陈述研究结果与对策。

4. 摘要只表明个别内容

有的摘要只阐明论文的主旨和研究方法,或只表明论文的主旨和结论,或对论文要点不提,或对研究方法不作说明。这主要是由于论文的侧重点不同。

例11

① This paper addresses the training of entry-level engineers for civil engineering and design consulting practice. ② A survey was conducted for both managers and engineers representing 26 firms in Alaska. ③Managers rated the entry-level engineer's skills/knowledge of design elements within the consulting-engineering business, and the entry-level engineers rated themselves in these areas. ④The discrepancies between the managers' and engineers' ratings are highlighted to provide focus areas for a consulting firm's internal training program and university civil engineering program curriculum. (**Training Entry-Level Engineers in Civil Engineering And Design Consulting Firm**, *Journal of Management in Engineering*, 1996)

分析：
第①句陈述研究主旨，第②、③句表明研究方法，第④句阐明研究意义。结论从略。

5. 小结

在摘要各要素中，研究主旨必不可少，研究方法次之，根据论文内容和性质，研究要点或意义可以体现在表主旨或表方法的语句中，有时也可略去；研究结论有时可视情况略去不予说明。

（二）英语学术论文摘要结构的标记性

英语学术论文摘要的文体特点除了基本要素的结构模式外，还有表现这些结构要素的特定语言，具有明显的标记性（markedness），用特定的词语标识出来。基于对以下英文学术期刊的调查，*Journal of Management in Engineering*，*Journal of Civil Construction Engineering*，*American Economic Journal*：*Applied Economics*，*American Economic Review*，*Journal of Macroeconomics*，*Journal of Finance*，*Economica*，*American Journal of Preventive Medicine*，*Architecture Review*，可概括表述如下。

1. 阐明研究主旨的表达形式

This paper approaches (addresses)（分析、论证、探讨）the issue of …

This paper offers an approach（提出解决方案）to the problem of …

This paper proposes (suggests, presents the arguments) that（本文提出/论述……观点）…

This paper reviews（本文综述了）/ defines the concept of（界定……概念）…

We (aim to) make an analysis of …（笔者旨在对……进行分析，……）

We (attempt to) address/approach the issue of …（笔者拟对……的问题进行讨论）

This paper develops …（本文旨在对……作一拓展，……）

This paper analyzes …（本文旨在对……进行分析）

This paper reconsiders …（本文对……的问题作进一步探讨，……）

This paper investigates (reveals, explores) …（本文对……进行了研

究，……）

This paper undertakes a comprehensive description of…, to…（本文通过对……综合性描述，以便/目的在于……）

2. 说明研究方法的表达形式

In comparison with … (we attempt to …)（通过与……的比较研究，……）

The structural X approach is used (applied, employed) to …（本文从运用 X 结构分析方法入手，……）

The approach taken in this paper is to introduce …（本文所采用的研究方法是……引入……）Using the non-parametric approach …（通过运用非参数变量方法研究模式，……）

We employ a …framework to compare …（本文采用……理论框架对……）

Our approach to … is to …（本文所运用的研究方法是……）

We use a (squad of three structure) to decompose …（本文运用……对……进行分解/解构）Using the traditional X model ….（we aim to analyze …）（通过运用传统的 X 模型……）Quantitatively, we attempt to …（通过数量分析，……）

Qualitatively, we aim to …（通过质量/定量分析，……）

Through quantitative (qualitative) analysis, it (we) arrives at the conclusion that…

3. 阐述研究的要点与意义的表达方式

The study/investigation/research suggests/indicates/shows that…（研究表明/显示）

The significance of the research is…（本研究的意义/作用在于……）

4. 陈述研究结论的表达形式

This paper concludes that …（本文的结论是……）

We come to a conclusion that …（笔者的结论是……）

The results show (indicate, demonstrate, illustrate, reveal) that …（研究表明……）

It is shown that …（研究说明……）/ It suggests that …（文章提出……）

We find (or argue) that …（笔者认为……）

This study has promising implications for…（本研究对……有积极意义/启示）

相比之下，中文论文摘要没有严格的写作规范要求，有些摘要行文比较简略随意，英译时需要按照英文摘要的行文规范进行必要的补充和完善。

运用上述英语学术论文摘要的基本结构模式及其特定语言表达方式，只要用户提供准确的专业术语，就能将专业性很强的论文摘要译出。有些理工类学术论文摘要看似简单，其实不然，其中的概念与逻辑关系环环相扣，翻译时需要仔细分析和理清各种概念和术语之间的相互关系，逐一译出。

例 12

原文：

基于连续介质理论的单壁氮化硼纳米管的振动研究

根据连续介质圆柱壳模型，推导了单壁氮化硼纳米管的三种振动频率公式。结合三种手性，分析影响氮化硼纳米管振动基频的因素。结果表明：手性对振动频率几乎没有影响。振动频率随纳米管的半径、管长和长径比的增大而减小。并且，在长径比相对较小时，纳米管主要表现为扭转振动；在长径比相对较大时，纳米管主要表现为弯曲振动。

专业术语：

连续介质 continuous medium；圆柱壳模型 cylindrical shell model；单壁氮化硼纳米管 single wall boron nitride nanotube；振动频率 vibration frequency；手性 chiral；长径比 draw ration；扭转振动 torsional vibration；弯曲振动 flexural vibration

原译：

On the Vibration of the Single Wall Boron Nitride Nanotube Based on Continuum Theory

Based on the cylindrical shell model of continuous medium, three kinds of vibration frequency formula of single wall boron nitride nanotubes are derived. Combined with three kinds of chiral, the factors affecting the vibration fundamental frequency of boron nitride nanotubes were analyzed. The results show that the chiral has little influence on the vibration frequency. The vibration frequency decreases with the tube radius, length and draw ratio to increase. And, in the aspect of minor draw ration, the main performance of the nanotube is torsional vibration. In the aspect of lager draw ration, the main performance of the nanotube is flexural vibration.

改译：

This study derives three vibration frequency formulas of the single wall boron nitride nanotube, based on the cylindrical shell model of continuous medium, <u>and addresses the factors that affect</u> the vibration of fundamental frequency of boron nitride nanotubes <u>by means of three approaches</u>. <u>The study concludes that</u> the chiral has little <u>effect</u> on the vibration frequency. The vibration frequency decreases <u>with the increase of</u> the tube radius, length and draw ration. <u>In addition, when draw ration is comparatively smaller</u>, the nanotube <u>performs</u> torsional vibration. <u>While</u> draw ration <u>is comparatively larger</u>, the nanotube <u>presents</u> flexural vibration.

分析：

通过添加 This study derives…, and addresses the factors…, by means of three approaches 引出研究主旨与方法，补充 The study concludes that…, In addition…, While draw ration is…依次陈述研究结论。结构完整，主题信息突出，表达更趋专业化。

例 13

原文：

水平地震运动作用下剪切杆的波动解

通常情况下，求波动方程解的解析表达式是困难的。本文通过合理修改定解条件，采用分离变量法求得水平地震运动作用下剪切杆的波动解，并和模态叠加法求得的解进行比较，分析两者的异同。

专业术语：

水平地震运动 horizontal seismic motion；波动解法 wave propagation method；；模态叠加法 modal superposition method；定解条件 definite condition；分离变量法 variable separation approach；剪切杆 shear rod

译文：

**Wave Propagation Approach of the
Shear Rod under Horizontal Seismic Motion**

① As the analytical expression of wave propagation equation is hard to achieve in normal condition, this paper <u>adopts</u> variable separation approach to achieve wave propagation approach of the shear rod under horizontal seismic motion, <u>by means of</u> appropriately modifying the definite condition. ② <u>In addition</u>, the solution of the wave propagation approach is compared with that of the modal superposition approach to demonstrate their similarities and differences.

分析：

句①陈述研究背景、研究主旨与方法 this paper adopts… by means of appropriately modifying。句②陈述研究要点与结论。

例 14

原文：

本文研究了 3D 虚拟环境如何支持团队的相互理解与决策过程。基于同步性理论，我们提出，通过 3D 虚拟环境创造的共享环境和阿凡达式的互动，有助于团队在决策的过程中意见集中，增加团队成员之间的相互理解，提高团队的业绩。本研究通过一个实验，对 70 个三人组合的团队在空间布局方面的决策过程进行调查。团队的互动采用三种形式：基于文本的同步聊天形式，在一个 3D 虚拟决策室进行，在一个反映空间布局的虚拟环境中进行。实验结果表明，在虚拟决策室或虚拟环境中，团队的相互理解高于基于文本的聊天形式，而且，在达成一致意见、获得满足感和形成凝聚力方面取得的业绩更高。研究表明，与传统的基于文本的合作技术相比，3D 虚拟环境为团队合作提供了更大的潜力。

专业术语：

同步性理论 synchronicity theory；阿凡达式的互动 avatar-based interaction；text-based chat 基于文本的聊天；虚拟决策室 virtual decision room

译文：

This study investigates how three-dimensional virtual environments (3DVEs) support shared understanding and group decision making. Based on media synchronicity theory, we pose that the shared environment and avatar-based interaction allowed by 3 DVEs aid convergence processes in teams working on a decision-making task, leading to increased shared understanding between team members. This increases team performance. An experiment was conducted in which 70 teams of three participants had to decide on a spatial planning issue. The teams interacted using synchronous text-based chat, a 3D virtual decision room, or were present in the virtual environment (VE) mirroring the spatial planning task. Results revealed that in the virtual decision room and the VE, shared understanding was higher than in the text-based chat condition. This led to higher task performance in terms of consensus, satisfaction, and cohesion. Our result show that 3DVEs offer potential for team collaboration over more traditional text based collaboration technologies.

四、摘要修改

摘要是学术论文的一个重要组成部分,是经过概括化了的宏观结构语篇,有其特定的信息传播方式,目的是方便读者快速检索和获取信息,加速研究成果的交流与传播。然而,许多作者不熟悉英语摘要的写作要求,有的摘要主旨不明、层次不清、要点不突出、行文冗长繁复;有的摘要完全按照中文摘要逐字对译,其结果是信息结构混乱,影响了研究成果的交流与传播。

然而,要做到结构合理、层次清晰、信息要点突出,作者应根据英语表达习惯做相应的处理,以符合英语读者的阅读与表达习惯。

例 15

原文:

当今社会,企业间的竞争,不可能只停留在商品质量和销售数量上拉开距离,而要在企业的知名度、美誉上展开争夺。良好的企业形象,有利于企业参与竞争,有利于扩大与延伸,有利于融资与吸收人才,有利于保护、发展民族工业。为达到强化企业形象的目的,则在广告宣传中,应注重突出企业独特的个性、独特的精神、鲜明的宗旨、民族的品质。("强化企业形象广告意识")

分析:

这篇中文摘要平铺直叙,与一般文章"引言"部分的行文风格没有区别,而且,论文的主旨、内容、方法和结论不清晰,不利于读者快速检索,掌握信息内容。因此,在摘要译写时可以做适当增删调节,使信息表达清晰,主题信息突出。例如增译<u>研究主旨</u>和<u>内容</u>,得出<u>结论</u>,压缩与删略意义重复的表述,如"独特的个性""独特的精神""鲜明的宗旨"。

译文:

<u>This paper addresses</u> the importance of enhancing enterprises' popularity

and fame under the current competitive environment of the market economy. <u>It points out that</u> good corporate image is of great advantage in the aspects of competition, financing, elite-attracting, protecting and developing national industries. <u>It concludes that</u>, to create a distinctive corporate image, the promotion campaign / advertising is designed to highlight enterprises' unique entrepreneurship, and the national characters. （曾利沙）

注意：使用惯用的表达方式：a distinctive corporate image, to highlight, promotion campaign。

例 16

原文：

本文重点论述了提升粤港经贸合作水平的问题，认为扩大分工领域、创新分工形式和内容，调动和发挥私营企业的积极作用，优化进出口商品结构、提高营销技巧，充分利用香港转口优势以及加大力度发展粤港服务领域等是有利于把粤港经贸合作提高到更高水平的措施。（"把粤港经贸合作提高到更高水平"）

分析：

这篇中文摘要将数个动宾结构统一放在一个长句内，对这种句式的英译宜先予以概括提示，然后分列陈述，使其层次清晰，论文的主旨、要点和结论一目了然。

译文 1：

<u>This paper aims at addressing</u> the issue of promoting economic and trading cooperation between Hang Kong and Guangdong Province. <u>Based on an analysis of the current situation</u>, <u>the paper holds that</u> to bring the cooperation to a new high demand efforts are to be made on the <u>following measures</u> such as <u>diversifying</u> the economic dimensions in both the first-and second-industries; <u>expanding</u> the coordinating dimensions; <u>mobilizing</u> and <u>motivating</u> the private enterprises' initiative; <u>optimizing</u> the imports and exports; <u>taking advantage of</u> Hang Kong's geographical position as an ideal transit basis and <u>expanding</u> trading services in both districts.

译文 2：

<u>This paper addresses</u> the issue of promoting economic and trading cooperation between Hong Kong and Guangdong Province. <u>The paper proposes that</u> specific measures are to be taken so as to enhance the prospect of the

cooperation. The measures suggested are as follows: diversifying the economic dimensions in both the first- and second-industries; expanding the coordinating dimensions; motivating private enterprises' initiative; optimizing the structure of imports and exports; improving marketing strategies / techniques; taking advantage of Hong Kong's geographical position as an ideal transit basis and expanding trading services in both districts. （曾利沙）

注意：使用惯用的表达方式：to enhance the prospect of the cooperation, the measures suggested are as follows

例17

原译：

A Study on Teaching Pattern of English + Specialty
(International Building Contracting)

①English is a tool, or a specialty, which is still a question to be differed. ②As for the teaching research of English study, we've taken it as specialty for years. ③We used to think that English major should embody liberal education only. ④ However, the entry to the WTO and the change of the conception of qualified personnel made us thinking that what kind of teaching pattern should be more suitable to train the students required by the building industry and to meet the needs of reform and open-door policy of our country, as well as internationalization of construction market. ⑤ The paper, according to the surveys of some building companies in foreign construction market and the requirement of the internationalization of the construction market in our country, puts forward the teaching pattern of English + specialty (international building contracting), which tries to integrate English learning with specialty and to solve the problem of "speaking English without understanding building engineering or understanding building engineering but unable to speak English".

分析：

对前4句的内容进行概括与改写，压缩关联性不强的陈述，突出研究内容和要解决的问题。①和②陈述研究背景，③陈述研究内容、目的和意义。

改译：

On Teaching Pattern of English + Specialty
(International Building Contracting)

① The entry to the WTO and the changed conception of qualified personnel are challenging the traditional idea that English major should focus on liberal education. ② It is arguable what teaching pattern should be adopted to train the students required by international construction market. ③ Based on the surveys of some building companies involved in international construction market and the requirement of the construction market open to the world, this paper puts forward the teaching pattern of English + specialty (international building contracting), which aims to integrate English learning with specialty in order to solve the problem of "speaking English without understanding construction engineering or vice versa".

例 18

原译：

Research on Form of Government Investment in Enterprises

This paper prove the limitedness of behavioral ability of government investment in enterprises from the definite "authorized contracts" signed by both government agents and individuals and characterized by aversion of risks. However, this limitedness of government investment does not interfere with its investment in its own areas for production of public goods and for the greatest social benefits. The paper argues that along with changes in economic returns in enterprises, the right to control enterprises consists in the hands of those who are related to economic interests, that only when an enterprise goes bankrupt, can the creditors control it, and that contracts by creditors are capable of stimulating business operators and stock-holders to great effects so that creditors' rights involve fewer risks than stock-holders' rights. It can be seen from the above that it is feasible that government investments are based on creditors' rights in China's state-owned enterprises.

改译：

On the Form of Government Investment in Enterprises

①This paper approaches the limited performance of government investment in enterprises, with "authorized contracts" signed between government agents and individuals, which are characteristic of risks. ②The investigation reveals that the limitation of government investment does not interfere with its investment in the production of public goods to achieve the greatest social benefits. ③ It suggests that with the changes in investment returns in enterprises, the control over enterprises lies in the hands of those who are related to economic benefits, and that only when an enterprise goes bankrupt, can the creditors get the control of it, and that contracts by creditors are capable of stimulating business operators and stock-holders to greater efforts so that creditors are exposed to fewer risks than stock-holders. ④ It concludes that government investments are based on creditors' rights in China's state-owned enterprises.

分析：

修改后的译文更加条理化，结构清晰。句①研究主旨，句②和③研究要点，句④得出结论，并且使用固定搭配，表达简洁准确。例如，be characteristic of risks 具有典型的风险特征，creditors are exposed to fewer risks than stock-holders 债权人面临的风险比股东小。

学术论文摘要与论文正文写作本身一样，有其特定的文体特征和结构模式，是一高度概括浓缩了的宏观结构体。作为论文的一个有机部分，摘要的写译应注意有效性和规范性。

第十章 简历、求职信写译

一、什么是个人简历

根据 *Cambridge Dictionary* 的定义：个人简历是 "a written statement of your education and work experience, used especially when you are trying to get a job"。

但是，技术写作专家 Jack Molisani 却不这么认为。在他看来，个人简历既不是对个人职业技能和职业经历的概述，也不是对个人能力的概括，更不是对人生故事的浓缩。(A resume is not a summary of your skills and professional experience. It's not a capabilities overview. It's not your life story condensed into a few pages.) 个人简历是一个展示申请人正好与所申请的职位要求匹配的工具。(A resume is a vehicle that shows that you match what the reader is looking for.)

Jack Molisani 是美国技术交流学会会员（Society for Technical Communication, Fellow），ProSpring Technical Staffing 公司总裁，在技术写作培训和项目管理方面颇有建树。

Jack Molisani 认为，作为申请人，你必须弄明白，你的简历为谁而写？谁是简历的读者？他们为什么要读你的简历？他们想要知道什么？——他们想要知道你是否与他们的需求匹配。然而，多数申请人并不知道如何运用这个工具增加自己的面试机会。

Jack Molisani 根据自己多年的实践经验对 *Webster's Dictionary* 的定义作了补充：

个人简历是对某人职业生涯和职业资质的简述，专为申请某个特定职位而定制，用于说明申请人与简历读者的要求（也就是岗位需求）的匹配程度。(A resume is a short account of one's career and qualifications, prepared typically by an applicant for a position, which shows how the applicant matches what the reader is looking for.)

二、如何制作个人简历

Jack Molisani 总是提醒求职者，面对雪片般飞来的简历，你不要奢望有人会从头到尾地阅读你的简历，他们只会匆匆浏览一下，或是瞄几眼，或是找出几个关键词，每份简历在人事部得到的关注非常有限，因为他们没有时间，任何关联性不强的文字信息都会让他们放弃阅读你的简历。在这里，简历被迅速分为两类：否或也许（No and Maybe）。

即便求职者的自身条件已经达到要求也不能保证他就能获得面试机会。Jack Molisani 曾经为休斯敦一家公司推荐一名有专利文献写作经验的职业写手，不料十几分钟后，对方回复邮件说"他没有专利文献的写作经历"。其实，此人确有专利写作经历，但是他把这个技能写在了简历的第 2 页，而人事部经理没有看到第 2 页。每年都有大量的求职者因为种种原因被拒。为此，Jack Molisani 提出如下建议：

（1）制作简历要有针对性，为达到某一特定岗位的要求而写作，使自我介绍与岗位要求相匹配。

（2）要想让自己的简历与招聘岗位要求相匹配，申请人需要预先调查发现招聘人的需求，根据岗位需求调整或制作自己的简历，这样才能增加自己的面试机会。

（3）尽可能将与岗位要求相匹配的职业资质与经历放在简历的第 1 页，甚至第 1 段。招聘人总是希望申请人目前的工作或研究与招聘岗位相符。因此，可以在简历的第 1 段概述你目前的工作与研究内容，说明你正是他们要找的人，这样才能避免迅速被拒。

（4）如果申请人目前的工作或研究与招聘岗位不符，可以简述或弱化自己目前的工作内容，强调和重点介绍申请人曾经做过的与招聘岗位相符的工作经历或研究内容。

（5）陈述你的工作内容或岗位职责比陈述你的岗位名称更重要，便于招聘人了解你的能力和工作经历，因为同一个工作可能会有不同的岗位名称。例如，"专业技术写手"（technical writer）在有些机构被称之为"信息工程师"（information engineer）"用户体验指导"或"产品经理"（user experience advocate）。

（6）简历要尽可能简短，最好将长度控制在 1 页之内，自我介绍要恰到好处，去掉废话，如果工作经验丰富，最长不超过 2 页。

（7）消灭拼写错误，版面设计要醒目，方便读者查找信息。

例 1

Curriculum Vitae

Bill Peterson (male, born on: 09/10/1953)
Experience
　· Over 20 years proven expertise in industrial purchasing, manufacturing, logistics, business development, marketing, sales and service. Experienced and innovative with sophisticated sales, customer service and business administration skills.
　· Background in a wide range of industries, including construction, plant hire, pharmaceutical, hygiene services and industrial process control.
　· International General Manager since 1991. Highly articulate, confident and persuasive team-builder, dependable and reliable in supporting and enabling team effort to produce genuine long-term sustainable development. Able to motivate and communicate to achieve exceptional business performance.
　· Implementation of modern management practices, concerning personnel, IT, reporting systems, and partnership customer-supplier relations, etc. Persistent and flexible approach to the mutually beneficial achievement of business plans and personal goals of staff, suppliers and customers.

Achievements
　· As production control executive with XYZ Corporation, introduced PC-based systems to reduce lead-times from 7 months to 3 days, and inventory by 80% from $4.7 million to $750 thousand.
　· As materials manger with ABC Inc., introduced systems to reduce lead-times from 3 months to 7 days, and inventory from $6 million to $2.5 million, and 12% reduction in procurement costs.
　· As operations manager with CDE, a 10% reduction in procurement costs.
　· As general manager for FGH, business achieved growth form $800 thousand to $5 million, increased new customer growth from 20 to 600 per year.

Career History
　　1996—present　XYZ Corp. General Manager
　　1988—1996　ABC Inc. International Operation Manager
　　1973—1988　Early career development with WER, ASD, CED Ltds

Education
    1973—1977   University of Wales
    1972—1973   Hertstone College

Contact Information
    Tel：0208 971 xxxx
    27 Hill Lane London NW 250 DB

简 历

比尔·彼得森（男，1953年10月9日出生）

工作经验

  ·在工业采购、生产、后勤供给、企业发展、市场营销、销售与服务等方面积累了20多年的专业知识和实际工作技能，经验丰富，锐意创新，掌握高级销售、客服和商务管理综合技能。

  ·工作阅历广泛，涉猎的行业领域包括建筑、厂房租赁、制药、卫生服务、生产流程控制。

  ·自1991年起担任国际部总经理。自信、有亲和力和感染力的团队建设者，值得依靠与信赖的领导者，支持与鼓励团队的长期、可持续发展，能与员工良好地沟通，调动他们的积极性，取得突出业绩。

  ·采用现代管理模式，包括人事、信息技术、汇报机制、建立客户和供货商之间的伙伴关系等方面。既有原则性又不失灵活性地处理企业与员工、供货商和客户各方利益之间的关系，实现多方共赢的局面。

工作成就

  ·作为XYZ公司的生产总监，引进了电脑管理机制，将生产准备时间由7个月减少到3天，库存从470万美元降至75万美元，费用减少了80%。

  ·作为ABC公司的物资经理，通过引进机制将生产准备时间从3个月减少到7天，库存从600万美元降到250万美元，采购费用降低了12%。

  ·作为CDE公司的项目经理，降低了10%的采购费用。

  ·作为FGH的总经理，业务量从80万美元增至500万美元，发展新客户由每年20个增加到每年600个。

工作经历

    1996—现在   XYZ公司，总经理
    1988—1996   ABC公司，国际项目经理

1973—1988　早期事业发展阶段，就职于 WER，ASD，CED 等公司

教育背景

1973—1977　威尔士大学（University of Wales）

1972—1973　赫特斯通专科学校（Hertstone College）

联系方式

电话：0208 971××××

住址：27 Hill Lane London NW 250 DB

（引自《商务汉英翻译》，有所删减）

分析：

(1) 这份简历的<u>工作经验和工作业绩十分突出，因此，分别置于第一、第二部分</u>，相比之下，工作经历和教育背景处于次要地位。对个人的工作职责、业务范围、工作业绩作了具体陈述，并且用数据说明，很有说服力，令人信服。

(2) 在竞争日趋激烈的职场环境下，简历的版面设计十分重要，需要<u>将自身的优势放在最显著的位置，才能吸引人事部门的注意</u>。此外，<u>版面的设计要方便读者查找信息</u>，因此，信息要进行分类，每一部分信息的标志性要强。

(3) 这份简历说明，申请人在陈述自己的工作经验时，不仅要历数自己所从事的相关或主要工作的名称，<u>更重要的是说明工作职责、内容和取得的成绩</u>，这样的简历才有实际意义。

（一）个人简历的翻译

Jack Molisani 的建议对简历的翻译具有切实的指导意义。此外，在翻译和制作简历时，译者可以通过网络查询，获得所要申请求职或留学机构的工作人员简介（Faculty Profiles）的模式、常用的表达方式、关键词，并以此为参照，制作个人简历。

英语简历属于职业写作或技术写作的范畴（Professional Writing/Technical Writing），针对特定读者，具有明确的目的性：确保读者快速准确地掌握和运用所传递的信息。在格式固定的语篇中，英汉简历的差异突出表现在结构和时间的顺序上。英语简历往往格式相对固定，多使用表格式的行文方式，句子通常不必很完整，文体干净利落。汉语简历对格式的要求不是很严格，可以用完整的段落和句子。

在时间顺序上，英语简历的行文一般是逆时的，而汉语简历通常是顺时的。英语简历是从现在到过去，汉语简历一般是从过去到现在。但是，

现在也不尽然，随着国际交往的加深，国外通行的文本模式不可避免地会对中文文本产生影响，要实现简历的文本目标，关键是要突出实时信息、重要信息或主要信息。在地名的翻译上，英文习惯是从小到大，从房间号或门牌号到大街再到区最后城市名，而中文习惯正好相反，即由大到小。翻译时，要注意使用符合译语习惯的表达方式或作相应的改写。

简历的结构主要有两种：一是按照时间顺序（chronologically）陈述，二是按照功能与技能（by function or skill area）分类陈述。采用何种方式视个人的实际情况而定，对于工作经历丰富、工作成效显著的申请者，功能型简历更能突出地展示个人能力，如例1所示。

例2

×××
联系方式

教育背景

2008.09—2012.07	××大学　建筑学本科

获奖

2009.07	●全国大学生建筑设计优秀作业（别墅），全国建筑学专业指导委员会主办
2009.12	●第十一届全国大学生"挑战杯"，三等奖
2012.07	●全国大学生建筑设计优秀作业（城市设计），全国建筑学专业指导委员会主办

实习经历

2012.04—2012.06	●上海睿舍建筑事务所实习
	●参与项目——成都置地商业综合体
	本人承担部分：
	●独立完成建筑立面设计，本人的设计方案被业主选中（事务所提供3个方案，本人完成其中1个方案）
	●完成3个方案的分析
	●参与设计理念的形成、绘图、模型研究全过程
	●负责项目中期规划汇报和翻译工作

调研项目

2012.01	●西安卧龙寺历史街区调研（城墙内历史街

区）——尺度对历史文化街区居民的互动与交流的意义

（这个调研包括这个城墙内的历史街区的尺度与规模、居民的分布、环境心理等因素）

2012.11
- 生态小学改造设计　陕西户县太平乡紫峰小学
- 调研目的：实践生态与可持续建筑技术理论，并对一所小学建筑提出可行性改造方案
- 调研方式：实地测量、访谈、问卷、照片资料
- 调研内容：小学周边基本情况（地理位置、村落规模、自然条件、气候、自然资源、当地文化）

　　　　　　村落小学变迁

　　　　　　村落小学现状（校园测绘、校园存在问题分析、能耗分析与测量）

　　　　　　与当地教师学生进行访谈

综合技能　　熟练使用设计软件：SketchUp/sketching，Adobe Premiere，Photoshop，Indesign，Illustrator

擅长：模型制作、摄影

Name
Contact information

Education	09.2008 – 07.2012	Bachelor of Architecture ××University
Awards	07.2009	Excellent Design Work（villa）organized by National Supervision Commission for Higher Education in Architecture China
	12.2009	Third Prize The 11th National Challenge Cup for College Students
	07.2012	Excellent Design Work（urban design）organized by National Supervision Commission for Higher

		Education in Architecture China
Internship	04.2012 – 06.2012	Intern at Rasier Architect, Shanghai

Work on the project — Chengdu Zhidi Commercial Complex

My work involves:
- Independently design the facade of the project, and my design was chosen by the project owner (the firm offers three options and I undertake one of them)
- Complete the analysis of the three optional plans
- Help to develop design concept, produce diagram and also work on study model
- Mid-term Presentation Layout and Translation

Research & Interaction   01.2012   Investigation on Xi'an Wolongsi Street Block (historical district Investigation within the city wall) — The Significance of the Scale to the and Communication within the Neighborhood with its Cultural Environment

(This investigation involves the scale and size of the streets within the ancient city wall, the distribution of residents, and the environmental psychology)

11. 2012   Redesign of Zifeng Primary School, Huxian County Shaanxi — Updating the Eco-environment of the School

Project Goal: Application of eco and sustainable technology and theory, offering a feasible plan to improve the school building

Approach: Surveying, communication, questionnaire, picture-taking

Information collection: General condition (location, size of the village, natural condition, climate, resources, and local culture), the development of the school, present condition (site

	survey, analysis of the problems on the campus, analysis and measurement of the energy consumption)
	Communication with the teachers and students
Skill Proficiency	Proficient in SketchUp/sketching
	Adobe Premiere, Photoshop, Indesign, and Illustrator
	Strong competence in wood model making, Photography

分析：

这份简历将申请人的工作与科研能力、自主完成的设计任务、实习内容、在项目中扮演的角色等重要信息表述清楚而具体，真实可信。版面设计便于查找信息，综合能力展示较为充分，适合用于申请设计工作或读研机会。

例3

×××
联系方式

教育背景

2008.09—2012.06　　哈尔滨工业大学　电气工程及其自动化　本科
　　　　　　　　　　哈工大实验学院（全校排名前5%）
　　　　　　　　　　平均学分绩：3.8/4.0

科研经历

2010.09—2012.04　　乳房手术图像导航系统（跨学科项目）哈工大生物医学工程研究中心
　　　　　　　　　　本人承担部分：
　　　　　　　　　　在图像建模与配准技术上实现两项创新
　　　　　　　　　　提高亏格为零的曲面 Guyau 算法的稳定性
　　　　　　　　　　熟练使用有限元分析软件 Abaqus
　　　　　　　　　　与项目组成员合作撰写项目研究论文

2010.09—2011.01　　数字化运动控制研究（独立完成）　哈工大微特电机研究所
　　　　　　　　　　熟悉 DSP 的基本原理及应用

熟悉电机驱动的基本技术与实现方法
成绩：96／100

实践活动
2010.03—2010.05　哈工大实验学院学生会宣传部　部长/首席平面设计师
日常管理与运作，负责平面设计培训
主持设计海报等宣传品近50份
曾为一汽轿车、沃特体育等知名企业设计宣传产品

获奖
2011年全国大学生英语能力竞赛二等奖（排名：14／1550）
哈工大新生奖学金5000元（全校排名前3%）
哈工大一等人民奖学金（全院排名前20%），两次

综合技能
英语水平：GRE：1320　TOEFL：101
熟练使用编程语言：C，C++，Matlab
熟练使用软件：Simulia Abaqus，AutoCAD，Solidwork

Name
Contact information

Education
2008.09 – 2012.06　Electrical Engineering, Harbin University of Technology (HUT) B. Eng Honors School student (Top 5% of HUT)
GPA：3.8/4.0

Research
2010.09 – 2012.04　Development of Image-guided Navigation System for Breast Surgery
(interdisciplinary research project) BME Research Center, HUT
My Role in the Project：
Achieve two innovations in modeling and registration respectively

	Improve the stability of Guyau algorithm for genus zero surface
	Proficient in finite element analysis with the application of Abaqus
	Work at the papers on the research in collaboration with the team
2010.09 – 2011.01	Digital Motion Control
	Micro Special Electrical Machinery Research Institute, HUT
	Proficient in basic principles of DSP and its applications
	Proficient in basic methods of electrical machinery control
	Project score: 96/100

Extracurricular Activities

2010.03 – 2012.05	Dept. of Publicity, Student Union, Honors School Administrator & Chief Graphics Designer
	In charge of the department operation, graphics design training
	Complete nearly 50 graphics design projects
	Product promotion design for large enterprise such as FAW, CAR CO., LTD and Voit Sports.

Honors and Scholarships

2011 National English Contest for College Students, the 2nd Prize

(ranking 14th among 1550 participants)

Entrance Scholarship of HUT (top 3% of HUT)

1st Prize of Academic Scholarship of Hut, twice

Skill Proficiency

English Proficiency: GRE: 1320 TOEFL: 101

Proficient in C, C++, Matlab, Simulia Abaqus, AutoCAD and Solidwork

分析：

这份简历突出了申请人的学业成绩和科研能力，用数据证明自己的实力，对研究内容描述具体可信，很有说服力。

二、如何写求职信

求职信（Application Letter 也称之为 Cover Letter）和个人简历是求职者申请职位的必备文件。个人简历与求职信的不同之处在于：个人简历是对某人的工作经历、工作业绩、教育背景、综合技能等方面信息与数据的总结、提炼与编辑，根据不同的职场需求，个人信息的选取、排列组合、突出重点会有所不同；求职信是营销自我的工具，更加个性化，其作用是将简历中列举的与某一特定岗位要求相关的信息做出具体说明，目的是向雇主说明求职者的职业资质和个人优势与岗位要求匹配，以便获得一个面试机会，针对不同的雇主需求，申请人需要撰写与之相适应的求职信。

但是，求职信的写作还是有规律可循的。求职信要做到言之有理，动之以情，申请人首先需要查询主管部门的负责人，以便将求职信直接发给该负责人，从而避免使用"To Whom It May Concern"、"Dear Sir or Madam"，or "Director of Human Resources"这样的称谓，使之更加人性化；申请人要学会换位思考，从人事主管的视角来审视自己，描述与陈述自我，使求职信更易于被接受。

求职信一般由三个部分构成。

1. 起始段

为了吸引雇主的眼球，起始段需要回答以下问题：

（1）写信的目的。
（2）获得岗位信息的渠道。
（3）满足岗位要求的自身优势。

如果这个岗位信息是由某位教授，或是求职机构的员工介绍的，可以直接说明，充分发挥人际关系的作用，因为他们对申请者能力的肯定有助于他获得面试机会。

例 4

At a recent meeting of the County Services Council, a member of your staff, George Azmar, told me that you will be hiring a public affairs coordinator. Because of my extensive experience in and commitment to community affairs, I would appreciate your considering me for this opening. I expect to receive my B. S. in Public Administration from Mid-Michigan College later this year.

2. 正文

正文一般由两个段落构成,每段 3 ~ 5 句话,简单易懂。正文需要回答两个问题:
(1) 教育背景。
(2) 工作经历与成果/业绩。

刚毕业或实践经验不足的申请者可以强调实习经历(说明实习内容、工作职责、独立完成的工作)、所学专业知识或课程、取得的专业资格证书或掌握的实用技能与所申请的岗位的关联性。

如果申请者的工作经历和研究成果与工作岗位关联性很强,能够充分证明申请者的专业能力和综合素质足以胜任欲求职的岗位,比教育背景更有说服力,可以将工作经历置于教育背景之前,如例 1 所示。

例 5

With a special interest in the publishing industry, I have completed more than 40 credit hours in courses directly related to layout design, where I acquired experience using QuarkXPress as well as illustrator and Photoshop.

3. 结尾

结尾要简短,两三句话结束,作用有三:
(1) 再次强调自身优势。
(2) 提出面试要求。
(3) 说明联系方式和联系时间。

例 6

I believe you will see in my resume that I possess an excellent skill set which matches your requirements perfectly. If you have any further questions or require additional documentation, please feel free to contact me. Thank you for your time and consideration.

例 7

                                                Maria H. Lopez
                                                1725 Brooke Street
                                                Miami, FL32701-2121
                                                Cell: 707-555-6390
                                                mlopez@eagle.com

Mr. Marvin Henrady
Human Resources Manager
×××Publishing Company
1001 Heathcliff Row
San Francisco, CA 4123-7707

Dear Henrady,

    I'm writing to express my interest in the Web Content Specialist position listed on Monster.com. I have experience building large, consumer-focused health-based content sites. While much of my experience has been in the business world, I understand the social value of the non-profit sector.

    With a BA degree in Professional Writing at MSU, my responsibilities included the development and management of the site's editorial voice and style, the editorial calendar, and the daily content programming and production of the web site. I worked closely with health care professionals and medical editors to help them provide the best possible information to audience of patients. In addition, I helped physicians learn to utilize their medical content to write user-friendly, readily comprehensible text.

    Experience has taught me how to build strong relationships with all departments at an organization. I have the ability to work within a team as well as cross-team. I can work with web engineers to resolve technical issues and implement technical enhancements, work with the development department to implement design and functional enhancements, and monitor site statistics and conduct search engine optimization.

    I would appreciate the opportunity to talk with you about the position and my interest in website development and design. My phone number is 707-555-6390. After June 12, I will be available for an interview at any time that is convenient for you.

Sincerely yours,
(signature)
Maria H. Lopez

Encl. Resume

四、留学申请

关于留学申请书（Application Letter，Cover Letter），不同的学校有不同的提法和要求，如 个人陈述（Personal Statement）、求学动机（Motivation）、求学目的（Statements of Purpose, Academic Statement, Academic Objectives）、研究计划（Study Plan, Research Proposal）等。尽管提法不同，侧重点也有所不同，其目的只有一个：通过它对申请人各方面的情况进行综合评定，有助于对是否录取做出判断。

留学申请的功能主要有三：一是展示申请人的英语表达能力，由此判断其用英语进行学习与完成实际任务的能力；二是展示申请人对所申请的学科的了解和投入程度，由此判断其学习和科研能力；三是展示申请人的个人特色、实际技能和综合素质。

因此，留学申请不是对个人简历的详细补充，而是向评审人推销自己的自我包装工具。留学申请的主要目的是向评审人说明申请人选择该专业有明确的动机和强烈的愿望，同时具备完成学业的能力。因此，留学申请必须围绕所申请专业的主题展开，思路清晰，通过个人的视角和经历表达自我，切不可落入俗套，千篇一律。因为，对于大多数申请人心仪的学校来说，每年的求学申请堆积如山，花在每份申请上的时间不过两三分钟。为了吸引评审人的眼球，让自己从众多申请者中脱颖而出，申请人必须突出展示个人的亮点，具有说服力。

不同专业有不同特点，所以申请书的侧重点也不尽相同。申请人需要根据自己的专业特点、自身条件、教育背景等方面的优势，突出自己扎实的专业知识及文献检索与分析论证能力，还要涉及科学实验、田野调查、研究报告、发表论文、社会实践、分析与解决问题的方法与思路等等。

同时，留学申请要根据所申请的学校的具体要求来写。一般来说，学校对字数都有限制，通常800～1500字，因此文章要短小精悍，内容充实丰满，语言流畅。有些学校对具体内容也有要求，因此文章的针对性要强。申请人可以从自己的成长经历、家庭影响、教育背景、兴趣爱好、学业成绩、经济状况、社会实践等方面，选取最有说服力的实例说明这些因素对申请人选择专业、制定学习研究计划的影响与帮助，紧紧围绕主题展开，事例要真实可信，语句要诚恳具体。

留学申请的写作要求同样对其英译有着切实的指导作用，要以实现译语文本功能为主要目标。

例 8

Motivation Statement

1 In my memory, I have never seen my father seeing a doctor since my childhood—not because he is very healthy and strong, but because of the fact that he couldn't afford it. As a girl from a poor family in a rural area, I'm quite clear that for most rural residents there is no escaping when a severe disease comes along, which is no less than a disaster to the whole family.

2 The moment I got to know the program of Erasmus-Mundus Master PhoenixEM Dynamics of Health and Welfare, my father's miserable condition came to my mind. Every time I got home, I would painfully see him suffering from multiple illnesses, and his ceaseless coughing made my heart ache. This hopeless situation not only occurs to my family but also presents a severe social problem for hundreds of millions of rural residents who are excluded from the welfare of medical and health care in China. It reminds me of C. Wright Mills, a famous American sociologist who prominently made sociology the study of the public issues. Now the program offers me an opportunity to associate my family trouble to a public issue. Maybe I can do something for folks like my father.

3 Obviously, the program of Erasmus-Mundus Master seems very appealing to me. Since late 1970s, Chinese government has insisted medical reform should be market-oriented. As a result, the issue of public health welfare is ignored to a large extent, which leads to social unfairness. One striking evidence is that rural residents do not have basic medicare. It is the responsibility of our generation to integrate successful medicare practice of developed countries and China's reality, and create a public medical system that can benefit all Chinese people, particularly the rural residents accounting for the

major part of the population. It is universally acknowledged that European medical system is remarkably successful and inspiring for the medical reform in China. I believe the success of Chinese medical reform will in turn contribute to new breakthroughs in European system.

4　The program provides me with an opportunity to get a better understanding of European public medical systems, while my four-year college education has laid a solid foundation for me to obtain the opportunity. In the first two years, I took many courses in humanity and social science, including sociology, political science, economy, history and philosophy. This comprehensive education has broadened my horizon. Then in the third year, I took philosophy as my major and have dramatically developed and enhanced my critical thinking. Furthermore, as my CV illustrates, I have actively participated in academic research, in which I have learnt to apply the methodology of social science into practice.

5　Now I'm fully prepared for an opportunity to fulfill the prospective study in Europe. I hope in a few years, with the sound ideas of European medical welfare, I will work together with my colleagues and devote ourselves to the health welfare in China, and build a fair, efficient health welfare system that may benefit all people across the country. （引自《成功留学写作指南》，有所删改）

分析：
　　申请人通过描述自己父亲的不幸遭遇，陈述个人对社会学研究的认识以及投身研究与解决社会问题的志向。全篇结构严谨，论述逻辑性强。
　　第1段用父亲的病痛引入申请该研究生项目的原因，以情动人。
　　第2段引用西方社会学家 C. Wright Mills 的理念说明中国农民医疗保障问题的实质，对这个项目的意义与作用的理解，同时表现申请人对社会学的理论也有所涉猎。
　　第3段介绍中国近30年来的医疗改革情况，需要解决的问题，欧洲福利制度对中国的借鉴作用。
　　第4段说明申请人知识面广，具有从事社会研究的实践经验，能够胜任此项目的学习研究工作。而且，从这里我们可以看出，当申请人本科所学专业 philosophy 与研究生项目 EM Dynamics of Health and Welfare 不一致时，可以列述本科所学的相关课程，在两个不同学科项目之间建立联系。
　　第5段表达渴望获得这个机会去欧洲学习的愿望。

例 9

Personal Statement

1 It was at primary school that I first became fascinated with making model planes. Under the instruction of my teacher, I chose paulownia (泡桐木) as the basic material of the frame of my glider models. I was impressed by this light and strong wood that makes itself the best choice to construct the plane models. In order to improve its texture, I learnt to brush a coat of resin (树脂) onto the material to make it stronger, and then cut the wood hollow and add a thin-film paper to make the construction even lighter. This experience of making model plane vaguely aroused my interest in developing and improving materials. Who would have then expected that my career is to be irrevocably committed to material science 10 years later?

2 I began my independent school life at 12, and performed exceedingly well and kept the first place in my grade for six years running. Consequently, I became the only student of my school to be recommended for immediate admission to Tsinghua University without taking an entrance examination, majoring in material science and engineering—a rare privilege for the top high school graduates in China.

3 At Tsinghua University, I distinguished myself with GPA for Basic Courses reaching 3.788/4.0 and GPA for Specialized Courses 4.0/4.0. Therefore, I was awarded a First-grade Scholarship of Tsinghua University in the first academic year, and the top Scholarship of our department in the 2nd academic year. These rewards not only have encouraged me but also stimulated my potential greatly.

4 Noticing that computers are widely used in many domains of study and research, I'm not satisfied with the fundamental courses of computer science offered by the university, such as Fortran, C, Hardware techniques, etc. I spent plenty of my leisure time teaching myself computer skills, like Delphi, Visual C^{++} and other advanced softwares. Meanwhile, I've managed to apply these skills in my specialized subjects. For instance, while attending Studies of Crystals, I found that the crystal lattice (水晶格) structures of rutile (金红石) are too difficult to analyze in a plane figure. Applying 3D Studio MAX, I

simulated the crystal structure with a three dimensional graphic. I have also achieved some success in drawing XRD graphs and doing data analysis with the aid of computer.

5 For all my academic undertakings, I am by no means a bookworm in daily life. In order to achieve all-around development, I am constantly engaged in a host of extracurricular activities. Thanks to my easy-going character as well as the ability of organization and management, I entered the Student Science Association and became vice-president in the following year. I was awarded Excellent Student Leader Scholarship for my devotion to the services for the Association. Another thing for me to feel proud of is that I participated in the project of designing and constructing the Student Dormitory LAN System, in both hardware and software items. Currently I am the team leader in charge of LAN Management & Maintenance and help to provide the students with BBS, WWW, FTP services via LAN.

6 Three years ago, I made a good start academically by entering Tsinghua University, the best engineering university in China. The motto of "to be the best" is what I am pursuing all the time. I have been following the research frontier of material science in a global sphere. Gradually I come to find that the United States holds the leading position in both material science research and education, and your school is universally acknowledged for excellent teaching, rigorous scholastic studies and great scientific breakthroughs. What's more, you provide students with easy access to the best facilities and laboratory equipment, which create the opportunity for students to fulfill their dreams and goals. These advantages are hardly resistible for any ambitious young scholar like me who is thirsty for knowledge and eager to see his dream come true. In brief, I desire to study at your university, and I would appreciate it if you could take my application into favorable consideration.

(引自《成功留学写作指南》,有所删改)

分析:

这份申请沿着学业成绩、自学能力、科研实力、课外活动组织管理能力这条主线展开,环环相扣。

第1段通过介绍童年时代做模型的乐趣以及对材料加工处理的过程,说明申请人与材料科学有着不解之缘。

第2段通过介绍申请人被保送清华,说明中学时代的学业成绩出类拔萃。

第3、4段介绍大学时代的学业成绩，自学电脑技术，并将其用于专业设计。

第5段介绍自己参与和负责的主要课外活动项目，特别是网络管理与维护。

第6段介绍选择去美国留学的原因，表达去该学校的强烈愿望。

例10

有些学校的要求比较宽泛，申请人可以根据自己的具体情况，选择最能表现自我的素材来写译。鉴于字数限制，申请人要时刻牢记文本目标和读者的信息需求，加强信息的关联性，避免空话套话。

下面是加州大学伯克利分校建筑学院的 Personal History Statement 要求：

This essay (500 words, maximum) is a narrative description of your life background in terms of how it has prepared you for this next stage of your studies. It should describe relevant aspects of your life story and achievements, as well as educational and cultural opportunities or circumstances that supported or deprived you of such achievements; family background; economic circumstances; special interests and abilities; and community or social service involvement. Throughout, be selective in describing things that specifically relate to your academic goals and intellectual pursuits. In particular, please be sure to focus on details of your research experience, and how your background has prepared you for the next stage of your studies.

Personal History Statement

1 In May 2012, when I was working as an intern at Rasier Architect Shanghai, I attended lectures and project presentations at Tongji University. At the conclusion of one project presentation, Professor Dong Yao mentioned UC Berkeley with outstanding advantages in urban design program.

2 Then I bought a book, *Vertical Cities Asia-International Design Competition* 2012: *Everyone Ages*, in which Plan B proposed by Berkeley has impressed me. This design has something similar to my design assignment in 2012—Design of the Historical neighborhood featuring Qinqiang Opera in Xi'an (a famous local opera). This project involves investigation of the scale and size

of the streets within the ancient city wall, the distribution of residents, and the environmental psychology. I have made some investigations in the ancient city of Xi'an at college, and have developed an interest in urban study.

3　I've read 2012 – 2013 MUD Program Statement. The description of the Urban Design Program just fits my interest. My interest concerns the connection between architecture and city, mixed use architecture, and urban transformation.

4　Architecture and urban design produce a sense of place, representing the unique feature and main attractions of a place and reflecting the aspiration of the residents. Now, China is going through a process of urbanization, which produces severe problems. With more land being developed in patterns that are dehumanizing and wasteful, the new-developed areas with large scale buildings and squares remain vacant, while the existing urban areas are over-crowded, with no space for public activities. The one-child policy makes many parents feel lonely while their only child is away at college or work. With no other choice, the only thing for them to do is to join square-dancing, which is a disturbance to the neighborhood. At the same time, cities all over the country look alike with little attractions. As an architecture major, I feel I should do something to improve the situation.

5　This is an interdisciplinary program instructed by faculty members from three departments, which is both challenging and inspiring for me. Especially, some studio is led by one of the MUD faculty with part-time involvement of two or three others. It seems that this well-structured program has created an ideal opportunity for the comprehensive development of students, I'm sure I'll be benefited from the instructions of several professionals at the same time, if I'm given the opportunity.

分析：

第1段说明了申请人如何获得MUD（Master of Urban Design）的信息，从而引起对该项目的关注，描述真实自然。

第2段描述了申请人对MUD项目的一个城市设计竞赛获奖方案的认识以及自己的城市设计实践，描述客观真实。

第3段介绍了申请人自己的研究兴趣。

第4段介绍了正在中国兴起的大规模城市化进程以及城市建设中出现的众多问题，作为建筑师应尽的责任。

第 5 段说明了申请人对这个跨学科项目的组织结构、教学模式的喜爱，表达了希望获得这个学习机会的愿望。

例 11

有些学校的要求非常具体详细，申请人需要严格按照要求来写译。以下是（荷兰）代尔夫特理工大学建筑学院的 Motivation 要求：

A clear and relevant essay in English（1000 – 1500 words）addressing the following：

· Your motivation for taking the MSc programme of your choice.

· Why you are interested in TU Delft and what you expect to find here.

· If there are optional specializations in the MSc programme of your choice: which specialization(s) interest you most, and why?

· Describe your hypothetical thesis project; what kind of a project would you prefer if you were free to make a choice? Also briefly explain what you would want to explore in your thesis project. Provide a maximum of three hypothetical thesis topics and elaborate on your particular interests in them.

· A brief summary (maximum 250 words) of the thesis work or the final assignment (to be) done for your Bachelor's programme, including information on the credits earned, grade, and full workload.

Motivation for Taking the MSc-program

Motivation for Taking the MSc-program of Architecture

My first knowledge of architecture came from my grandparents, who taught architecture design at a university in Xi'an. With detailed arrangement, their compact home ($70 m^2$) in 1990s appeared spacious and comfortable, which was much admired in their neighborhood. For Chinese, housing is important that it is their aspiration and hope, reflecting their taste for and quality of life. Since I was enrolled in College of Human settlements and Civil Engineering ××× University (listed in the top 15 universities in China) in 2008, I find that I cannot give up architecture to take up another major. Architecture is about to design and improve people's life and environment. In the process of learning architecture, I find myself improving in many aspects, such as broadening knowledge, keeping balance among various elements, cooperating with different people, leadership in teamwork and etc. To get myself better prepared to face the challenge of building a better living environment, I want to pursue the MSc-program of Architecture.

Why you are interested in TU Delft and what you expect to find here

First, I have leant some knowledge of western architecture. Studying abroad can broaden my horizon, and especially, I can live and work in the environment I have seen in architecture books and magazines, so that I can understand it better.

Second, in the process of globalization, the design market in China is open to the world and competition for project is becoming severe. How to apply the cutting-edge design concepts and technology into the resolution of local problems is a big challenge to Chinese architects.

Two years ago, I bought a book "From Berlage to Koolhaas: A Hundred Years of Dutch Architecture 1901 - 2000", written by Leen Van Duin and S. Umberto Barbieri of TU Delft. In this book, I've learnt the achievement of Dutch architecture and its impact on western architecture. I notice that most architects mentioned in the book come from TU Delft, which suggests the important role TU Delft is playing in architecture world.

From this book, I get to know a new concept of what is design: Design by Research. Dutch architects are discovering potential problems in the process of their design, and solutions to each specific problem, which makes their designs unique in the architecture world featuring uniform style and form. Another distinctive feature of their designs is the detailed arrangement of every part, which contributes to the quality and signature style of Dutch architecture. Their approach is inspiring for Chinese architects to deal with the challenge of the cities with similarly built environment and densely populated urban area. In addition, I visit TU Delft website and see many students' works, reflecting the design principle of "design by research", which is just what I admire and pursue.

In 2011, I initiated a discussion on "Beautiful Render vs Ugly Project" at an architecture forum. Over one hundred people participated in the discussion, and we found many examples of projects beautifully presented in renders but ugly built in China. I think the main reason is that most of the designs stop at the overall concept stage, without further detailed design conducted.

Consequently, the form of the project conflicts with the construction methods, e. g. using concrete to imitate wood structure. At the TU Delft website, I see architecture education emphasizes on laying a solid foundation, detailed design of every section, e. g. detailed design of joints of different parts. This approach will guarantee the design in graphics coming into reality, which impress me most.

Which specializations interest me most, and why

Among the nine optional specializations in MSc-program of Architecture, I take great interest in Architecture & Public Building and Materialization & Design Development.

(1) Architecture & Public Building

As mentioned in the curriculum introduction: this program "focus on the question of how new architectural and urban models, typologies, programs, and design strategies can be developed to meet a diverse and open society's cultural, social and political needs…" From this description, I think this approach will address many problems such as: "What is the meaning of public domain?" "Is it the image project of government's effort?" "How should we deal with the situation of urban areas with uniform public buildings?" Public buildings are the main attractions of a community and reflect the aspiration and spiritual life of the community. They produce a sense of place, representing the unique feature of a place. This specialization is of great significant to the present world.

(2) Materialization & Design Development

The curriculum introduction states: "Materialization emphasizes the importance of the craft to develop ideas from paper to material reality. Ultimately, the shape of the building, the chosen materials and their assembly determine the appearance of the building." This specialization involves detailed design process and will determine the quality of built environment. It will develop the knowledge and skills in architects to realize their designs. However, this approach is often overlooked in the large scale construction going on in China, which contributes to many examples of "Beautiful Render vs Ugly Project". I feel that I have the responsibility to do something to improve the situation.

Three themes for Master thesis:
(1) Transformation and Revival of Old or Deserted Space

In China, with the development of industry and updating of production methods, some communities and factories become deserted. The demolishing of these facilities produces huge cost and construction wastes, which are threatening to environment. I am interested in transforming these deteriorated facilities. How to make the transformation fit in with new life or become a highlight in new life? How to integrate the old and new?

(2) The Significance or Possibility of Public Realm

For the citizens of developing countries, a public space with distinctive feature and attraction will be the highlight for their everyday life. It will help to create the urban environment with the quality of culture and taste, and become the center of focus. It will also develop the feeling of pride in citizens. I'm interested in how to create a public space that will create activities and appeal to citizens, how to create the spirit need of the public by design.

(3) The Transition between the Old and New Urban Areas within a City

With the increase of the population, urban area is expanding rapidly. The transition between the old and new areas becomes abrupt, causing a lot of problems, such as traffic flow, life circle, distribution of business, environment protection, cultural environment, and etc.

Graduation Design Project:

Caotang Elderly Care Complex (project planning and design)

(1) Brief Introduction

This is a real project to be built for the purpose of taking care of the elderly. The project is initiated by the local government in Xi'an, and is under hot discussion, as it involves a large scale land development and no agreement is made. The purpose of taking the program as the graduation design project is to encourage students to explore more potential solutions.

The proposed elderly care complex is a comprehensive project occupying a floor space of 60,000 m^2, plus medical, convention and service facilities of 40,000 m^2. The site is located in a piece of wasteland, occupying a land area of 120,000 m^2, in southern suburb of Xi'an, with a river passing through southeast corner of the site, faced by Caotang Temple (historic building, tourist destination) to the east, having a beautiful view of the Qingling Mountains (tourist destination) to the south. The site has different elevations, with the south higher than the north, the section in the center being the lowest, dotted with water pools.

(2) Specific Features of the Design

The site planning conforms to the landscape, taking advantage of the water pools in the center, drawing water from the river flowing down from the Qingling Mountains into the pools. A water system is formed, acting as a unifying force to connect different sections and create a series of scenery.

Based on the field investigations of large nursing homes for elderly, the architecture design focuses on creating apartments for elderly with home-style environment, providing sufficient sunlight, various forms of living spaces, encouraging communication among elderly.

Conclusion:

As I have a clear motivation and goal to study at TU Delft, I am confident of having the ability, accumulation and passion to finish the study. I am looking forward to having the opportunity to study in your school.

分析：

第1部分说明了家庭环境与选择建筑设计专业的关系，表达了对建筑设计的认识以及继续学习深造的愿望。

第2部分说明了从书中获得的有关对荷兰建筑以及代尔夫特理工大学建筑学院的认识，特别是"通过研究做设计"的理念（Design by Research），对细节与节点的精确设计，这些设计理念与技术对中国建筑设计的启示，说明了选择该学校的原因，而不是俗套空洞的 TU Delft is a famous university in Europe with a long history，表现了申请人的学习兴趣与学习能力，对荷兰建筑教育的理解与向往。

第3、4部分说明了申请人对该项目的理解、研究兴趣以及完成学业的能力。

第5部分说明了申请人所在学院对毕业设计的要求，项目的规模与工作量，从而展示了申请人的研究与设计能力。评审人由此可以了解申请人所在学院的教学质量。

参考文献

[1] 贾文波. 应用翻译功能论. 北京：中国对外翻译出版公司, 2004.
[2] 曾利沙. 应用翻译讲义. http://www1.gdufs.edu.cn/jwc/bestcourse/kecheng/04.asp.
[3] 常玉田. 商务汉英翻译. 北京：对外经济贸易大学出版社, 2010.
[4] 陈小慰. 新编实用翻译教程. 北京：经济科学出版社, 2011.
[5] 彭萍. 实用旅游英语翻译教程. 北京：对外经济贸易大学出版社, 2010.
[6] 衡孝军. 对外宣传翻译：理论与实践. 北京：世界知识出版社, 2011.
[7] 修月祯等. 首届全国旅游暨文化创意产业翻译研讨会论文集. 北京：知识产权出版社, 2008.
[8] 许建平. 成功留学写作指南. 北京：外语教学与研究出版社, 2011.
[9] 菲利浦·科林. 工作中的英语写作. 北京：人民邮电出版社, 2011.
[10] 李长栓. 非文学翻译. 北京：外语教学与研究出版社, 2009.
[11] 吴建, 张韵菲. 企业外宣英译：一个多层次重构的过程. 上海翻译, 2011 (1).
[12] 卢小军. 中美网站企业概况的文本对比与外宣英译. 中国翻译, 2012 (1).
[13] 曾利沙. 论投资指南的翻译原则. 国际经贸探索, 2000 (2).
[14] 李德超, 王克非. 平行文本比较模式与旅游文本的英译. 中国翻译, 2009 (4).
[15] 王银泉. 非文学翻译：翻译教材建设和翻译教学的思维转向. 外语界, 2009 (2).
[16] 黄友义. 坚持"外宣三贴近"原则，处理好外宣翻译的难点问题. 中国翻译, 2004 (6).
[17] 袁晓宁. 以目的语为依归的外宣英译特质——以《南京采风》翻译为例. 中国翻译, 2010 (2).
[18] 陶友兰. 翻译目的论观照下的英汉汉英翻译教材建设. 外语界,

2006 (5).

[19] 文秋芳. 输出驱动假设与英语专业技能课程改革. 外语界, 2008 (2).

[20] 陶友兰. 翻译专业汉英翻译教材的建构模式新探. 外语界, 2008 (2).

[21] 苗菊, 高乾. 构建 MTI 教育特色课程—技术写作的理念与内容. 中国翻译, 2010 (2).

[22] 封一函. 探究式翻译之偶得. 中国翻译, 2012 (6).

[23] 王刚毅. 政治文件翻译的几点思考和建议. 中国翻译, 2014 (3).

[24] 冯晞. 语言服务是战略. 2016. 12 http://mp.weixin.qq.com/s/A1Rxu7QIDv8GKcc5F_TUjw.

[25] 蒋好书. 文化走出去和翻译服务. 中国译协网 http://www.tac-online.org.cn/ch/tran/2013-08/05

[26] Devoss, Danielle Nicole and Julier, Laura. Profile of professional writing at Michigan State University [Z]. 2009.

[27] Jack Molisani. Resume Secrets That Might Surprise You. 2010 http://www.prospringstaffing.com/Resource/Resume Secrets That Might SurpriseYou.pdf

[28] 龚露. 爱因斯坦都办公司了. 南方周末, 2010-20-21.